TOWARD THE RENEWAL OF CIVILIZATION

Toward the Renewal of Civilization

Political Order and Culture

Edited by

T. William Boxx
and
Gary M. Quinlivan

with a foreword by

Archabbot Douglas R. Nowicki, O.S.B.

WILLIAM B. EERDMANS PUBLISHING COMPANY
GRAND RAPIDS, MICHIGAN / CAMBRIDGE, U.K.

© 1998 Wm. B. Eerdmans Publishing Co.
255 Jefferson Ave. S.E., Grand Rapids, Michigan 49503 /
P.O. Box 163, Cambridge CB3 9PU U.K.

Printed in the United States of America

03 02 01 00 99 98   7 6 5 4 3 2 1

Library of Congress Cataloging-in-Publication Data

Toward the renewal of civilization: political order and culture /
    edited by T. William Boxx and Gary M. Quinlivan
        p.   cm.
    Based on lectures delivered in a conference at Saint Vincent College, April 10-12,
1997.
    Includes index.
    ISBN 0-8028-4534-7 (paper)
    1. Postmodernism — Social aspects — Congresses. 2. Postmodernism — Political
aspects — Congresses. 3. Politics and culture — Congresses. I. Boxx, T. William,
1953-   . II. Quinlivan, Gary M., 1952-
HM73.P593 1998
306 — dc21   98-4448
                                                                                CIP

In Memoriam
Donald C. McKenna

Contents

CONTENTS

Acknowledgments

THIS collection of essays is based on lectures delivered in a conference at Saint Vincent College, April 10-12, 1997. The conference was sponsored by Saint Vincent College's Center for Economic and Policy Education (CEPE) which was named to the 1997-98 Templeton Honor Rolls for Education in a Free Society. There are several individuals, foundations, and institutions that we would like to thank for their help, advice, and financial support.

The editors would like to thank Saint Vincent College which provides the academic and physical setting for the Center's events. Since 1992, Saint Vincent College has been recognized four times by *U.S. News & World Report* as one of the Top 10 Best Regional Liberal Arts Colleges in the North.

Our strongest appreciation goes to Rt. Rev. Douglas R. Nowicki, O.S.B., the archabbot of Saint Vincent Archabbey and chancellor of Saint Vincent College and Saint Vincent Seminary, for authoring the forward for this book; to Rev. Martin R. Bartel, O.S.B., president of Saint Vincent College, for providing the welcoming message which began our April 11-12 sessions; and to James L. Murdy, chairperson of the Saint Vincent College Board of Directors and Executive Vice President of Finance and Administration at Allegheny Teledyne Incorporated, for introducing Hilton Kramer's lecture.

We thank the following administrators and faculty members at Saint Vincent College for their organizational help and the additional hours they worked: Christine M. Dumm, M.P.A., CEPE's program manager; Andrew R. Herr, Ph.D., CEPE's fellow in economics and policy; Donald A. Orlando, director of public relations; Br. Norman W.

ACKNOWLEDGMENTS

Hipps, O.S.B., provost; and Brent D. Cejda, Ph.D., academic dean. In addition we especially thank Fr. Thomas Devereux, O.S.B., director of special events; and Joseph F. Reilly, director of Saint Vincent Theatre and instructor of film, for technical assistance with the Hilton Kramer lecture.

Our gratitude is extended to the following students who volunteered their time and efforts to ensure the success of the conference: Elizabeth M. Appel, C'99; Ronald J. Baker, C'98; Melissa D. Blough, C'98; Jorge F. Cardona, C'99; Faye L. Carpenter, C'97; David Gaito, C'98; William M. Garrett, C'97; Adam D. Gasper, C'97; Matthew A. Halloran, C'97; Aaron B. Hinde, C'97; Elizabeth M. Kaczmarski, C'99; Jaime M. Kochis, C'98; Anthony T. Kovalchick, C'99; Amy Leonardo, C'97; Ann M. Lund, C'98; Anthony R. Marciano, C'00; Robert C. McBride, C'99; Siddhartha Namasivayam, C'98; Nicholas M. Racculia, C'99; Andrei S. Romaniouk, C'98; Gregory S. Thome, C'97; and Anthony S. Zito, C'98.

We thank our indexer, Sandra S. Quinlivan, M.A. We thank the contributors to our book for the numerous drafts they labored over. In addition a special thanks to our reviewers whose comments appear on the cover of this book: William Kristol is the editor and publisher of the *Weekly Standard;* Michael Novak, former U.S. ambassador, is the George Frederick Jewett Chair in Religion and Public Policy at the American Enterprise Institute in Washington, D.C.; and William E. Simon, Secretary of the Treasury from 1974 to 1977, is president of the John M. Olin Foundation. Our appreciation is also extended to William B. Eerdmans, Jr. for reviewing and publishing our book.

Finally we are in debt to the following foundations and organizations that made the conference and this book possible: Aequus Institute, Curran Foundation, Earhart Foundation, Intercollegiate Studies Institute, the J. M. Foundation, Massey Charitable Trust, Philip M. McKenna Foundation, PNC Bank Charitable Trust Committee, and the Alex C. Walker Educational and Charitable Foundation.

Foreword

THIS volume and the conference at Saint Vincent College upon which it is based, was designed by the editors to address the troubling state of American civilization and to explore grounds for renewal. The twelve renowned authors here presented, consider various aspects of the political and cultural foundations of America and the West and the ideological and institutional changes and challenges of contemporary life. That the intellectual and moral heritage of our civilization, a civilization drawn from the best of Athens and Jerusalem, has lost social force in modern times is manifestly apparent. That the principles and propositions of this heritage must in some manner be revitalized for the preservation of a free and well-ordered society is the underlying premise of this work. It is a worthy and compelling undertaking that will hopefully spur a broad dialogue on the problems of our times and help renew civil society.

It would be hard to imagine living in a time which could witness the crucial changes that have occurred in our lifetime: revolutionary changes in political and economic systems as reflected in the collapse of the Soviet Union; and radical changes in human consciousness as a result of the explosive developments in communication technology. Yet, it was not too many years ago that human consciousness was characterized by a great optimism and self-confidence. This was the mentality of modern man — the maker of the modern world that originated in the seventeenth-century Enlightenment.

It is not difficult to understand what engendered this optimism and self-confidence. The great accomplishments in science and technology created a new world; and, perhaps even more significant, these accomplishments promised human control over nature and a future of inevitable and unending progress. Human reason and technology would create the perfect society — a society which would be emancipated from religion and ethical systems based on religion. What a tremendous shock it was when this dream of the modern world of rationalism, romanticism, individualism, and idealism collapsed before our eyes. The slaughter of millions in the Great War, the holocaust, environmental challenges, fear of nuclear annihilation, the social and political chaos rooted in ethnic conflict which has emerged with the collapse of communism, the breakdown of our social structure (especially the family), have brought with them a climate of cynicism and despair.

The modern age was the age of optimism; our postmodern world has been called the age of anxiety. For the postmodern person, instead of the belief in the inevitable progress of civilization, there is a growing fear that our science-fiction technology, despite its great achievements, in the end may destroy its maker; that worldwide unresolved political and economic chaos will result not in winnable wars but in nuclear holocaust or in a gradual disintegration of society through terrorism and violence.

Is not our experience of the human condition, with its great accomplishments, its great tragedies, its ever-changing understanding of the vision of the future, similar to the reality that Saint Benedict confronted with the collapse of the Roman Empire? Roman law and language, Roman army and administration, Roman bureaucracy and trade — all helped to create the illusion that a utopian society had been created. But soon the illusion began to be exposed. Optimism gave way to pessimism. Saint Benedict lived in the sixth century when the Roman Empire was in a state of disintegration; and he fled the paganism and pessimism of Rome.

Saint Benedict, however, had a profound understanding of the reality of the human condition and human history. Our world is not a world of inevitable progress. Any ideology based on the illusion that we can create a perfect world, whether it be the Roman Empire or the utopia of Karl Marx, will collapse. Such utopian vision of optimism will gradually give way to the hopelessness of despair. Saint Benedict's affirmation of hope in the midst of chaos was based not on his vision of a new world order, but on his trust in the reality of God's promise.

It is the promise that, ultimately, chaos and evil will not prevail. The often hidden, gentle power of God's loving presence is stronger than the blatant power of evil; God's love is completed, when nothing is perfect. Because of our hope, however, we, like Saint Benedict, will not give in to the despair and anxiety of our postmodern age. We will live in the hope that God is with us to complete what is now unfinished and at times nearly overcome by evil.

No one could predict what the post–Roman Empire world would become or who would define its nature. As it turned out, this world became the Christian civilization that was created in no small measure from Benedict and the monastic movement.

Today we do not know what the postmodern world will become or who will define its nature. That is why the struggle of competing forces to define its values has been referred to as a "cultural war." Our responsibility is to bring the values of our heritage to this struggle.

In the Benedictine tradition, there are two fundamental elements: to pray and to work. It is true that authentic hope is rooted in prayer and the ensuing trust in the promise of God's presence. It is equally true, however, that authentic hope must be coupled with work. We cannot do it alone; yet it will not happen without our intense efforts, without our bold action. We must enter the struggle that is now going on to shape the values of our post-modern culture. How should we approach our task?

The challenge is twofold: (1) we must seriously study the heritage and values that provide the foundational underpinnings of our nation; and (2) we must seriously study our contemporary cultures and determine what is helpful and what is harmful to human development.

If the monks of Medieval Europe turned swamps into rich pastures and wastelands into flourishing centers of civilization, why not now on the threshold of the twenty-first century? The dialectic between faith and culture is of prime importance to an institution like Saint Vincent College, which is firmly rooted in the teachings of the Catholic faith and the 1500-year heritage of the Benedictine Order. Deepening the understanding of faith and culture is at the core of our educational mission.

The received wisdom of Western civilization and the best of America's heritage, from which this volume draws, teaches us that the well-being of the human community depends upon faith, freedom, and order. The insightful and accomplished thinkers herein call us to reflect seriously upon first principles for the revival of our age, and that is the hope in which I commend this reading to you.

ARCHABBOT DOUGLAS R. NOWICKI, O.S.B.
Chancellor, Saint Vincent College

1. *Institutionalizing the Counterculture*

HILTON KRAMER

THE topic of this volume presents us with a very tall order: to assess the state of the political order and culture at the present moment. It also signifies a very high hope to address the renewal of civilization at this particular moment. I tend myself to think of the immediate prospect as one in which we can, for the moment, hope to make an effort to retrieve some of the civilization we have lost before we can go on to think about the renewal of civilization. The particular subject I mean to address is the way the counterculture of the 1960s has been institutionalized in our political and cultural life. I want to describe some of the ground that has been lost, reflect upon some of the implications of those losses, and perhaps point to, in however modest a way, the ways in which we might begin to recover or retrieve some of the ground that has been lost to us.

I shall begin with some general observations on the subject of the political order and culture in the 1990s, and then go on to some specific examples — and also write from a personal perspective and experience as a writer, a journalist, and lately as a critic of the media. It is certainly one of the melancholy characteristics of political life in the 1990s — and not only in America but in what we have now come to think of as the whole developed world — that the gravest political issues confronting our societies are no longer susceptible to purely political solutions. This is a greater historical misfortune for us than is commonly understood, for when the political order is no longer capable of containing the really disruptive political forces that threaten it, we are likely to find ourselves — as we do more and more frequently today — having to deal with many questions that in happier times are properly thought to lie beyond

1

the providence of politics. To deal with those questions as political questions, we find ourselves having to think about such things as art and morals, education and sexuality, marriage and the family, even life and death, in largely political terms because our politics now requires us to do so.

For want of a better alternative, it is now our practice no matter what our political allegiance may be — whether we are radicals, liberals, conservatives, reactionaries, or some combination thereof — to regard such subjects as belonging to this mysterious realm we call culture. By this term, however, we no longer mean what we used to mean, we no longer mean what the word once signified when culture really stood for what we now are obliged to call *high* culture. We no longer mean high culture, though high culture may still be included in our use of the word culture if only for the purpose of deconstructing it and unmasking it for the many political meanings it may have. We certainly do not reserve the word culture for what Matthew Arnold had in mind in his famous formulation: ". . . culture being the pursuit of our total perfection by means of getting to know on all matters which most concern us the best which has been thought and said in the world." We may argue today about the exact date on which that use of the word culture lost its persuasive power for us. But there can be little argument about the role of the radical counterculture in the 1960s in effectively eradicating whatever remained of that once proud and honorific conception of culture. Since that really fateful turning point in our history, it has become commonplace for the word culture to denote every kind of thing imaginable. We speak of a racing car culture, a drug culture, a culture of classical music, the culture of rap music, the culture of garbage disposal — and considering some of the things that are considered as culture today, I suppose garbage is not too strong a term for some of the things that are proposed to supplant what Arnold called, ". . . the best which has been thought and said in the world."

Culture was always perhaps a less precise and more open-ended concept than Arnold and the Arnoldians felt any need to acknowledge. And when the time came to challenge the Arnoldian conception of culture, there was already at hand an alternative idea of culture ready to take its place — a more leveling idea of culture waiting to be appropriated, the idea of culture fostered by the social sciences. The Arnoldian conception of culture was still tethered to an idea of virtue that derived from both Christian tradition and Classical learning. It was an idea of culture that, for better or worse, was meant to serve as a secular alternative to or substitute for religious faith as a source of what we now call "values." The idea of culture fostered by the social sciences, however, was and is something quite different. It is strictly an instrumentalist idea of culture that in principle abjures all inherited judgments about art and morals, marriage and the family, life and death, and all the most imperative issues that govern our experience. It abjures all inherited judgments in order to demystify them as mere social constructions masquerading as venerable traditions and renders them susceptible to deconstruction. From the perspective of this more instrumentalist and deconstructivist idea of culture — which is the culture we admire today — there are no sacred traditions to be honored, no inherited standards to be transmitted to future generations. There are only competing interests vying for power and preferment. It is a radically debased version of this idea of culture that we have inherited from the counterculture of the 1960s — a conception of culture that consigns the discussion of all the most fundamental questions of life to the arena of political debate, exempting none. What we have come to mean by culture, in other words, is the institutionalized version of the 1960s counterculture that now governs — and indeed misgoverns — at nearly every level of our society. It is the force that has corrupted our morals, destroyed our universities, ruined our public schools, coopted the churches, debased our popular entertainments, subverted our arts institutions, debauched the media, and — let's see, have I left anything out? — Ah yes, and with the election of Bill Clinton, has given the nation its first countercultural President and First Lady.

It is worth recalling what the characteristic attributes of the counterculture were when it first emerged in the sixties. It has turned out that the antiwar movement in the sixties, although a highly dramatic historical occurrence at the time, was not really the basic issue of the counterculture. If it had been, the counterculture would have disappeared when the government stopped drafting draft-age men. But the counterculture did not disappear, it prospered even in the aftermath of the war. It was one of the fundamental tenets (perhaps *the* fundamental tenet) of the counterculture that all hierarchies — social hierarchies, moral hierarchies, aesthetic hierarchies, all hierarchies that suggested that some things were more perfect than others, some things represented a greater achievement than others, some things represented a higher value than others — that all hierarchies were inherently evil, authoritarian, oppressive, and therefore undemocratic. There was a fierce animus against the whole idea of hierarchy, particularly in the

3

realm of literature, the arts, and what was still regarded as high culture. The very notion of making a distinction between high culture and low culture, or what came to be known as popular culture, or what the Marxist sociologists used to call mass culture — the very idea of making a distinction between high culture and popular culture was suddenly looked upon as politically and morally invidious, and therefore had to be destroyed in our schools, in our criticism, in our cultural life. The distinction between high and low culture has not only been eliminated but has been supplanted at many levels of graduate and undergraduate education by the aggrandizement of popular culture at the expense of high culture. More liberal arts students today study the history of the movies and fewer study Shakespeare's plays than ever before in the history of higher education in America or indeed in any country in the world. This attack on hierarchy, this campaign to establish a kind of parity between high culture and low culture — but not a real parity because all the advantage, of course, is being conferred upon popular culture — was devastating in itself. But it was also accompanied in the counterculture by a parallel attack on the kind of moral hierarchy that had previously governed the conduct of sexual life. As a consequence, there was unleashed upon our society a sexual revolution the consequences of which we are still desperately and not very effectively attempting to cope with.

There was a countercultural attack in still another realm, and it has proved to be irreversible: an attack on language itself — a debasement of common speech, a debasement of language both spoken and written at every level of society. This is now something we have, reluctantly, come to accept as commonplace. I overhear conversations among people at museum exhibitions that consist of language that would have embarrassed the illiterate fishermen in the town where I grew up in Massachusetts when I was a boy. Now you can hear some of it on television. I do not follow the Internet, but I understand it is filled with such language. In the corridor of any grade school, any high school, any college, the debasement of common speech is pervasive and headlong, and as it gets worse and worse, it is remarkably seldom that it is even remarked upon. We have now become inured to it, our ears and our moral sensibilities have somehow learned to cope with it.

A further destructive impulse of the counterculture we have inherited — and, as you might say, domesticated and failed categorically to defend ourselves against — is what is commonly known as the drug culture. Quite apart from the consequences in the realm of crime, there

4

are also the moral consequences of the drug culture, which unfit its victims to live any sort of moral or useful life beyond a certain point. I was particularly conscious recently of the amazing eulogies and obituaries lavished on Allen Ginsberg when he died at the age of seventy, because Allen Ginsberg was one of the principal figures who made drugs fashionable in this country. Those of us who are old enough can remember those great slogans about dropping out and turning on: that was one of the Allen Ginsberg's war cries, and he was amazingly effective in enlisting disciples, most of them very young. It was a small group of writers advocating moral degeneracy in the name of personal emancipation that introduced the great popularity and acceptability of drugs into our society in the sixties. Its pervasive influence on more vulnerable segments of our society among the uneducated has had devastating consequences.

You would not find, in any of the obituaries of and eulogies of Allen Ginsberg in the mainstream press, any reference to that particular legacy of his discussed in any detail. Mainstream culture in this country — and it is another example of the debasement it has suffered — has made its peace with the legacy of that drug culture, however much we may in Washington and in other places spend huge sums of money and arrest this or that drug kingpin. We all know that our society has proved that it lacks the moral fortitude to address this menace, which is not only a physical and social menace, but a moral menace. We know that our society lacks the will and the fortitude to really deal with it.

It has followed from the attack on hierarchy — from the sexual revolution that was part of the attack on the hierarchy of the family as an institution and especially the middle-class family — that marriage and the family became targets for deconstruction by the counterculture. Those of us who are old enough to have been witnesses to this devastating transformation in American life in the sixties and seventies, who can judge it from a perspective of an earlier period, found the most astonishing, and in some respects the most melancholy, aspect of this attack on the family that took place under the banner of the counterculture, to be not only the way it influenced the children who dropped out of those middle-class families but also the way it influenced parents to emulate, so often, the behavior of their drop-out children. In this radical transformation of middle-class life, the collapse of the family as an institution was a collaborative effort between middle-class parents and middle-class children. And these middle-class exponents of the

5

counterculture have passed on their radicalism as a legacy to the people at the bottom of our society who are even more vulnerable and less capable of dealing with the moral consequences than the middle-class itself. In the town where I live in Connecticut, a very prosperous town filled with people who are in the advertising business and work in Wall Street and other highly paid professions, you could see from one week to the next, one month to the next, this radical change in the people getting on the train to go to their jobs in Manhattan in the morning. In September they might be wearing a three-piece suit, but by December they were in jeans. In September their hair was cut quite short; by spring it was down to their shoulders. You could see the beards, the sneakers, the affected unwashed look, which at times was not merely affected. It was a real revolution in middle-class life. These parents in their forties and fifties suddenly felt that their children should be taken as models in the way they might transform their own lives. Of course, this meant the breakup of marriages, the increase of divorce, and everything that followed from that.

It was impossible for education to escape the evil consequences of all of the assaults that I have enumerated here. It may be in the end, when we come to make long-term assessment of the damage the counterculture has caused us, that the destruction of the public educational system in this country will be found the most devastating consequence of all. For the moment, this breakdown of the public schools certainly looks like the most irreversible consequence of the counterculture. That was another destructive transformation people of my own generation were able to witness firsthand. In 1966 and '67 my wife and I were living in Brooklyn in an area that was contiguous to the Bedford Stuyvesant section, where the movement for what was called "community control" of public schools in New York had its origin. The idea of community control was that each local community should be empowered to appoint school officials, to govern the school budget, to determine the curriculum, and so on. It has to be understood by those who are unfamiliar with the history of public school education in New York City that, until the Sixties, the educational standard of the public school system in New York City was one of the highest in the nation. I know that when I went to Syracuse University as an undergraduate — and I had had a wonderful public school education in Massachusetts, an education that determined my whole career as a reader and as a writer — I felt tremendously intimidated by the students I met at Syracuse who came out of the New York City high schools. They knew so much more, they had to work so much harder, they were trained in a much more disciplined manner. Some of them came from the elite schools like the High School for Music and Art and the Bronx High School of Science, but many of them came from high schools that were not regarded as elite schools, and the standard was tremendous. City College, which attracted so many of the children of immigrants because it was a free undergraduate program, had standards as high as any of the greatest private universities in the country at that time. Today City College is a scene of devastation. Under the direct impact of the politics of the counterculture, the college surrendered to the idea of open enrollment, breaking down the distinctions between people who are equipped to do college work and people who are not. The attack on an idea of hierarchy had that kind of specific consequence, and suddenly City College went from being an institution where you could really acquire an intellectually elite education to become a kind of high school for intellectually retarded students. The grade schools collapsed too, and as a consequence of this breakdown the whole problem of living in New York and sending your kids to school induced a great wave of moral panic in middle-class and working-class parents. There are now parents in New York at every level of the economic and social scale who are working almost beyond their physical capacity to find some way to pay for their children to avoid going to public school. Many of these parents, particularly children of newly arrived immigrants, will work at two or three jobs a day to send their kids to parochial school — not only for the standard of education they know their children will receive there but for the protection their children will receive against all the evil things that are out there in the public school and in the public school classrooms.

It is unquestionably the effect of the influence of the counterculture that we are now living with in our mainstream culture in the 1990s. Those young barbarians, who were banging on the university doors demanding their "rights" back in the sixties, are now sitting in the president's office. They are the deans, they are the tenured professors, they are the people presiding over the foundations — Ford, Rockefeller, MacArthur — they are the people who are the curators in our museums, the people who are making decisions at Random House and Knopf and Simon and Shuster about which books are to be published, and indeed those are the people who are putting out the *New York Times* every day. I worked for the *New York Times* for seventeen years; now I only write about it. Of course the paper that I worked for from 1965 to 1982 was very far from being perfect. But compared to what has befallen the *Times* in recent years, the paper I worked for was a very different publication. In 1976, for example, I wrote an article called "The Blacklist and the Cold War." The occasion for it was the publication of Lillian Hellman's scandalously mendacious memoirs called *Scoundrel Time*, which had a rousingly favorable introduction by Gary Wills; the movie called *The Front*, in which Woody Allen starred as someone who fronted for a blacklisted writer in the television business; and a documentary movie called *The Hollywood Ten*, about the ten Hollywood screenwriters who had taken the Fifth Amendment and refused to say whether or not they were Communists. (Of course, all of them had been Communists.)

These were not the usual subjects that I wrote about for the *New York Times*. My principle task there was writing about art. I was the chief art critic and the art news editor. But I had a wonderful editor there at that time, Arthur Gelb. Arthur, insofar as he thought about politics at all, was a kind of old-fashioned New York liberal. More important to him than politics, however, was a very vivid sense of what in journalism constitutes an event, a journalistic event. As soon as he had seen an advanced screening of the movie *The Front*, he came to see me and said, "There's a movie I want you to see and I think you might consider writing an article for the *Times* around it." I had worked very hard during all of my years at the *Times* to avoid becoming a movie critic. So I said, "Well, I'm not going to review movies." He said, "No, I'm not asking you to review movies. You go to see this movie. There will be some other things that will connect with it, and see if there is an article in it." And he was right because, by an accident of fate, I was very closely acquainted with many old-time Communist writers, some who had reformed, some who had not. I had acquired quite an extensive understanding of the Communist movement in this country, particularly its literary and cultural aspects. So I wrote this piece called, "The Blacklist and the Cold War." It was very long and it started on the front page of the Sunday arts section. It was the first time I ever showed something to my wife that I had written for the *Times* before I turned it in. I knew it was going to cause a tremendous uproar. My wife was born and raised in New York, and pretty much knew what the score was about the Communist party. She read the article and said, "Well, I think it's wonderful, but I think we should leave town for a couple of weeks." And there was a tremendous uproar. It was said to have brought in the largest volume of mail that any piece in the Sunday arts section had ever brought in. For weeks afterwards the letters poured in. Some of them were quite remarkable, some from people who today would be very embarrassed to be reminded of the enthusiasm they showed for my article — Arthur Schlesinger, for example, Alfred Kazin among others. Arthur Schlesinger wrote: "For every American under the age of forty, this should be mandatory reading."

I cite this article on "The Blacklist and Cold War" because it was rare for me to write about political subjects in the *Times*. In writing it, I had total support from everybody; from the publisher on down there was never a whisper that maybe my article should be toned down. That article today would be totally unpublishable in the *New York Times*, where everything — the way the headlines are written, the way the stories are written, the way the photos are chosen, the size of the photos, where they are displayed, how Page One is made up, even the sports pages — is now politically determined by the publisher and his thought police. The *Times*, alas, is still an indispensable paper. But now it is a torment to read, particularly if you know anything about the subjects they are writing about. But this is largely true across the entire spectrum of the liberal media today; *Time* magazine, the *New Yorker* — these mainstream journalistic institutions have been totally transformed by the values, practices, and general ethos of the counterculture.

It is for all of these reasons that, before we can speak of "renewal," we have to speak of retrieval. What we have witnessed in my adult lifetime is a phenomenon that certain writers of the past have hinted at and correctly predicted in small ways. None that I know of predicted a disaster on anything like the scale that has actually occurred. What we have seen happen is that what the political Left in this country lost on the field of political battle, it has more than regained in the culture wars. It is for this reason that I think we have to learn from the Left that many of our political battles cannot be won unless we can win back the ground we lost in the culture wars. It is not that electoral politics do not count. I am not saying that. But a fundamental retrieval of the intellectual, artistic, and moral territory that has been lost under the assault of the counterculture is now the crucial task. This is fundamental not only to a renewal of civilization but to a restoration of the kind of politics that allows us to separate politics from all those other questions we have come to think of as cultural.

2. Cultural Origins of Politics: The Modern Imagination of Escape

CLAES G. RYN

To assess realistically the prospects for renewal of our old civilization we need to consider carefully the origins of our troubles and the preconditions for overcoming them. The troubles are widely blamed on so-called "modernity." In that respect, traditionalists and postmodernists are in agreement. A problem is that both groups typically define "modernity" in a reductionistic manner, as if the modern world were moving in a single general direction. Modernity actually contains opposing potentialities. It includes, among other things, the continuing and evolving influence of ancient beliefs and practices. Sometimes modernity is arbitrarily assumed to be ending or to have been superseded. Yet what is called postmodernism is easily shown to share important elements with what it is believed to be supplanting. For example, it has much in common with a figure like Jean-Jacques Rousseau.

Although the complexity of historical reality must be kept in mind, one may, for certain analytical purposes, usefully isolate currents of thought, imagination, and morality that bear a marked family resemblance and that can be described as distinctively modern, as distinguished from "classical" or "medieval." The purpose here is to identify and examine one particular cultural dynamic within the modern world that has been a powerful source of change in the last two centuries and that is an important origin of our current difficulties. The aim in analyzing that dynamic is to indicate how we might extricate ourselves from problems it has created.

The cultural force in question has profoundly changed the way in which Western man sees himself and the opportunities of human existence. It had gained sufficient power more than two centuries ago to begin transforming societies. The dynamic has manifested itself somewhat differently according to time and place, but its basic characteristic pattern has remained the same, and it continues to affect Western society. Understanding this cultural force is a key to understanding the history of the last two hundred years and the social crisis in which we find ourselves today. The following analysis will suggest the great importance of this force but is not intended to deny the significance of other formative influences.

In current academic debates modernity is generally associated with the Enlightenment and rationalism. That these have profoundly affected the modern world is beyond dispute. What needs to be better understood is that we move closer to the heartbeat of modernity if we look behind its *ideas* to the kind of imagination they express. What is replacing the classical and Christian outlook in the West is certainly a new *Weltanschauung*, one often rationalistic in appearance, but we miss its main source of power if we focus narrowly on abstract ideas. What most deeply shapes modern man and guides even his more strictly philosophical efforts is a new way of *imagining* the world. Examining the imaginative basis of theoretical formulations is always important to discerning their meaning, but in the case of the dynamic here explored, the imaginative component is prominent and especially illuminating. It is in the arts that we find some of the best evidence regarding the nature of the evolution of Western society in the last two hundred years. The transformation of the imagination most relevant here is intimately connected with a transformation of the moral life, so that we may refer to the dynamic in question as moral-imaginative.

We look in vain for a historical turning point, after which it might be said that this new cultural trend had acquired decisive influence. The old classical and Christian outlook is deeply rooted and has not entirely disappeared even today. Neither can we point to particular individuals in the modern world whose personalities are entirely clear-cut embodiments of the new moral-imaginative momentum. All human beings contain both old and new. Much of the neurosis of contemporary society is intrinsic to the cultural dynamic under investigation, but additional anxiety and confusion come from individuals harboring not only it but other personality traits with which it is incompatible.

To establish what is distinctive to this moral-imaginative impetus, let us recall a few prominent characteristics of classical and Christian man. These may perhaps, for convenience's sake, be called "pre-modern," "classical," or "religious." It goes without saying that Greco-Roman civilization was very different in important respects from Christianity, but as one contemplates what is now replacing them both, one is struck rather by what they have in common regarding the understanding of human nature and society.

Premodern man, especially Christian man, had modest expectations of life. The Greeks thought it possible to elevate human existence through effort, especially moral-intellectual effort, but the Delphic admonition to know thyself included a reminder that man is not a god. What humans are able to achieve is limited by ignorance and other flaws. Wisdom, said Socrates, is knowing how little you know. Christianity stressed original sin. Due to man's fallen state, life on earth is inevitably full of trials and tribulations. For St. Augustine, happiness was possible only through divine grace and was reserved largely for the life to come. In emphasizing the ravages of sin, he seemed at times to discount the higher possibilities of human existence. St. Thomas and others put more stress on the potential for worldly perfection, but sin continued to limit man's capacity. Conscience mercilessly exposed man's moral weaknesses, calling for repentance.

Given the awareness of sin and the inclination to be self-critical, religious man did not regard suffering as unexpected or even undeserved. According to St. Augustine, sinful human beings had no reason to be indignant about such misfortunes as bad government. Who were they to complain? Feeling himself not undeserving of misery or damnation, the Christian considered such well-being and happiness as came his way as examples of divine grace, reasons for gratitude.

If premodern man felt acutely his own weaknesses, it was partly because he measured himself by high moral standards. To compound his burden, he tended to blame himself for problems around him. His moral shortcomings were his own, and he knew that no one but himself could improve his character. He should strain to the utmost to do so. And even if he made some progress, plenty of remaining imperfections would require yet more effort. Christians believed that moral-spiritual betterment was possible only by divine grace, but they also felt a deep personal obligation to make the best of their own lives and to shoulder responsibility for neighbor.

We turn now to the kind of person who exhibits the mentioned modern moral-imaginative dynamic. Although modernity contains other and contrasting elements, it may be permissible here to call that person simply "modern man." His demeanor is very different from that of premodern man. Far from discounting the opportunities of a worldly existence, this person entertains great expectations. Francis Bacon was only one of the first to believe in endless progress. He thought that, with the disappearance of old superstitions and a full application of the methods of experimental science, a vastly improved human existence was possible. The Enlightenment extended these expectations. The hope for a new and better world was not necessarily based on faith in science and reason. The most fundamental longing, discernible behind scientism itself, was for a basic transformation of human existence, for a great liberation, expansion, and deepening, making life infinitely more satisfying. Rousseau is but an early and prominent example of one who believed that classical and Christian civilization was based on a profound misconception and who also believed that the resulting oppression can be ended and mankind achieve a new, superior existence.

Modern man does not regard a good life as an undeserved gift. He is more likely to see it as an entitlement. Human beings, so it is asserted, have rights. The "natural rights of man" proclaimed by such theorists as Locke and Rousseau have been made more elaborate and specific in our own century by the United Nations. For taking the trouble to be born, human beings have rights to food, housing, health care, and so forth. There has been no announcement of corresponding duties.

Although demanding his rights, modern man is placing no particular demands on his own person. He is not inclined to see anything wrong with self. In the words of that familiar and reassuring slogan, "I'm OK, and you're OK." Rousseau proclaimed the goodness of man already in the eighteenth century, dismissing the doctrine of original sin as an affront to human nature. What is to blame for life's deep and numerous disappointments is not some flaw or perversity within man or nature but oppressive, distorting social institutions and conventions. The remedy, Rousseau argues, is for humanity to cast off the chains that harness its goodness.

We come here to a great problem facing modern man. With all his rights and his expectation of happiness, modern man must still live in the actual, historical world, and that world stubbornly remains the kind of place it has always tended to be. It is a mixture of ups and downs and full of imperfections. The difficulty for modern man, given his high hopes, is that he will experience the disappointments of a typical human life — for example, suffer his share of unfairness, economic pressures,

13

and illness. People close to him will die. Society will display greed, intolerance, ruthlessness, and crime. There may be wars or other painful disruptions. Much of life will be merely boring.

Having been led to expect a satisfying life, happiness even, modern man looks in vain for the world to deliver on the promise. His daily life is painted in grays and other drab colors, sometimes in black. Since his actual existence falls far short of his dreams, he begins to feel mistreated, cheated of his due. He soon nurses a grudge against life. He starts to suspect, and is encouraged by various ideologues to believe, that he is being deprived of his entitlement. Each new disappointment intensifies a feeling of betrayal. The time comes when society, indeed, all of human existence, appears to him unjust and oppressive, as if manipulated by sinister forces. Rousseau gives early and paradigmatic expression to the modern feeling of disappointment and defeat. Toward the end of his life he writes, "I was created to live, and I am dying without having lived." He bemoans having to give back to his maker a host of "frustrated good intentions."[1]

If we wish to understand the kind of outlook that is replacing classical and Christian civilization in the West, we do well to study Rousseau. He is convinced that he has seen more deeply into human nature than any previous observer and that he has discovered the secret of happiness. But the world, as it is, is unfriendly to that truth and to him personally as the messenger. Especially in his later autobiographical writings, Rousseau expresses his deep hurt at being wronged by life in general and at having been "cast out" from society, this despite his being, by his own account, "the most sociable and loving of men."[2] He has not been treated as he thinks befits a person of his deep insight and benevolence but feels himself the victim of cruel persecution. He takes to a paranoid extreme a dissatisfaction that was to become chronic in the modern world.

Starting in the eighteenth century, a mood of daydreaming develops into a richly orchestrated theme in the cultural life of the West. With others in tow, artists begin to escape from a world increasingly perceived as depressing. In poetry, fiction, painting, music, and so forth, one can study a growing tension between what exists and the desire for something more satisfying.

1. Jean-Jacques Rousseau, *Reveries of the Solitary Walker* (London and New York: Penguin Books, 1979), II, pp. 37-39.
2. Ibid., p. 27.

In the imagination, as opposed to the historical world in which we act, anything is possible; the dreamer can make for himself an existence according to his own wishes. Humanity has always sought relief in daydreams from the pressures or the boredom of the moment, but now daydreaming ceases to consist of short and transient flights of the imagination. It expands into elaborate and permanent visions of life transformed. Daydreaming becomes an almost constant reminder of the dreariness of daily existence, repeatedly luring the person away. The dream begins to overflow the all-too disappointing world where action takes place. The vision comes to seem more important — more real. Modern man would rather live in his dream than in the world of practice. What begins in the imagination of the artistically inclined soon is translated into schemes for transforming society. The imagination having revealed the possibility of a wonderful existence, why put up with life as it is?

The imagination becomes for Rousseau an almost constant refuge from what he considers the tyranny of society. He repeatedly recalls two months spent on an island in the lake of Bienne in Switzerland. It was, he writes, a time of "blissful indolence," of drifting according to the impulse of the moment. Now mankind is persecuting him and "will never let me return to this happy sanctuary," but he consoles himself that "at least they cannot prevent me from being transported there every day on the wings of imagination." "Were I there, my sweetest occupation would be to dream to my heart's content. Is it not the same thing to dream that I am there?" Starting a powerful trend in Western culture, Rousseau attributes greater significance to life lived in the imagination than to the world of action. "I abstain from acting," Rousseau writes.[3] He gets to taste real life in his pastoral reveries.

Modern man's flight from the concrete responsibilities of the here and now assumes different forms depending on the personality of the particular dreamer. What is common and constant is the longing for glorious fulfillment, and the theme: "Life would be so much better, if only . . ." "If only I could get a fresh start, real life would finally begin." Artists in the last two centuries have provided a sense of new possibilities, a change of scenery, transporting us, for example, to sunny fields, delightful picnics in the grass, glittering water, flowers, beaches, palm trees, mild breezes, lightly clad women. Who does not want to follow?

3. Ibid., pp. 90-91, 103.

CLAES G. RYN

Rousseau's notion of a new society is based on an imagined human past when life was truly "natural." That past bears little resemblance to what is known of human history. Significantly, the author of the immensely influential *Discourse on the Origins of Inequality* tells his readers in one of the opening paragraphs that his "investigations" into the past "should not be taken for historical truths, but only for hypothetical and conditional reasonings." He writes, "Let us therefore begin by putting aside all the facts, for they have no bearing on the question."[4] Rousseau's readers are invited to change their view of man and society in the light of an imaginative construction of the past that is unencumbered by demands for accuracy and respect for actual human experience. Uncomfortable facts must not interfere with beguiling possibilities.

Rousseau's deep alienation from existing society permeates all his writing. Already in the *First Discourse* he attacks the "vile and deceitful uniformity" that condemns man to "perpetual constraint." Everywhere society suppresses naturalness. "Without ceasing, politeness makes demands, propriety gives orders; without ceasing, common customs are followed, never one's own lights."[5] Such comments are indistinguishable from Rousseau's ubiquitous autobiographical theme. In the words of the *Reveries of the Solitary Walker:* "I have never been truly fitted for social life, where there is nothing but irksome duty and obligation."[6] Happiness is possible only if the individual can be freed from burdensome restraints and live according to the impulse of the moment. He writes of a short period of happiness in his youth: "I was perfectly free, or better than free because I was subject only to my own affections and did only what I wanted to do." He remembers with joy "when I was myself, completely myself, unmixed and unimpeded, and when I can genuinely claim to have lived."[7] Since being "unmixed" and free of all restraint is out of the question in the world of action known to man, Rousseau has constructed the sharpest possible contrast between his vision of happiness and what now exists.

The new society about which Rousseau dreams will not receive its cohesion from difficult and protracted moral struggle and self-dis-

4. Jean-Jacques Rousseau, *Second Discourse,* in *The Basic Political Writings* (Indianapolis: Hackett, 1987), p. 38.
5. Rousseau, *First Discourse, Basic Writings,* p. 4.
6. Rousseau, *Reveries of the Solitary Walker,* p. 103.
7. Ibid., pp. 153-54.

cipline on the part of citizens. That notion belongs to an ancient but wholly mistaken conception of human nature. The political order that he envisions will flow spontaneously from man's true nature once society has been cleansed of traditional structures and refounded on the basis of equality. Liberated, "unimpeded" nature will then shape society, as once it formed the happy but primitive state of nature. It will give the people a common purpose, a "general will." True popular rule is incompatible with constitutionalism. As the spontaneous force of nature, the general will can manifest itself only in uninhibited freedom.

Before illustrating further the modern mood of daydreaming, it should be underscored that of course humans have always sought solace in the imagination. It is hard to be always handling the pressures and responsibilities of life. There is a time and even a need for relaxation. We look out the window, think ahead to dinner with a special friend, take some time off from work, have a drink. We take little vacations from ordinary life. But then, back we go to our obligations, perhaps refreshed and reinvigorated. In the eighteenth and nineteenth centuries, escape from the present ceases for many to be a brief interlude and becomes a steady accompaniment of daily life. The daydream becomes the vantage from which to judge existence.

In all of the arts we may study modern man's deepening disgust with things as they are and his desire for radical relief. One of the best literary examples of the modern moral-imaginative dynamic is the central figure in Gustave Flaubert's novel *Madame Bovary* (1857). Flaubert tells the story of Emma, a young pretty woman who marries Charles, a physician. They live in small-town northeastern France. She has long been a reader of romantic novels, which have fed a dreamy personality. Charles is not the kind of dashing person that is depicted in her novels, but she married him willingly, and he loves and is utterly devoted to her.

Still, Emma feels from the very start that her married life does not satisfy her deepest longing. Charles tries in every way to please her, yes; he has steady character, and the townspeople like him, yes. But she finds him plodding, unimaginative, stolid. He passed his medical examinations only with difficulty. He practices very cautious medicine, afraid as he is of killing his patients. In comparison with dreams that begin to flood her mind, Charles and her life in general are a growing disappointment. He is of a piece with the stifling provincial life that surrounds her. Charles and the local yokels are an affront to her fine sensibilities. How very different life might have been. Soon she is thinking about "meeting some other man." She imagines what the husbands of her old friends at school must be like. Why is Charles so much less? He "might have been handsome, witty, distinguished, attractive, as, doubtless, were all the men her friends from the convent had married." While she is stuck with Charles in a rural town, they are undoubtedly living thrilling lives. "In the city, with the street noises, the hum of the theaters, and the lights of the ballroom, they were living lives in which the heart expands, in which the senses blossom. But her life was as cold as an attic with northern exposure, and boredom, that silent spider, was spinning its web in all the dark corners of her heart."[8]

Emma exhibits just the moral-imaginative disposition that, in one form or other, would permeate Western culture. As Flaubert's novel describes her: "Everything that immediately surrounded her, the dull countryside, imbecilic petty-bourgeois people, the mediocrity of exis- tence, seemed to her an exception in the world, an unusual accident in which she found herself trapped, while beyond it the immense world of happiness and passion extended itself as far as the eye could see." In her imagination the world beyond, represented by Paris, seems to her "something sublime" — a "world of ambassadors," "gleaming par- quet floors," "salons paneled with mirrors," "vast intrigues," "dresses with bustles," and on and on.[9]

The more Emma lives in her daydream, the more darkly disap- pointed she becomes when Charles appears. The greater her desire to escape, the deeper her disgust with actual life; and the deeper the alienation, the greater the need to flee yet again. Precisely because of her hopes for consummate fulfillment, the imperfections of the present fill her with bitterness. Even Charles's loving kindnesses become intol- erable. His belief that he is pleasing her seems "an imbecilic insult." "Was he not the obstacle to all happiness, the cause of all this misery, the sharp buckle, as it were, of the intricate strap that was binding her on all sides?" Emma's sense of life is that of myriad modern individuals: "At one and the same time she wanted to die and to live in Paris."[10]

The rest of the novel need not be summarized here. Emma looks to other men for fulfillment. What should be added is that, contrary to the predisposition of an earlier Western personality type, it does not occur to Emma to have modest expectations or to blame herself for her

8. Gustave Flaubert, *Madame Bovary* (New York: Signet, 1979), p. 63.
9. Ibid., pp. 75-76.
10. Ibid., pp. 118, 77.

misery. She looks everywhere except self for the source of her unhappiness. Her lover Rodolphe, a local squire, is more calculating and cynical than she has yet become, but in voicing his resentment against society he is also expressing hers and that of countless others in the modern world. He says to Emma: "Doesn't this conspiracy of society revolt you? Is there one ounce of feeling that it does not condemn? The most noble instincts, the purest emotions, are persecuted and slandered, and if two poor souls finally meet, everything is organized so that they cannot unite."[11]

Is then Emma entirely to blame for her own misery? Or is she the victim of a misbegotten marriage and a stultifying society? It is not necessary to determine the precise extent of Emma's culpability to recognize her moral-imaginative inclination as an impediment to making the best of life as it is. Even if it is granted that Emma finds herself in a less-than-desirable marriage, despite society's and her own original judgment, and that her social environment is uninspiring or worse, these factors by themselves do not adequately explain her growing despondency. It is her own personality that makes it virtually inevitable. Disinclined to accepting and coping with disappointment and to seizing chances for happiness available to her within the traditional setting that she has chosen, she will be satisfied only with a life that places no obstacles in the way of glorious satisfaction. She fluctuates between dreams of euphoric, permanent fulfillment and dejection in the face of what exists just around her. It is in the very nature of her desire for liberation that it should be defeated by life, whatever her actual circumstances.

It might seem far-fetched and paradoxical to connect the modern dream of a marvelous new world with cynicism and bitterness. And yet the interplay between these seeming opposites form the essence of the moral-imaginative dynamic under examination. On the one hand, modern man uses his imagination to an unparalleled extent to evade the hard and painful task of moral responsibility up close: he always dreams of happiness on entirely different, far easier terms, of a life that can satisfy all of his pent-up desires. As long as he indulges this imagination he is intoxicated, inspired. But just as often the dark side of life seems to him to be all there is, and he despairs of happiness. Bitterness and pessimism torture him.

The coming together of these two moods should not seem para-

11. Ibid, p. 150.

doxical or puzzling. On the contrary, they are inseparable, two sides of one and the same modern personality. That personality moves for fully intelligible reasons between euphoria and dark depression. The person is up, or he is down, rarely in-between, and the swings tend to get more violent. This is because every romantic-utopian flight of imagination aggravates resentment against the world as it is. And the more disappointing the actual world appears, the greater is the desire for imaginative solace. Modern man becomes — in fact, he makes himself — a manic-depressive, using that term philosophically. To see how and why this is the case, one need only ask: who *is* the cynic, that person who sneers at life and suspects all others of having the foulest motives? Who is he but the disillusioned, repeatedly disappointed dreamer, a person who bears life a deep grudge for defeating his cherished longings? The artificial exhilaration created by the romantic imagination must inevitably bring on grim resentment. Rousseau is as usual paradigmatic, going from euphoric raptures to paranoid fits. Persons of similar temperament may tearfully sympathize with his suffering, as has been the case with many generations of readers. From the vantage of an older Western moral and aesthetical sensibility his pain looks rather self-inflicted and even well-deserved.

Unfortunately, these mood-swings have meant suffering not only for a few beautiful souls of literary orientation. They have become the hallmarks of a new culture, which has given rise to new ideas, including political ideologies. One does not have to look far for examples of the manic-depressive temperament in politics. Rousseau himself sets the pattern. The manic or utopian strain in his political thought comes through in his vision of the release of man's true nature and the transformation of life. His famous phrase "man is born free" suggests the possibility of a glorious new society, but the very next words about man's current predicament express the depressive dimension of Rousseau's ideology: "everywhere he is in chains."[12]

Convinced of the purity of his own heart, Rousseau becomes ever more convinced that only a conspiracy can explain his being subjected to endless suffering. He writes of himself that, although he is the best of men, he has been "cast out by all the rest." Exhibiting in advanced form the paranoia that later appears in Emma, Rodolphe, and so many others, Rousseau writes of his fellow men: "With all the ingenuity of

12. Jean-Jacques Rousseau, *The Social Contract*, in *Basic Writings* (Indianapolis: Hackett, 1987), p. 141.

hate they have sought out the cruellest torture for my sensitive soul."[13] It is Rousseau against an unfeeling, perverse world, as it is Emma against the constrictions of society.

In the French Revolution the manic-euphoric mood is manifest in the vision of a future society: "freedom, equality, and brotherhood." The depressive side concerns, among other things, the vile oppression of traditional French society. And because the monarchy and the aristocracy conspire against the oppressed, the guillotine must do its work.

In our own century communism has inspired its followers with the dream of a coming classless and stateless society in which human beings will finally develop the full range of their potential in perfect freedom. The drudgery of boring, mechanical, routinized work will have been overcome. But that wonderful future stands in sharp contrast to a darkly depressing present: ever-worsening exploitation, greed, cruel competition, immiserization, and alienation. So abominable is capitalist society that revolution is inevitable. In Marxism the conspirators against liberation are the owners of the means of production, the bourgeoisie. Needless to say, realizing the dream will necessitate suffering. Something so great cannot be born without birth-pangs. The communists turn ruthlessly against opponents. "If you want to make an omelette, you have to break some eggs," says Lenin. The paranoia that forms an integral part of the manic-depressive dynamic leads to the discovery of enemies not just among the capitalists. Stalin comes to see enemies of the people everywhere, even within the Communist Party. Never-resting vigilance against counterrevolution sends millions to the Gulag. As is typical of the manic-depressive ideological movements, their inspiring vision is all benevolent concern for the downtrodden, but their practice is almost unbelievable inhumanity.

National Socialism rejects the egalitarian assumptions of Rousseau and Marx, but it seeks its own kind of liberation from what exists historically, and it follows the same manic-depressive pattern. Its inspiring vision, its great Daydream, is the Thousand Year Reich, the future reign of the Aryans. The Aryans will inspire a national renewal, restore racial purity, and dominate inferior peoples. But the present situation is radically different, depressingly so. The German-Nordic race and culture are everywhere being polluted. We come here to the Nazi version of the sinister conspiracy. Behind all the perversity and

---

13. Rousseau, *Reveries of the Solitary Walker*, I, p. 27.

decadence is an inferior but cleverly scheming alien race. Again, the paranoia permits no respite in rooting out enemies.

One could go on at length illustrating how the modern moral-imaginative dynamic has affected various aspects of society. The "split" personality of modern man manifests itself across the religious, moral, intellectual, aesthetical, and political landscape. Often it is masked or moderated somewhat by lingering older attitudes and beliefs, but it is ultimately incompatible with the old classical or Christian view of the human condition.

Western man has not learnt much from all of this evidence, not even from the great man-made disasters of this century, including two world wars and the extermination of many millions of human beings, disasters which are substantially related to the moral-imaginative disposition under discussion. We remain strongly attracted to the temperament in question. We continue, for example, to attribute moral superiority to people with ambitious and allegedly beautiful visions for remaking human existence. Despite that fact it is often asserted today that we are entering upon an era of greater realism and sobriety and that we are moving beyond ideology. Intellectual strife will peter out, assert many intellectuals, for we have finally discovered the form of sociopolitical existence whose superiority and salvific powers will soon be recognized by all: democracy. But no special powers of discernment are necessary to recognize here another ideology — call it democratism — and to recognize yet another manifestation of the modern daydream. Especially the more dogmatic forms of democratism reveal a familiar pattern: "The world would be such a wonderful place, if only . . ." Remaining obstacles to a democratic world must be removed. Away with all conspirators!

Among those who shape our culture it seems as common as ever to deny in one form or other the real preconditions of social harmony and individual happiness and to indulge the imagination of escape. Postmodernism, for instance, is typically shot through with a Rousseauistic desire for liberation. Because this general pattern remains strong in universities, entertainment, media, and the arts, we probably face worsening troubles.

What then could make a difference? The imagination is pulling us away from that without which no real and lasting improvement is possible — a revitalization of character and a renewed willingness to confront the self and the world as they are. Since it is the imagination, in service to moral lassitude, that is luring Western man away from the urgent but demanding responsibilities that are personal and immediate, is the solution to try to suppress the imagination? Plato took a dim view of the imagination and trusted only what he called reason. Puritan and other iconoclastic Christians condemned imaginative distractions, preferring the pure word of God. Modern rationalists advise that we rely on reason alone. But reason, whatever we mean by that term, does not operate in an imaginative vacuum. It is oriented by an underlying imaginative view of human existence.

Rationalism is usually a close ally of escapism, in spite of the claim of many rationalists that they are sober critics of illusion. From the time of Francis Bacon one may study how dreams for the transformation of society and the world blend with a strong belief in human intelligence and science. For example, a utopian desire for change has often sought expression in a belief in social engineering. The inspiring vision, which is obviously marked by escapist imagination, subtly affects also the understanding of reason itself, producing a faith in Science as the solution to the problems of mankind. True, some rationalists scoff at the gullibility of utopianism. For them, real intellect is quick to unmask dreamy vision. But are not rationalists of that kind often romantics themselves, only romantics of the disillusioned, defeated kind? Is not their understanding of intellect colored by the cynicism of an imagination that is increasingly stuck in the depressive mode? Hiding behind the intellectualism of this type of rationalist is a deeply disappointed romantic who has come to expect only the worst from human nature. Efforts to improve life appear futile. No less than the utopian does the cynic feel himself excused from the kind of personal moral effort that begins with making the best of self and one's own circumstances. Both types of rationalists are unwilling to recognize the real limits and opportunities of man's historical existence.[14]

Ideas give conceptual expression to a basic intuition of what life is and can become. Really to change a person's mind means changing his imagination. What is needed today, on a large scale, are efforts to expose the modern imagination of daydreaming for what it is. For too long those who set the tone in our intellectual and cultural life have gotten away with presenting their panaceas and dreams of liberation

14. For a discussion of the connection between the imagination of "sentimental humanitarianism" and belief in science, see Irving Babbitt, *Literature and the American College* (Washington, D.C.: National Humanities Institute, 1986 [first published in 1908]).

as benevolent and noble. It is essential to expose their inhumane and potentially diabolical nature. Far from deserving admiration, these visions should fill us with foreboding. Democratism is no exception. At its core, the modern moral-imaginative dynamic is a willful evasion of the real terms of human existence, a neglect of our primary responsibilities as human beings. The longing for liberation often expresses an ominous drive for uninhibited power. That drive stands fully revealed in some who barely bother to deceive themselves regarding their innermost motives but advance their noble-sounding schemes for improving the world in a blatant, cynical pursuit of power.

But intellectual criticism, though indispensable, is insufficient. It is not possible to defuse escapist imagination with no imagination. This is the case whether the escape is predominantly of the utopian or the cynical variety. Human beings, including self-described rationalists, live in the end according to hopes and anxieties that formed in the imagination. It is their concreteness, their experiential texture that makes them powerful. What we cannot do without, therefore, is the non-escapist imagination, which vividly expresses the actual higher possibilities and the actual dangers of human existence. Truly great art is never didactic, but it attunes us to the real world and to acting within it. Without that kind of imagination, intellectuals claiming to remedy our present difficulties will merely spin abstractions that do little to wean us off our escapism; indeed, their ideas may be only a new version of the problem. For instance, much traditionalist-sounding theorizing today — advocating a return to "virtue," "justice," "values," and the like — is suffused with romantic avoidance of the historical world and provides a good example of the need for reorienting the imagination.[15]

The great art of the past sometimes reacted against degradations and indignities in the present, and it conveyed man's true humanity in some way, but it did not do so in a spirit of escape. It affirmed life's higher potential in acute awareness of the limits of our historical existence. The present arbiters of culture often do their best to discredit works of that kind, but such art can, if made accessible again, still have a cathartic effect.

15. For an extensive philosophical discussion of the epistemological issues of the argument here presented and the systematic definitions of key terms, see Claes G. Ryn, *Will, Imagination and Reason*, 2nd ed. (New Brunswick, N.J., and London: Transaction Publishers, 1997).

Yet our greatest need may be for art from our own time that speaks powerfully to our predicament. There is one problem: great art cannot be ordered up the way think tanks and foundations may order up policy studies, conferences, and research projects. Real art is a miracle, which may appear when and where we least expect it. But we need and wait for such miracles.

3. Christianity and the Spirit of the Age

JOYCE A. LITTLE

WILLIAM Butler Yeats, in his poem "The Second Coming," which seems more prophetic and is quoted more often with every passing year, spoke of how his sight was "troubled" by an image of "Spiritus Mundi," a rough beast "with lion body and the head of a man," slouching towards Bethlehem. More recently, Robert Bork has pointed out that this beast has found a new home, Gomorrah, towards which to slouch.

We know that the spirit of our age is, on one level at least, manifested by a desire, indeed even a demand, for, as Bork also notes, radical egalitarianism and radical individualism.[1] In fact, these two things are inseparable. The demand for unrestrained freedom of choice requires that the same range of choices be open to everyone. This, in turn, requires that all differences among human beings be minimized, trivialized, or eliminated, as the case may be. We cannot insist, for example, that the sexual differentiation between males and females is in any way substantive, because to do so would imply, indeed require, that in the very nature of things the range of choices open to a woman be different from the range of choices open to a man. But such a proposition is unacceptable to the cultural elites of our society, constituting, as they see it, a clear case of sexism.

All of this has produced an enormous transvaluation of all values, to borrow from Nietzsche, though not perhaps in quite the sense he meant or in what seems the most obvious sense today. It is obvious, for example, that a transvaluation of the value of such things as abortion,

---

1. Robert H. Bork, *Slouching Towards Gomorrah* (New York: ReganBooks, 1996), xiv.

26

homosexuality, and euthanasia is in process and has been for some time now. But this is not the most important sense in which the traditional way of viewing things has been overturned. It is but its symptom. More seriously, we have seen a transvaluation of whole sectors of our lives and an alarming reversal of the values we attach to those sectors.

In the traditional scheme of things, religion and morality were recognized to make absolute claims upon us. Religious and moral absolutes defined the bedrock of our personal lives and of our culture. Politics, on the other hand, was understood to have a *relative* value and to involve the acceptance of compromise. Today, these things are reversed. Religious and moral relativism are not only common but are thought to be essential to our freedom, freedom being understood as the right to do what one desires to do. How can one be bound to all of the Ten Commandments all of the time and still be free? From the point of view of modern man, the question answers itself.

At the same time, politics has become the arena in which the absolutes of modern life are established. Absolute tolerance for all points of view, all lifestyles, all forms of expression, is demanded. Political correctness will brook no exceptions to its rules. Radical egalitarianism and radical individualism demand that all choices be regarded as equally good. Hence the insistence that "the personal is political and the political is personal."

If one protests that the demand for absolute tolerance does not really seem to tolerate all points of view, one is told that the only views not tolerated are those views which are themselves intolerant. This is not consoling, however, when one reflects that all major religions and moralities are intolerant, to one degree or another, of those things they deem false or evil. Our new tolerance rules out of court at the outset almost everything that almost everyone believed prior to the advent of the modern world. And this new tolerance, we have now been told by the highest authority in the land, is in fact essential to that liberty guaranteed us by the Fourteenth Amendment to the Constitution. To cite the now famous (or infamous) "mystery passage" from *Planned Parenthood* v. *Casey:* "At the heart of liberty is the right to define one's own concept of existence, of meaning, of the universe and of the mystery of human life."

Because so many Americans seem willing to follow our cultural elites into the abyss of religious and moral relativism which even our Supreme Court now tells us is demanded by the Constitution, we have to ask ourselves how it is that so many people have been seduced by this new view of things, where all of this is leading, and what we might do about it.

The Destruction of the Contexts of Our Lives

How have so many been seduced and why are so many more on the path to that same seduction? By way of answering this, I would like to ask what all of the following have in common: O. J. Simpson, the movie *Mission: Impossible,* the Heaven's Gate cult whose members committed mass suicide, the folks who embrace cryogenics, and the folks who see in the cloning of human beings a boon to mankind? What all of them have in common is that they manifest the primary strategy by which the citizens of this country have been disarmed by the spirit of this age. That strategy is the stripping away or destruction of context.

Almost twenty years ago, George W. S. Trow wrote a book entitled *Within the Context of No Context,* in which he noted "the powerful urge that flowed into this century from the nineteenth century and is only now beginning to recede — the urge to shed any context perceived as inhibiting and in conflict with the possibility of personal satisfaction."[2] He targeted television as a medium which, by its very nature, destroys context. What television employs, he pointed out, is "the use of ad-hoc contexts. Just for the moment. We're here together, in a little house. It makes such good sense. Just for the moment."[3]

And that brings us to O. J. Simpson. Almost everyone who watched the slow-mo chase of Simpson in the Bronco across the freeways of L.A., and who attended to subsequent events and revelations about Simpson's private life, was taken aback by the revelations, even apart from the question of whether or not he had murdered two people. The O. J. Simpson we had come to know and love, on the gridiron, on the sidelines, in the broadcasting booth, in the commercials and movies, bore no resemblance to the man we got to know during those days and weeks following his arrest. The false context of television had given us a very distorted understanding of the man. And it was a shock.

Granted that television uses ad hoc contexts, those contexts also

2. George W. S. Trow, *Within the Context of No Context* (Boston/Toronto: Little, Brown and Company, 1978, 1980, 1981), p. 39.
3. Ibid., p. 28.

are not immune to destruction. To anyone who had grown up with and enjoyed the television series *Mission: Impossible,* the movie was, as Greg Morris, one of the stars of the original series, put it, an abomination. Under cover of the television title and music, the movie trashed the series and its main character, Jim Phelps. Yesteryear's hero turned into today's villain. And the successors to yesteryear's good guys, in the person of Ethan Hunt (the character played by Tom Cruise), are today's sleazes, as was so clearly displayed at the beginning of the movie when Ethan Hunt, the man clearly designated to head up future Mission: Impossible teams, cold-bloodedly murders another man, kicks his dead body and demands, "Get rid of that scum." My own polls, conducted among friends, acquaintances, and students, revealed that, by and large, those who liked the movie knew nothing of the television series, whereas those who disliked it did so because they knew its context and were appalled that its context was trashed. The lesson: knowing the proper context of a thing plays an essential role in our ability to make intelligent judgments.

And thus do we arrive at the Heaven's Gate cult. What happened to the members of this cult is a micro-lesson in the dangers visited upon people who have no context out of which to live their lives and judge the world around them. The members of this cult left home, family, possessions, and the larger society behind. They lived in isolation from everything that might have supplied them with a context for judging the rationality, not to mention the sanity, of Marshall Neff Applewhite. One of the network commentators reflected that a part of this tragedy lay in the fact that this cult had no religious tradition to fall back on. Very true. What he neglected to mention is the fact that the cultural elites of this society, including those in charge of network news and programming, have been undermining religious and all other traditions for sometime now.

Having no context out of which to live their lives, the members of this cult were persuaded to accept a context cobbled up by Mr. Applewhite. Their belief that the Hale-Bopp comet masked the approach of an alien spaceship come to whisk them off to a higher plane of existence seems absurd to most of us, but then we have not been stripped of our religious faith and tradition and the means they give us for making reasoned judgments about the claims of an Applewhite. As G. K. Chesterton observed, when a man no longer believes in God, it is not that he believes in nothing but that he believes in anything.

People enthusiastic about cryogenics, even to the point of plunking down cold cash now to have their bodies frozen later, offer perhaps the extreme example of the radical individualist for whom context no longer matters at all. One woman I saw featured on a news story about cryogenics is paying $40,000 to have her head frozen. Her reasons for doing this? She loves life, does not believe in God or heaven, and thinks $40,000, which after all is what some cars today cost, is a small price to pay for another chance at life in this world. What was particularly striking is the fact that she cares not at all, apparently, about where, when, with whom, or in what body (from the neck down, at least) she enjoys that life. Bereft not only of religious faith, she is also bereft of any context, any ties to any person, place, or time. It matters not at all to her that she will live in another body, another century, another civilization, among strangers. If, as Walker Percy said, the disease of our age is "abstraction,"[4] this woman could be its poster person.

It is, of course, no secret that those engaged in the dismantling of our culture are our cultural elites — in religion, education, politics, the arts, the media — those whom one would expect to maintain the institutions of this culture within which they have achieved preeminence and from which they have been entrusted with so much responsibility. As Christopher Lasch has pointed out, a view widely shared in the past was that "the value of cultural elites lay in their willingness to assume responsibility for the exacting standards without which civilization is impossible. They lived in the service of demanding ideals."[5] Whatever their value today, this is not it.

My first year studying theology in graduate school, I met the dismantling of context head-on in my Introduction to the New Testament course. The Church has always insisted that, in order to understand Jesus Christ, we must engage in a kind of triangulation. That is, we must understand him in three contexts — in relationship to the Father as his Son, in relationship to the people of Israel as their Messiah, and in relationship to the Church as her Head and Bridegroom. However, the professor of my course, a disciple of Bultmann and thoroughly immersed in historical-critical method, set us firmly on the path to decontextualizing Jesus Christ. This is routine in biblical studies today. And while our class did not go quite as far as the Jesus Seminar, we

4. Lewis A. Lawson and Victor A. Kramer, eds., *Conversations with Walker Percy* (Jackson: University Press of Mississippi, 1985), p. 83.

5. Christopher Lasch, *The Revolt of the Elites and the Betrayal of Democracy* (New York/London: W. W. Norton & Company, 1995), p. 26.

were introduced to the notion that, in order to sort out from the Gospels those sayings of Christ which we can rest assured are authentic, we must eliminate everything he said which sounds like something either a Jew or a Christian would say. In the hands of the Jesus Seminar, this has led to the conclusion that the only thing we can be really sure he said was "Abba." It took me years to recover sufficiently from the effects of this course to be able to read the New Testament once again as the word of God, the "book of the Church," and the divinely-appointed sequel to the Old Testament.

This destruction of context, of course, serves the agenda of those who would like Jesus Christ to be able to say the sorts of things we want to hear today. Stripped of context, he is turned into a cipher now capable of being filled with whatever it is we wish to find in him. No longer related to Israel and the Church, his relationship to God is also rendered ambiguous at best, leaving us able to put our own "spin" on what that might be.

Much the same sort of thing has been happening in other areas dominated by the cultural elites. What we have witnessed in recent Supreme Court decisions, especially with and since *Roe* v. *Wade*, is what Bork calls "constitutional nihilism."[6] The "mystery passage" in *Planned Parenthood* v. *Casey* is the logical outcome of that process. And what that passage underwrites is the view that liberty is the right to make up one's own context for living and, even more alarming, act upon it. For it must be remembered that this decision is not just about a pregnant woman deciding for herself whether or not she is carrying a human being, but also about her right to act upon her decision, that is, to kill the unborn child if, according to her particular concept of the mystery of human life, she deems that child not to be human.

Everywhere we look today, the traditional context for understanding things has been or is being stripped away. Hence, we confront new definitions of marriage to accommodate same-sex marriage, new definitions of family to accommodate almost any arrangement of people living under the same roof, and new definitions of sex and gender to accommodate the rights, now virtually absolute, for sexual freedom and control of one's reproductive organs. The traditional view of sex and babies as appropriately located within the context of marriage has been shattered, producing sex without babies, sex without marriage, babies without sex, babies without marriage, marriage without babies,

---

6. Bork, *Slouching Towards Gomorrah*, p. 321.

marriage without sex (a national organization recently came into existence to bring together people who want to marry but do not want to have sex), and the demand for same-sex marriages. Can anyone doubt that cloning will be claimed as a reproductive right of the future? For, having stripped away the traditional contexts of marriage and family, on what grounds might we protest this novel technique for bringing new life into the world, having already adopted so many techniques for engendering a child which stand outside the context of marriage, of family, of sexual intercourse, and of love?

Although its advocates dress religious and moral relativism in layers of language suggesting that something substantive is bound up with it, it is in the final analysis thoroughly nihilistic. No God exists apart from whatever concepts of him we might cobble up, no moral demands are made on us beyond those we choose, or do not choose, to make. Liberty itself is annihilated, for while the choices arrayed before us may seem virtually unlimited in scope, we have no particular reason for choosing one thing over another except as our own impulses dictate. Indeed, the annihilation of liberty is a necessary consequence of religious and moral nihilism, for, as Ortega y Gassett well understood, "Without commandments, obliging us to live after a certain fashion, our existence is that of the 'unemployed.' "[7] Anything we might choose to do under these circumstances is simply make-work designed to pass the time but getting us literally nowhere. It is not surprising, therefore, that passing the time as pleasantly as possible should become our primary concern. The seductions of immediate gratification, however, have set us on a path leading beyond Gomorrah and into a future far more terrifying and ultimately far more ruinous than God's destruction of that city.

Beyond Gomorrah: The Politics of Totalitarianism

Modern societies have rejected the contexts supplied by both nature and religion. As a result, and as Hannah Arendt put it in her classic work, *The Origins of Totalitarianism*, "Our new difficulty is that we start from a fundamental distrust of everything merely *given*, a distrust of all laws and prescriptions, moral or social, that are deduced from a

7. José Ortega y Gassett, *The Revolt of the Masses* (New York: W. W. Norton, 1957), pp. 135-36.

given, comprehensive, universal whole."[8] This is why modern liberty is construed as the right to define one's own concept of existence, the universe and life, and the right to act upon one's own view of reality.

Our refusal of the givens of nature and religion, however, is not mere distrust. It has become, as Arendt also noted, downright resentment.

> For the first disastrous result of man's coming of age is that modern man has come to resent everything given, even his own existence — and to resent the very fact that he is not the creator of the universe and himself. In this fundamental resentment, he refuses to see rhyme or reason in the given world. In his resentment of all laws merely given to him, he proclaims openly that everything is permitted and believes secretly that everything is possible.[9]

This explains why the worst among us "are full of passionate intensity" while so many of the best "lack all conviction." But in this combination of passionate intensity among those who resent the God-given nature of things and apathy among those who know, or at least suspect or desire, better, lies the greatest danger of our age. For unless the best among us intervene, the worst shall bring to fruition that technological totalitarian tyranny which Aldous Huxley called *Brave New World* and C. S. Lewis recognized to be *The Abolition of Man*.

Jacques Monod, Nobel prize-winning French biologist, asserted two things in *Chance & Necessity*, his famous work on the implications of science in today's world, which we ignore at our peril. First, "Modern societies, woven together by science, living from its products, have become as dependent upon it as an addict on his drug."[10] Second, these societies are morally weak because they still try to cling to religiously-informed value systems which have been totally undermined by science. "The contradiction is deadly. It is what is digging the pit we see opening under our feet. The ethic of knowledge that created the modern world is the only ethic compatible with it, the only one capable, once understood and accepted, of guiding its evolution."[11]

8. Hannah Arendt, *The Origins of Totalitarianism* (New York: Harcourt, Brace and Company, 1951), p. 435.

9. Ibid., p. 438.

10. Jacques Monod, *Chance & Necessity*, trans. by Austryn Wainhouse (New York: Alfred A. Knopf, 1971), p. 177.

11. Ibid.

Jacques Ellul, French Christian sociologist who has spent decades studying the impact of technology on modern western societies, agrees that scientific technology has overwhelmed our societies, undercut their cultures, and absorbed everything into the orb of technique pure and simple. "Everything now depends on technique. We live incontestably in a society that is totally made by it and for it."[12] Indeed, as Ellul has observed, technique is challenged neither from without, for it absorbs everything in its path, eliminating anything that might stand on the outside, nor from within, for "No particular technique challenges or opposes the global movement of technique. Even the most dazzling innovations are within the system."[13] As a result, what we discover today is "the profound and widespread conviction in developed countries that everything is ultimately a technical problem."[14]

Thus, the solution to the problems caused by technological damage to the environment is the development of new techniques to repair that damage. The solution to the threat of nuclear annihilation is the development of the technique of a Star Wars defense. The solution to AIDS is the technique of a cure. The solution to excessive fertility (as some see it) is contraceptive and abortifacient techniques. The solution to infertility, whether natural or induced by contraceptive techniques, is new reproductive techniques that would allow the infertile to acquire the children they desire. The solution to disease is new techniques for curing disease. The solution to suffering is new techniques to eliminate suffering. The solution to suffering which proves intractable to technique is a wide array of techniques for committing suicide, as outlined in Derek Humphrey's *Final Exit* or Dr. Kevorkian's "death machine."

When technique, however, is sought as the solution to other than technical problems, religion and morality must necessarily seem absurd unless their claims can be tailored to the technological imperatives of

12. Jacques Ellul, *The Technological Bluff*, trans. by Geoffrey W. Bromiley (Grand Rapids: William B. Eerdmans Publishing Company, 1990), p. 12. Ellul recognizes that technique has always played a role in culture, but points out that today "the problem is that size, number, speed of development, omnipresence, and omnicompetence now make it impossible to insert techniques into a stable culture. On the contrary, techniques are now encircling and swallowing up all that has constituted culture from the beginnings of human history" (Ibid., p. 138). Furthermore, "Once technical operations are in billionths of a second and even the best machines are out of date in a few years, no distance, no reflection, or criticism is possible" (Ibid., p. 145).

13. Ibid., p. 14.
14. Ibid., p. 48.

our day. Nothing makes this clearer than the fact that while the Catholic Church condemns both the practice of contraception and the exportation of that practice to every corner of the world, American Catholics are by and large untroubled by these things. Practicing contraception themselves, they find Church prohibitions against the practice incomprehensible and government efforts to export such practices laudable. Those in the thrall of technique necessarily end up estranged from their own religious traditions.

It is true, of course, that most people to one degree or another want the technologies modern science has to offer us. But what most people do not understand is that the reasons why our elites welcome these technologies differ considerably from the reasons ordinary citizens desire them. First, our cultural elites are more susceptible to technique, because they are less attached to religion and tradition. Every poll indicates that the ordinary American is far more conservative about abortion, reproductive technologies, same-sex marriages, and doctor-assisted suicide than are those in high places. Second, devoid of religion and tradition, our cultural elites are deeply imbued with the Marxist mandate to stop studying and start changing the world, and they recognize that technique is ultimately about the power to do that. As Ellul puts it, "In all technique . . . knowledge means power. We should never forget that its only objective is to enhance power."[15] We have reached that point where "[t]he legitimacy of power is no longer religious or democratic. Power affirms itself scientifically."[16] And our cultural elites know this, even if we do not.

Here, however, we arrive at the crux of our crisis and at the central reason why technique threatens everything man has ever been, known, or done. For science, and the techniques it spawns, are devoid of any notion of final causality. Monod recognized this to be the primary dividing line between scientific and religious knowledge: "The cornerstone of the scientific method is the postulate that nature is objective. In other words, the *systematic* denial that 'true' knowledge can be got at by interpreting phenomena in terms of final causes — that is to say, of 'purpose.' "[17] Or as Ellul puts it, the primary features of technique are "autonomy, unity, universality, totality, automatic growth, automation, causal progression, the absence of finality."[18]

15. Ibid., p. 25.
16. Ibid., p. 103.
17. Monod, *Chance & Necessity*, p. 21.
18. Ellul, *The Technological Bluff*, p. 15.

The absence of final causality means two very sobering, even frightening, things. First, since no purpose can be assigned to anything, no nature can be assigned to it either. Things become nothing more than potter's clay at the disposal, not of God, but of technique. Second, without final causality, there is no defined end toward which technique could be said to be moving. Thus, there is literally no end to the things it can do and no intrinsic controls on what it does do. This means, as Ellul warns us, that "it does not know where it is going"[19] and that "Scientists will not accept philosophical, theological, or ethical judgments. Science simply leaves by the wayside those scholars who have scruples of conscience. It goes its inexorable way until it produces the final catastrophe."[20] Thus do we operate under a scientific imperative which demands that if we can do it, we should do it. There are no exceptions to this rule, which is why everyone knows that the cloning of human beings inescapably lies ahead. As Ellul rightly counsels, "[w]e should stop pretending that research is neutral, that only its applications are good or bad. Can we find a single example of nonapplication of a discovery when it responds to an existing need or to one that it creates itself? It is prior to discoveries that ethical choices should be made."[21] Therefore, although one might characterize the spirit of our age in terms of radical egalitarianism and radical individualism, the real spirit of our age is other and much worse: knowledge is unlimited power, and unlimited power is unlimited technique. Thus, while ordinary citizens may be seduced by egalitarianism and individualism, our cultural elites are seduced by the promise of unlimited power.

Technique pursued as unlimited power over the givens of God and nature seals that transvaluation of sectors previously discussed. Religion and morality are necessarily relativized, because technique establishes itself as the only absolute. As Ellul says: "If technique makes everything possible, it becomes itself absolute necessity."[22] And allied with the state, the absolute necessity of technique will eventually sweep away all traditional notions that politics is the realm of the relative and the realm of compromise. The absolute tolerance demanded today will sooner or later give way to the absolute necessities dictated by technique. China's policy of forced abortion after one child and our own

19. Ibid., p. 39.
20. Ibid., p. 187.
21. Ibid., p. 186.
22. Ibid., p. 218.

"culture of death" are but the tip of the iceberg. Beneath the icy waters, but not so far that we cannot see their shadows, are the designer children of the future, shaped on the potter's wheel of scientific technology to serve whatever purposes our future political masters desire to see served.

For centuries now, science has held out that promise that man might acquire knowledge to dominate nature. And, for as long as man himself remained outside the nature he sought to dominate, the promise seemed fulfilled. Once, however, man placed himself within the category of nature, the situation radically changed. And man made that quantum leap with contraception, by which he yielded his body to the domination of technique. The path this put us on has already produced reproductive technologies and genetic engineering experiments along the way, and promises cloning around the next bend; but at its end, if we pursue it there unchecked, lies that "brave new world" which C. S. Lewis characterized as "the abolition of man."

Fifty years ago, C. S. Lewis reminded us that man's power over nature is really only the power of a few men upon which all other men depend. Only a few men, for example, have conquered flight. The rest of us just pay for our tickets and board the plane, usually in a state of anxiety if not downright fear. Lewis also reminded us that contraception in particular is a two-edged sword, inasmuch as

> . . . there is a paradoxical, negative sense in which all possible future generations are the patients or subjects of a power wielded by those already alive. By contraception simply, they are denied existence; by contraception used as a means of selective breeding, they are, without their concurring voice, made to be what one generation, for its own reasons, may choose to prefer. From this point of view, what we call Man's power over Nature turns out to be a power exercised by some men over other men with Nature as its instrument.[23]

He warned us that those men who step outside what he called the Tao, that is, religious and moral tradition, have no basis for making decisions except their own impulses. And "impulses" is just another name for "nature." The result is inescapable as it applies to the leaders of the future, the Conditioners who have at their disposal all of the

---

23. C. S. Lewis, *The Abolition of Man* (Toronto: The Macmillan Company, Macmillan Paperback Edition, 1947), pp. 68-69.

power of technique. According to Lewis: "Nature, untrammelled by values, rules the Conditioners and, through them, all humanity. Man's conquest of Nature turns out, in the moment of its consummation, to be Nature's conquest of Man."[24]

The future with which technique confronts us is not some glorious earthly eschaton in which all men enjoy complete dominion over nature. The reality is quite otherwise. Lewis says:

> The real picture is that of one dominant age — let us suppose the hundredth century A.D. — which resists all previous ages most successfully and dominates all subsequent ages most irresistibly, and thus is the real master of the human species. But even within this master generation (itself an infinitesimal minority of the species) the power will be exercised by a minority smaller still. Man's conquest of Nature, if the dreams of some scientific planners are realized, means the rule of a few hundreds of men over billions upon billions of men.[25]

Thus, "Man's final conquest has proved to be the abolition of man."[26]

Conclusion

G. K. Chesterton defined civilization as "the full authority of the human spirit over all externals" and the civilized man as free to determine what he will and will not do. The barbarian, on the other hand, is "enslaved to Nature," and capable of going only where nature takes him. This led Chesterton to conclude that "scientific determinism is simply the primal twilight of all mankind; and some men seem to be returning to it."[27]

If we are to stave off the barbarism of unrestrained technique, we must, I think, do two things. First, we must recognize the fact that the line we ought not to have crossed but did, and beyond which no other reasonable line can be drawn, is contraception. Catholics have been agonizing over this issue for some thirty years and for good reason,

24. Ibid., p. 80.
25. Ibid., p. 71.
26. Ibid., p. 77.
27. G. K. Chesterton, *All Things Considered* (New York: John Lane Company, 1913), pp. 226-27.

because the philosophical implications of accepting contraception are enormous. In delivering our bodies over to the manipulations of technique, we have divorced the body from the soul and declared our own, not God's, dominion over ourselves. This, in turn, has produced three consequences which contribute directly to unrestrained technique, making it virtually impossible for us to stop the current plunge into catastrophe.

First, we accepted the practice of administering medicine to healthy bodies in order to suppress the normal functioning of those bodies. All of the doctors on the commission set up by Pope John XXIII to study the contraceptive pill opposed approving it precisely because they thought it to be bad, even unethical, medical practice. A society cannot embrace medicine as manipulation of healthy bodies without being drawn further down this path. A direct line can be traced from contraception to artificial insemination, in vitro fertilization, and surrogate motherhood. In the not-too-distant future, we shall be able to draw a direct line from contraception to cloning.

Second, we accepted a notion of "control," as in "control of our bodies" and "control of our reproductive organs," which is appropriate to animals but runs counter to the dignity of human beings invested with intellect and free will. We take our dogs and cats to the vet to acquire, through the vet, control of their reproductive organs. To take ourselves and our children to doctors for contraception and abortion is to treat ourselves as we treat our dogs and cats. The irony of the situation could not be more acute: those who claim as a right the extrinsic controls of contraception and abortion have actually ceded control of their bodies to the pharmaceutical companies and the abortionists, and they have done so because self-control, the only control consonant with our dignity as human beings, is precisely what they do not want to exercise. But this reliance upon control from without rather than from within is the very thing that enslaves us to technique.

Third, we accepted abortion as backup contraception. For abortion is, after all, not about babies but about sexual freedom. Abortion-on-demand was unthinkable prior to the advent of the contraceptive pill and its widespread use. So great is our desire for freedom from all constraint on our sexual behavior that, as Peter Kreeft has pointed out,

> We are even willing to *murder* to preserve our so-called sexual freedom. And we will murder *the most innocent* among us, the only innocent among us. And *the most defenseless* of all. And in the teeth

of *the strongest instinct:* motherhood. It is a miracle of black magic, a stunning success, explainable only by supernatural power and defeatable only by supernatural power.[28]

One of my colleagues at the University of St. Thomas tells the story of how her father, now dead but at the time a "non-practicing Southern Baptist," greeted the announcement on the evening news some thirty years ago of the availability of the contraceptive pill. He said to his wife that this pill would create a revolution in our society which would make all other revolutions pale by comparison, because it would transform our sexual behavior in such ways as to undermine both marriage and family and the responsibilities that attach to them. And he predicted that the day would come when we would regret having taken this fork in the road. Many people have pointed out, as Peter Kreeft most recently did once again, that the infinite passion for God, once deflected, finds its most immediate alternative in the infinite passion for sex. "Sexual passion is modernity's substitute for religious passion."[29]

And that brings me to my second point. We are currently losing this war to the worst among us whose passionate intensity has all along been driven by the desire for unrestrained sexual freedom. And the future promises yet more catastrophic losses, if one considers that sexual passion is not our greatest or most dangerous foe.

It is for this reason, I believe, that Pope John Paul II has warned us that we have reached a moment in history of supreme crisis. Reflecting on our situation at the end of *Crossing the Threshold of Hope,* he said, "André Malraux was certainly right when he said that the twenty-first century would be the century of religion or it would not be at all."[30] Modern technique wages war on all religions, all moral systems. It knows neither the laws of God nor the laws of the universe. And it seduces by playing to the one ungodly passion more powerful than sex, the passion for infinite power, the power to become like God.

Those who see in technology nothing more than a vehicle for radical egalitarianism and radical individualism have not yet seen the real face or real future of technique. For this reason beyond all others,

28. Peter Kreeft, *Ecumenical Jihad* (San Francisco: Ignatius Press, 1996), p. 17.

29. Ibid., p. 54.

30. Pope John Paul II, *Crossing the Threshold of Hope,* trans. by Jenny McPhee and Martha McPhee (New York: Alfred A. Knopf, 1994), p. 229.

those of us who recognize it for what it is must rediscover within ourselves and our faith that "passionate intensity" for God which conquered an empire and which alone can wage the war that must be fought against those driven by the twin passions for unrestrained sexual freedom and unlimited power. For, as Peter Kreeft has rightly observed with regard to our own society and its sexual passion, "Argument is insufficient; America needs exorcism."[31]

31. *Ecumenical Jihad*, p. 17.

4. Culture, Politics, and the American Founding

CHARLES R. KESLER

How can politics help to restore a healthy American culture? The question assumes that politics *can* shape culture — indeed, can conduct us "toward the renewal of civilization," in the noble words of this volume's subtitle — but that assumption is, of course, itself controversial.

Consider the character of the arguments in today's "culture wars." To begin with, American conservatives claim that the Left, from its parapets of power in Hollywood, the universities, the national media, the federal courts, and the National Endowment for the Arts, has waged, for decades, a "culture war" upon the American people — a war that the people have been losing. The conservatives' complaint is commonly put this way: the Left has set out to "politicize" American culture, to force it to conform to a new orthodoxy of political correctness in everything from sexual education to pronoun usage. The conservatives' point is that culture should be above, or at least separated from, the political order; that civil society — the realm of art, religion, family, and private property — should be protected, for the sake of liberty as well as culture, against political encroachment. Instead of politics trying tyrannically or arbitrarily to create culture, politics should devote itself to conserving culture (in the sense of the people's evolved sentiments, habits, and way of life). Thus in the conservative view, politics should grow out of culture and serve culture, not the other way around.

But at this point one sees that there are actually two conservative views of culture. They differ on the question of what it means to "conserve" culture: Does it mean to keep government's hands off it, to be neutral towards culture and allow it to develop however artists and citizens choose? Or does it mean a hands-on approach, an active promotion of "traditional American values" (not a traditional American phrase, by the way) against their would-be subverters in and out of government? Hands-off is the preference both of libertarians, who tend to take an indifferent or *laissez-faire* attitude towards culture, and of those neo-conservatives who defend high culture (and particularly one of its valuable prerogatives, academic freedom) against the public's attempts to influence it. The hands-on approach is preferred (in various ways, to be sure) by the so-called Religious Right, by most who refer to themselves as "cultural conservatives" or traditionalists, and by many neo-conservatives who are repelled by the prospect of American society's utter demoralization. Even conservatives who are prepared to use government to shore up American culture, however, typically reject the notion that they are "politicizing" the culture. They argue that they are only using politics to get beyond politics — that is, to overcome the culture's artificial or forced politicization by the Left.

Seizing upon this contradiction or ambiguity, the Left today charges that conservatives are prepared, when they are prepared, to take a *laissez-faire* attitude towards culture only because theirs — the white male bourgeois culture — is the dominant one. When its hegemony is challenged, liberal critics note, as it is being challenged currently, then conservatives cease to be defenders of a hands-off cultural policy and quickly become advocates of cultural protectionism.

Yet in challenging the supposed hegemony of patriarchal or conservative culture, most liberal intellectuals do not imagine themselves to be calling for the hegemony of their own culture. Today's liberals stand for "multiculturalism," for the replacement of ruling-class culture by the multiplicity of cultures belonging to oppressed, or formerly oppressed, classes and groups. In the past, white males had used their culture to justify and reinforce their rule over the rest of society; it was they who first "politicized" culture, according to the multiculturalists. Now, the rest of society — indeed, the rest of the world — can bring "historically excluded" cultures to bear in order to delegitimize the old "racist, sexist, homophobic" order and ordain a new, more inclusive one. Still, the new order will be "one," will be unified and organized around the idea of multiculturalism; so how will it escape the charge that it desires merely to substitute one ruling class for another — one ruling culture for another?

From the standpoint of traditionalist conservatism, every society or people is defined by its culture, and therefore every culture is more or less an exclusive one. In John O'Sullivan's words, "A multicultural society is a contradiction in terms and cannot survive indefinitely. It either becomes monocultural or runs into trouble."[1] At this juncture, we urgently need some clarity on the meaning of "culture." The oldest or fundamental definition of "culture" *(cultura)* is something that grows as a result of cultivating, tilling, or planting. In common speech, "culture" means either high art or an ethnic group with its characteristic customs. The word's two contemporary senses cohere, however, when combined with the first meaning of "culture" as a kind of growth: a culture is a living social organism that has particular ethnic "roots" and develops from those roots, often flowering into unique, that is, characteristic achievements of high art. To understand a culture means therefore to appreciate it in its particularity, to see it as a unique historical growth — not as a mere exemplum of a common and unchanging human nature, much less as an imperfect embodiment of the best political or social order.[2]

Reason has little to do with culture in this sense, therefore, because the modern concept of culture emphasizes the ethnic, the particular, the authentic at the expense of the universal; whereas reason strives, even in practical affairs, to see particulars in the light of universals. An authentic culture is natural in the sense of being an uncoerced growth, not in the sense of containing universal principles that can be grasped and perhaps manipulated by reason. Accordingly, an authentic culture cannot be designed or planned because it cannot be thought through; it is always in the process of slow change or adaptation. Ever since Edmund Burke, whose defense of the British Constitution became the model for the Right's thinking on the cultural roots of politics in general, conservatives have argued that culture is neither a goal that politicians can seek to achieve nor a product that they can make — let alone export.

Oddly enough, the multiculturalists agree with the traditionalists on the primacy of culture over politics, and to some extent even on the definition of culture. What the multiculturalists insist on, however, is

1. John O'Sullivan, "Reinventing the American People?" in Robert Royal, ed., *Reinventing the American People: Unity and Diversity Today* (Washington, D.C.: Ethics and Public Policy Center, 1995), pp. 275-84, at 278.
2. Cf. Harvey C. Mansfield, Jr., "The Twofold Meaning of '*Unum*,'" in Robert Royal, ibid., pp. 103-13, at 105-6.

that culture does not have to be exclusive, or more precisely, that Americans can participate in many cultures without succumbing to any one of them and without ceasing to be American. But this is to pile absurdity upon absurdity. If cultures are unique, it means that they disagree with one another; if they are to be taken seriously, it is because they disagree about serious things in serious ways. Multiculturalism must overlook or minimize these serious disagreements in order to make it possible for diverse cultures to keep house with one another; and to enable Americans to experience this homogenized "diversity" openly and sympathetically. In general, today's liberals diminish cultural disagreements to the level of differences in cuisine. So multiculturalism tries to view cultures as individual dishes on the great smorgasbord of America, but is unable even to distinguish between main courses and side dishes at this potluck feast, since this would imply that some cultures are more central or substantial than others. Of course, multiculturalists make no secret of their own taste for the unusual foods of the Third World, but their preference shows, in effect, how boring it is to have to eat in a cafeteria of bland cultures.

Multiculturalists do not shun every disagreement, however. Despite their facile assertion of the equality of all cultures, they are in fact children of contemporary American culture. Their relativism yields, in the end, to their liberalism. Any culture that rejects multiculturalism or modern liberalism is, therefore, in principle, intolerable. (Though non-Western cultures are largely exempt from public criticism — perhaps because their cuisines are so piquant.) The unholy trinity of what they call racism, sexism, and homophobia (which bears little resemblance to actual moral vice; for them, "racism" means insisting on colorblind law) is *not* relative: these attitudes are *wrong*, as they see it, and cultures that embody them are wrong, too. Since they regard America's traditional culture — that of the Declaration of Independence and the Constitution — as cursed by all three, they do not disguise their desire to replace it with a better one. Once the country has expiated these sins, however, the work of politics — of political correctness and "consciousness raising" — will be done, and a thousand multicultural flowers will presumably bloom freely.

For the contemporary Left as well as for the Right, therefore, the use of politics is to get beyond politics. In their own ways, liberals and conservatives alike assume that politics ought ultimately to reflect culture; that American politics, in particular, has always been based — and for the Left, ought increasingly to be based — on race, ethnicity, and

45

CHARLES R. KESLER

history. Both groups agree, loosely speaking, that American politics is essentially a legacy of white male bourgeois culture, though liberals deplore it and a few conservatives, at least, celebrate the (alleged) fact. But there is another way to look at the relation between politics and culture, an older way that is nonetheless familiar to us; in fact, it is assumed in the very charges that liberals and conservatives fling at each other. Each accuses the other of using politics to impose a culture on society. Each admits then, in so many words, that it is possible for politics to overrule — and thus to rule over — culture.

*   *   *

The fully worked-out and thought-through account of politics' ability to rule over culture may be found in Aristotle's *Politics.* For Aristotle, the highest theme of politics — and of political science — is founding. Founding a city or political association means to give it the law, the set of authoritative institutions, offices, and precepts, that chiefly makes the city *what it is* — that gives it its distinctive character as a democracy, aristocracy, monarchy, and so forth, but also as this particular democracy, say. This authoritative arrangement of offices and institutions is what Aristotle calls the "regime," which establishes who rules in the city and what ends or purposes their rule serves. The regime is the fundamental fact of political life; and because the character of those who rule shapes the character of the whole people, the regime imparts to the city its very way of life. So, for instance, Lycurgus and his famous laws made or formed the Spartans by commanding them to live the Spartan way of life. Similarly, the children of Israel became a unified, pious, and warlike people only as a result of the laws of Moses; without his laws (which were, of course, God's laws), the Jewish people would not be the same people.

The phenomenon of founding thus shows that politics can shape or rule culture — but not completely. Aristotle is careful to say that it is with regard to the regime "above all" that the city may be said to be the same or different; that is, the regime chiefly but not exclusively determines the character of a city.[3] In his account, Aristotle compares the regime's relation to the city to the relation between form and matter. As a sculptor combines the form or look of Pericles, say, with the matter of a marble block in order to fashion a statue of the Athenian statesman,

3. Aristotle, *The Politics,* trans. Carnes Lord (Chicago: University of Chicago Press, 1984), 1276b9-10.

46

so the founder or lawgiver combines the regime or form of government with the "matter" of the city, producing a democratic city, an aristocratic city, or whatever. By the "matter" of a city, Aristotle means its location, population, ethnic stock, customs, economic skills and resources, distribution of wealth, levels of education, and so forth.[4] Aristotle recognizes that, in any particular case, matter limits the forms that can be combined with it, even as the size, shape, and quality of a block of marble limit what a sculptor can create from it.

To be sure, in political life there are very few virgin blocks of marble, whatever their quality. Most foundings are refoundings or revolutions, in which legislators have to start from a pre-existing way of life or culture — as though a sculptor were to take a statue of Henry VIII and try to turn it into one of George Washington. Aristotle does not use the term "culture," but his notion of "matter" refers to much the same thing, and more. The essential difference is that for him, culture is really, or at least mainly, past politics, the residue of previous regimes, laws, and customs. By subordinating culture to politics, Aristotle emphasizes the capacity of men to shape their own destiny or govern themselves by *choosing* in politics; he emphasizes, in other words, that men are free, that they are not enslaved to the past or to their "culture." But this is not complete or existential freedom, in which men are free to disregard the past or recreate themselves however they will. For Aristotle, men are free enough to face up to, and thus take responsibility for, the limitations on their own choices — the cultural, economic, geographical, and other factors that may constrain, but cannot abolish, their freedom. No political choice is ever entirely free, therefore, nor completely determined. Yet against the dogmatic determinism of the cultural approach and of so much of contemporary social science — including cultural anthropology, "cultural studies," sociology, psychology, and other fields — Aristotle reminds us that man does have freedom, a freedom that is visible especially in politics or statesmanship; and within statesmanship, a freedom that shines most clearly in the phenomenon of founding.[5]

*   *   *

4. Consider Aristotle, *The Politics*, 1267a17-40, 1280b29-1281a7, 1281a40-1281b17, 1282a13-19, 1288b10-34, 1289b26-13, 1295a25-1296a12, 1296b13-40.

5. Cf. Harry V. Jaffa, "On the Necessity of a Scholarship of the Politics of Freedom," in Harry V. Jaffa, ed., *Statesmanship: Essays in Honor of Sir Winston S. Churchill* (Durham: Carolina Academic Press, 1981), pp. 1-9.

It is important to remind ourselves of these facts because the United States had a founding. The general theory of the American founding is expressed forthrightly in the Declaration of Independence, *The Federalist*, and other great documents of the era, which explain that American republicanism is based on the doctrine of the social contract. But what does that doctrine mean? In one Enlightened rendering, the doctrine holds that individual men, animated by self-interest or the desire for comfortable self-preservation, contract together to escape the terrors and inconveniences of the state of nature by entering into civil society and establishing government. Each individual then keeps his promise to obey the civil law out of fear of punishment and a sense of his enlightened self-interest. A more populist version of the contract doctrine, popular among some Americans in the founding period, holds that once individuals have contracted together to form a proper republican polity, a kind of spontaneous republican virtue would emerge to keep citizens faithful to the law and willing to sacrifice on its behalf.

James Madison, among others, thought that both of these accounts of the social contract were defective. In the first place, he doubted that such a calculated attachment to the law would be sufficient to institute republican government, or to sustain it in the long run. In the second place, he doubted that republican virtue could be counted on to arise spontaneously from democratic society — and during the Critical Period of the 1780s, in fact, such virtue had not emerged from the small republican polities of the states. Madison corrected these theories in the political science of *The Federalist*, which argued that a certain popular "reverence" or "veneration" for the Constitution and laws (not just enlightened self-interest) was necessary to perpetuate American republicanism; and that this reverence for the law would not arise spontaneously, but only as the result of a wisely structured Union and Constitution. Furthermore, *The Federalist* maintained that to institute good republican government required "some patriotic and respectable . . . number of citizens" to take the lead and propose to the people "some *informal and unauthorized propositions*," that is, the Constitution. There had to be lawgivers even in the modern setting of social contract theory, in other words. Neither the people's virtue nor their interests could lead them to write a good constitution, though they were certainly capable of deliberating on one once it had been proposed to them.[6]

6. *The Federalist Papers*, ed. Clinton Rossiter (New York: Mentor, 1961), No. 1, p. 33; No. 40, p. 253; No. 49, pp. 314-15.

The American people's reverence for the laws needed to extend to the lawgivers, too, and *The Federalist* did its best to honor and accentuate the Constitution-makers' wisdom, patriotism, and love of justice. The country took this lesson to heart — and for this very reason, there are in the popular imagination no "founders" of the Articles of Confederation — and surely it is important that "we the people" continue to trace our nationhood to the "founding fathers" of 1776 and 1787, to ancestral lawgivers as it were, somewhat in the manner of the ancient city. *The Federalist* itself, written under the pseudonym of a founder of the Roman republic, "Publius," functions as a perpetual oracle of our "ancestral" lawgivers' wisdom.

But of course America is not an ancient city — and it is by reflecting on this fact that we may gain some additional perspective on our present-day problems of politics and culture. What separates America from the *polis* is not merely such modern advantages as science, technology, traffic jams, and so forth, but also something that modern America lacks — the gods of the ancient city. In the ancient world, every city or people had its own gods, and every city had divine or semi-divine founders. America belongs to a world decisively transformed by the presence of universal religion, of Christianity; a world in which there is an endemic separation or conflict between the city of God and the city (really, the cities) of man, between religious loyalty and civic loyalty. In truth, however much God may bless the United States, He is the God of all mankind, not ours alone; but in the ancient world it would have been a poor people indeed who lacked their own local, special, and favoring deities or deity ("the Lord God of Israel"). Thereafter in the Christian West, the uneasy distinction between the temporal and the spiritual played itself out as the conflict between Pope and Emperor in the High Middle Ages, and as horrific wars of religion between Catholics and Protestants, and among Protestants, in the sixteenth and seventeenth centuries.

America in its founding attempted to resolve this problem. Our founders did not indulge the favorite methods of the preceding centuries — trying to impose a religious tyranny over politics, or a political tyranny over religion — but took the unprecedented course of separating church and state. At the national level, the First Amendment forbade Congress to establish a national religion or to prohibit religion's free exercise; and at the state level, a campaign to disestablish state churches began in the mid-1780s with Virginia and gradually spread throughout the Union, culminating in the disestablishment of Congregationalism

49

in Massachusetts in 1833. By these actions, America marked itself as a liberal or modern republic, in the sense that unlike the ancient city, the American republic would not try to prescribe a comprehensive or total way of life for its citizens. In America, each citizen would enjoy a realm of freedom of conscience in which he would be free to cultivate his relation to God, and over which government would have no direct authority.

Madison, writing on behalf of religious liberty in his great "Memorial and Remonstrance" of 1785, argued that freedom of conscience was an "unalienable" or natural right, not only because religion was a matter of "reason and conviction," and thus men must be free to follow their own "conviction and conscience," unconstrained by force or violence; but also because "what is here a right towards men, is a duty towards the Creator." It is every man's duty "to render to the Creator such homage, and such only, as he believes to be acceptable" to Him; and "this duty is precedent both in order of time and degree of obligation, to the claims of Civil Society."[7] In short, Madison argues that the natural rights of conscience derive from man's rational nature and from his status as a created being, born with duties to his Creator. What those duties comprise, however — what is true religion, in other words — is a question that every man's "conviction and conscience" must wrestle with, to his own satisfaction.

Human rights thus rest upon a prior human duty to God. And human government must acknowledge this duty by respecting a realm of private freedom for every man to discharge that duty conscientiously. Precisely from the highest point of view, then, government must be *limited* in order to be just; it would be impious for government to attempt to decide questions of ultimate religious truth by putting them up to majority vote. The problem of religion and politics that had bedeviled the West for so many centuries found a practical solution in America, then, a solution that required the limiting of government's scope and power, and the corresponding emancipation of "civil society" from what had been, in principle, comprehensive political control.

The independence and dignity of civil society depended, however, on its ability to remain "civil," that is, civilized or suitable for free men and women, for citizens *(cives)*. So civil society had to be capable of

7. James Madison, "Memorial and Remonstrance Against Religious Assessments," in Marvin Meyers, ed., *The Mind of the Founder: Sources of the Political Thought of James Madison* (Indianapolis: Bobbs-Merrill, 1973), pp. 7-16, at 9.

sustaining free government without itself being part of the government; put another way, in a free society there had to be a form of "government" in civil society that was not part of the state as such. To be sure, one great purpose of forming government in the first place was to enable it to restrain and punish lawbreakers; but if every member of civil society were a lawbreaker, there would soon be no civil society left and no limited government, either — a situation that America may be approaching today in certain areas of its largest cities. Civil society had then to be self-governing, by and large, if limited government in the political sense were to be viable. The independence and dignity of civil society, the home of "culture," depended on its containing high and noble purposes of its own, in light of which self-government made sense. These purposes — seeking the truth about God, worshiping God according to conscience, living a godly or virtuous life — to the extent that they gave a tone to civil society, helped to ensure that the "pursuit of Happiness" would be respectable, from the traditional or Aristotelian point of view of politics itself.

If the highest purpose of private freedom, however, were to be reduced to the love of money or the pursuit of bodily pleasure, then civil society would cease, *pro tanto*, to be very respectable; and the moral government that is essential to political self-government would devolve back to the state, and perhaps in the end, political freedom would prove simply impossible. Hence Madison's observation that if "there is not sufficient virtue among men for self-government," then "nothing less than the chains of despotism can restrain them from destroying and devouring one another."[8] But the other side of the American founders' solicitude for private freedom was their affirmation of a public morality that honored religious liberty — and civil liberty — as based on natural rights and natural law. This morality consisted of the commonsense teachings of reason and revealed religion alike, the overlapping precepts indicated by the very phrase "the laws of nature and of nature's God." The founders sought to incorporate this morality into American culture, or rather to make it the basis of American culture.

This they did not accomplish directly, by creating, let us say, a federal Department of Morality and Culture — an approach they would have regarded as unconstitutional, unwise, and unavailing. Nor did the founders attempt to order artists and writers around. They proceeded

8. *The Federalist Papers*, No. 55, p. 346.

CHARLES R. KESLER

indirectly, careful not to trample the very liberty they were trying to save, by a series of exhortations and legal encouragements at the national level, and by founding a new set of institutions at the state and local level. In the end, most of their efforts converged on this new set of institutions, namely, the public or common schools. At the time of the Revolution, only the New England states (Massachusetts, Connecticut, New Hampshire) had laws requiring youngsters to attend publicly financed common schools. But beginning in the 1780s, the great men of the Revolution began to turn their attention to the education of youth. The Northwest Ordinance, passed by the Congress under the Articles of Confederation and repassed by the First Congress, adjured that "Religion, Morality, and knowledge being necessary to good government and the happiness of mankind, Schools and the means of education shall forever be encouraged." Under its provisions, a sixteenth part of every township formed out of the Northwest Territories was granted to the new state governments for the maintenance of public schools. The same grant was made afterwards to most other new states; and beginning with California's admission in 1850, the grant's size doubled, and with the admission of Utah, Arizona, and New Mexico, quadrupled.[9]

By the early nineteenth century, the public schools movement had taken root in the majority of states. These schools were not only new — no other country in the history of the world had ever erected such a system — but they were new *kinds* of schools, dedicated to inculcating the skills, habits, and principles of republican self-government. Benjamin Rush, the Pennsylvania revolutionary leader who was one of the earliest supporters of public education, distinguished in 1787 between "the late American war" and the "American Revolution." The war is over, he wrote, but the Revolution properly so-called was just beginning: "It remains yet to establish and perfect our new forms of government, and to prepare the principles, morals, and manners of our citizens for these forms of government after they are established and brought to perfection."[10] The real "American Revolution" was the moral and intellectual education of her present and future citizens — the growth

9. See Charles R. Kesler, "Education and Politics: Lessons from the American Founding," *The University of Chicago Legal Forum* (1991), pp. 101-22, at 111.
10. Reprinted in G. Brown Goode, *The Origin of the National Scientific and Educational Institutions of the United States,* in *Papers of the American Historical Association,* vol. 4, part 2 (1890), pp. 82, 84.

of an American culture to confirm American independence and to fulfill
the promise of American republicanism.

*   *   *

But it is this American culture, and the education appropriate to it, that
have been under sustained attack for the past century. Strangely, many
conservatives attribute today's cultural crisis not to the abandonment
of our country's political and cultural principles, but to their victory.
Judge Robert H. Bork, for example, argues in his recent book that the
extreme egalitarianism and libertarianism of today are simply the
founders' premises of equality and liberty, victorious at last over the
traditions of law, inherited morality, and religion. These saving traditions had concealed the founders' radicalism from themselves, had
moderated it for many generations after them, but now have fallen
away, revealing the Enlightenment extremism that had been there all
along.[11] About the only hope he sees for America is in the ongoing
revival of revealed religion. This is a peculiar hope, inasmuch as the
Enlightenment cut its teeth on the critique of revealed religion in the
seventeenth century. If its critique was plausible then, why should it
not be more so today, given our cultural decline? Bork attacks modern
liberalism wittily and passionately, but he does so because he does not
think it can be attacked rationally or philosophically; he thinks liberalism represents the triumph of reason (that is, Enlightenment) over faith
and tradition. He does not think that Enlightenment radicalism can be
refuted on the basis of reason, and so he stakes his case on results: he
tries to show that extreme egalitarianism and libertarianism ("the Sixties") are bad because their consequences (the Seventies, Eighties, and
Nineties, roughly speaking) are bad. Bork thus implies that Americans
are not so far gone as to be unable to recognize bad social policy when
they see it; but surely this implies that they have access to some knowledge of good and bad, right and wrong, independently of legal and
moral traditions that many of them, alas, have never known.

Bork has no great confidence in the possibility of such natural
knowledge, that is, in what can be known by human reason as opposed
to "Enlightenment" reason. For him, the hope for religious revival is
not a reasonable one but a desperate, last-chance hope — a Hail Mary

11. Robert H. Bork, *Slouching Towards Gomorrah* (New York: ReganBooks, 1996), pp. 56-58, 66-67.

pass if there ever was one! Bork does not see that modern, multicultural liberalism is really an attack on reason, especially on the reasonable morality of the American founders, in the name of will and authenticity. For the contemporary Left, after all, culture is not something reasonable. The "cultures" of multiculturalism are rooted in ethnicity, race, and gender — in our bodies, in the subrational parts of human nature. But more important than the bodily origins of the self is the *will*, which must shape or assemble these bodily facts into an identity. It is nowadays possible to have a sex change operation, for example, which shows that the will can trump gender; but only in the name of gender, "the real you" who must have your bodily nature adjusted to match your authentic self. Everything, starting with personal identity, becomes "socially constructed," which means in turn that everything is ripe for social deconstruction.

Against liberal relativism and deconstructionism, religion needs the assistance of reason. Without reason's authority, revelation is prey to the same easy-going egalitarianism and relativism of which Bork complains. In its highest sense, divine revelation is the disclosure of something suprarational, of something that cannot be known by human reason alone. But if reason cannot by its own operations arrive at any important truths about good and bad, right and wrong, the purposes of human life and liberty, then the suprarational (that which is "above reason") becomes a vacuous category, capable of holding everything and nothing, waiting to be filled with anybody's "values," however frivolous, however evil. Without reason's support, in other words, the suprarational tends to deconstruct into the subrational.

It is certainly true that Christianity and Judaism must play an indispensable role in any moral-cultural revival in America. But we should not look for the salvation of our culture from religion alone or, for that matter, from culture alone. Politics has an important, indeed a crucial role to play.

*   *   *

Perhaps the single most compelling lesson that we can learn from the American founding is that we need to begin to think of ourselves as founders, or more particularly as refounders of our civilization. The founders spoke of "civilization" rather than "culture," because they took their bearings from nature not history, from reason not passion or will, from mankind not ethnic groups, from freedom not determinism, and from politics not sociology. Nonetheless, the founders may be said to have deliberately set out to shape, through the influence of laws, mores, and their own example, the first American culture. In doing so, they did not begin with a pristine block of marble; they began as Englishmen, the inheritors of centuries of constitutional, religious, and artistic development. This impressive inheritance deserves greater consideration than we have time and occasion for here, needless to say. But despite this inheritance — and partly, of course, because of it — the Americans of the founding generation chose to cease being Englishmen and become something else.

Becoming American was initially a political and constitutional choice, but finally it necessitated a series of profound transformations in business, speech, dress, literature, religion, education, heroes, holidays, civic ceremonies — in character. The public schools movement was one of the most important, as well as one of the most obvious, of these subsequent efforts to conform the American people to their new republican institutions. It is an old political observation, echoed in Montesquieu and countless other writers, that in the beginning men make the institutions, and after that the institutions make the men. The American founders had this maxim very much in mind as they built the institutions that would guide the nation's destiny, and today it is worth pondering anew. Perhaps it is time to build some new institutions, if we are to have a real chance to rehabilitate American culture.

The Left took this path, beginning in the 1870s and 1880s, when it began to build America's first research universities and graduate schools, mostly on the German model, which its intellectual pioneers knew and intended would have a close, symbiotic relation with the modern state that they would also construct eventually. Experts from one would baptize the other, for the modern welfare and administrative state would be constantly in need of scientific civil servants, and the modern research university would be constantly honing its sense of social justice and administrative expertness or ambition. Conservatives today have made a fair beginning at counterrevolution, establishing think-tanks and policy journals galore; but much more needs to be done to found new elementary and secondary schools, colleges, and graduate programs, taking the founders' own precepts as the intellectual point of departure. Without intellectual support and legitimation from such new or renovated institutions, conservatives have little chance of achieving lasting political and cultural reformation — much less the renewal of our civilization.

5. Radical Challenges
to Liberal Democracy

WILLIAM B. ALLEN

HISTORY's dodo germinates future failures in the euphoric celebration of recent triumphs. Thus did Athens squander in Syracuse what she won in Greece. Thus did Rome despoil at home what she had gained in Carthage and Europe. Thus did American statesmen welcome the greatest military victory in human history — the victory of the United States over the Soviet Union — with the invocation of a New World Order predicated on economic determinism: free markets make free men. The special insouciance of this blind reliance on capitalism is its notable failure to recognize the opportunity to convert a merely military victory into a moral triumph. The world, therefore, joined the United States in easy assumption that the fall of Soviet-directed communism and parties of the left in Europe, Africa, and Latin America had disproved rather than merely disapproved of socialism. No one paused to inquire whether the soul of socialism had crept so nearly into the core of western liberal democracies, including the United States, that only the parasite's host had fallen, while the parasite had successfully migrated to fatter kine.

We reason correctly when we argue that the most significant practical challenge to liberal democracy was socialist-sponsored totalitarianism. Before we close the door on the history of radical challenges to liberal democracy, however, we ought to take stock of the foundations on which those challenges emerged, the merits of their positions, and the reasons they at length failed. Such a project would exceed by a considerable space the occasion afforded me to launch this inquiry here.

56

I can, however, frame the question suitably to later investigation. To that end I recapture the origins of radical challenges to liberal democracy, as reflected in Tocqueville and Marx, in order to demonstrate that we have not yet responded to the weightiest doubts regarding the moral sufficiency of this form of life.

Among radical challenges to liberal democracy I distinguish three that are separate and distinct: the moral, the political, and the intellectual. I would wish to demonstrate — but here can only suggest — that there are just these three and no more. To put the matter most succinctly: Liberal democracy fails insofar as, morally, it diminishes the weight and authority of moral principle in the lives of ordinary people; insofar as, politically, it entrusts the safety and prosperity of society to the hands of the foolish rather than the prudent; and insofar as, intellectually, it destroys the habit of deference to reason in regulating practical conduct.

The argument in favor of liberal democracy must be strong indeed to command the assent of respectable intelligences in the face of such an arraignment. While I focus on the long-perceived weaknesses of liberal democracy (in order to achieve a better understanding of perceived cultural defects in the contemporary era), I also point out that liberal democracy emerged in its best form against a backdrop of similar reflections.

Remember that constitutionalism anciently won acclaim as a good, while democracy anciently won scorn as an ill. At the advent of the modern era, the two terms converged such that democracy became the only substantive content for the process called constitutionalism. This altered perspective did not merely evolve but was rather ushered forth through serious argument and long reflection on the part of thinkers and statesmen who eventually abandoned the ancient distinctions and came to view democracy as necessary at minimum and potentially even good. What we now call liberal democracy results from this process as much as any other, boasting modern architects schooled in the ideas of classical political philosophy right up through Machiavelli. Simultaneously and correlatively, with altered moral and political perspectives, the process engendered diverging conceptions of the nature of political and social study — political science. In these divergences we can locate the radical challenges to liberal democracy at the same time as we discover how constitutionalism and democracy came effectively to be synonymous. Indeed, it was far rather to be wished that United States policy, in the aftermath of the fifty-year war with the Soviet Union, had trumpeted constitutionalism and democracy rather than capitalism and democracy. It trumpeted capitalism and democracy, however, because radical challenges to liberal democracy still live.

*   *   *

We begin by taking John Locke seriously, rather than to dismiss him simply because we are the children of Rousseau. We grapple with the same problem Locke grappled with, the same problem Montesquieu grappled with. The problem is to know how to generate liberalism, which is that form of society in which the individuals count for themselves as well as for their relationships. Political power there is exercised within limits that must respect that individualism, that individual liberty. Moreover, that liberty must be compatible with efforts toward acquisition of material goods. Thus, liberalism grew from an argument that holds that everyone has a right to defend his life, his liberty, and his property.

To be sure, equality was not less implicated in the founding of liberalism. However, the very fact that Rousseau diverged from the individualism of Locke and others demonstrates that equality was a contested and often misunderstood component of liberalism. This divergence, indeed, ultimately became the foundation for the radical challenges to liberalism which emerged in full throat in the nineteenth century, and which Tocqueville and Marx make clear not only for that century but for all time since. Because it was pre-nineteenth-century liberalism that eventuated in the liberal democracy of the United States, that is the background we need in order to assess the implications and the propriety of the subsequent challenges.

E. S. Corwin wrote earlier in this century of The "Higher Law" Background of American Constitutional Law and thereby situated the founding in the context of debates that still prevailed in the eighteenth century.[1] Those debates preserved an awareness of various forms of law beyond positive law, including divine, natural, and customary. Moreover, the idea of various forms of law descending from the Latin lex and jus entails an inherent distinction between the mere command of law (lex) and right inhering in law (jus). At its origins, then, liberalism enjoyed a vocabulary that has largely been lost to us now.

The question for Locke was the same as it had been for others. He

---

1. E. S. Corwin, The "Higher Law" Background of American Constitutional Law (Ithaca, N.Y.: Cornell University Press, 1965, c1929).

speaks of law in the sixth paragraph of his *Second Treatise*, where he defines the law of nature, as reason.[2] The various forms of law depict the means by which human beings have sought to set limits on their engagements in the world or the terms of their organized pursuits. Law posits a quest for order against the threat of the arbitrary or chaos. Locke started humankind in the state of nature and introduced war right there in the state of nature. But raising the notion of law right there and at the same time suggests an inherent if not realized order in human life. When Locke identified reason as that law, he specified it rather as potential than enjoyed. Nature in some fashion prescribes to human beings certain ordered relationships in order to the attainment of certain specified ends. Those ends, though, are pitifully few, mainly turning around self-preservation. All of the terms Locke derived from this observation refer to things that exist in the way that they exist because of an order pre-existing or inhering in the constitution of humanity.

Locke then began with laws by definition distinguished from laws that human beings impose upon themselves — positive laws. Whether his definitions differ from customary law, and perhaps divine law, raises a separate but not trivial question. The more we entertain such quandaries, the more we veer away from the goal we imagined. Beginning with what appear to be necessary relations, we quickly meet with an assertion that a particular command is, say, divine law. Then the question becomes what is one's relationship to the law based on its source. That is a fundamental question — the human being's relationship to the law relative to the source of the law. Does one have more or less an option regarding laws depending on the source of the law? Is the law that derives from nature more exiguous than a law that derives from another human being or less exiguous than one coming from God? Is a law of greater import when written? Is it of greater import when evolved, as in the common law? Corwin places these questions in a perspective that serves as a form of shorthand to situate our conversations about liberalism in the entire flow of political philosophy in the western world.

We read in the first book of Montesquieu's *Esprit des Lois*, which is entitled, "About Laws in General," that "the laws in the broadest meaning are the necessary relationships that derive from the nature of things. In this sense, all beings have their laws; the divinity has its laws;

2. John Locke, *Second Treatise on Civil Government*, para. 6.

the material world has its laws; intelligences superior to man have their laws; the beasts have their laws; man has his laws."[3] That statement and the following argument produce more problems than clarity, since the notion that everything that is has a law fails to rise above the banal. Without some distance between the way things are and the laws that are appropriate to things, or that govern the conduct or the behavior of things, no leverage over human action can be obtained.

Consider the implications of the difference between the terms, "behavior" and "conduct." These words do not refer to the same things, even if parents will occasionally speak loosely to children when admonishing or praising them. Characteristically, we speak of the behavior of inanimate matter — a passive recipient of forces existing in a Newtonian universe of equal and opposite actions and reactions. On the other hand, the word "conduct" invokes the notion that the being moves as if it conducts itself. It might move this way or that way upon election, upon choice. Hence, when we speak of humans our tendency, if we want to blame them for what they have done, is to speak of their conduct — their bad conduct. If we want to praise them as noble, we also speak of conduct. If we speak of their behavior, we do one of two things. We address ourselves to children, whom we conceive not to know what they are doing, or we adopt the modes of social scientists, who have reduced human things to things that are subhuman, as if we were only inanimate matter or at best beasts.

Montesquieu's opening sentence forces us to ask whether we must make a distinction between things passive and active when speaking of laws. Is all the world constructed of things passive — of equal and opposite actions and reactions? Or, is there some part of the world that is not passive, but active, and therefore sets motion in being rather than merely receiving motion from others?

Montesquieu opens with a fairly Newtonian view of the world, but he quickly goes through his first book to show a more complicated picture. He wrote of "intelligent beings," in particular. He means primarily human beings and he realizes the implication of the title of the work, the "spirit" of the laws [which we may take to mean the mind or intelligence of the laws], by focusing on the laws of human community. He affirmed that "individual intelligent beings" have laws that they have made and laws that they have not made, meaning that they are subject to both kinds of law — subject to being acted upon and

3. Charles de Montesquieu, *De l'esprit des lois*, Bk. I, ch. 1.

capable of acting. It is important to discern, therefore, which spheres rely upon which of the varying kinds of law.

Montesquieu followed this introduction by making the claim that "relationships of equity" exist prior to positive law. This very special term derives from our law books — especially Anglo-American law books. Equity is the principle by which a judge may look at a particular case and decide it on the basis of what is right for the case rather than the literal terms of the law. This occurs for the reason that laws themselves are always general, and general language does not always address specific facts in the manner that lawmakers would wish. Judgment in equity may say of a case in which the law requires "x" that the facts of the case make "y" more appropriate. In order to have a judgment in equity based on fairness or what is right in the case, the one thing needful is manifestly a standard of right. Reason may disclose such a standard; something else may do so; but there must by all means be one.

Thus emerges the question of the relationship of human beings to the principle behind the law. That is also the relevance of Corwin's discussion of the "higher law background" of American law. The claim is that there exists beyond lawmakers, beyond constitutions, and beyond organized society a principle that animates all human law. Moreover, human beings have access to that principle even when they do not enjoy consensus around that principle. It has become in our time a hotly contested issue whether natural law — or any higher law principle — ought ever to enter the minds of the judges and others involved in the judicial process. On the other side, the point is urged that it is difficult to discern the source of law's authority absent some principle of right that establishes it. Advocates of civil disobedience, in the absence of an appeal to higher principle, stand nakedly on an insistence upon their own interest. Critics who arraign unjust law point to an emptiness where there exists no justice apart from the law's command. No one may judge the law apart from the law itself when positive law is the highest thing to which human beings can appeal.

The significance of this debate is what it reveals about our opinions regarding the current character of our political regime — what we think the Constitution is and what we think are our claims under that Constitution. Related to this problematic is the word most prominent, ultimately, in Locke's political philosophy, the word that anchors the claim that every man has a "right to life, liberty, and property." Locke introduced "right" in a different context than has characterized our discussion of the right behind the law. This right does not derive from a standard of justice, per se. For justice is invoked necessarily in judging differences between individuals. Locke's "right," by contrast, is applied to an individual without respect to any other particular individual.[4]

Take the right to life. In Locke's argument it is a "right" to life because it is a course of action required of the being and from which the individual cannot desist. One cannot fail to act on the basis of this principle of self-preservation. It is inherent in one's being. What one does, and what makes one what he is, is precisely to preserve one's life. Thus it becomes a right to life. The corollary is the "right" to liberty, because the action that preserves one's life presupposes the liberty to act for the purpose of preserving one's life. The "right" to property similarly becomes a right because property constitutes those things that one obtains with the end in view of preserving one's life. In the end it all comes back to the imperious necessity that we feed, shelter, and defend ourselves. Hence it is a right that no one can take from one, and it is a right that one cannot give away. Naturally, Locke is aware of suicide and self-sacrifice. He maintains, however, that in such cases people suffer from some disorder. For they cannot and have no right to take their lives. Thus, far from requiring judgment in the cases of conflict between individuals, a right is turned squarely on the individual himself.

Thinking through Locke's argument, we can discern the problem he aimed to resolve. That problem is not merely how to generate human society. That is the ultimate goal — what we may call state building. But the problem is to know the foundations, to know why it is that men do not simply live idly in what he called the state of nature. The principal reason he gave is that, in the state of nature they would be constantly in a state of war. It would be dangerous and insecure. Men would not be happy, and they would not live long. They leave the state of nature to preserve their lives.

But Locke is also mindful of locating the motivation of human action. He seeks a comprehensive, universal, scientific explanation. He seeks to eliminate external influences in order to identify the sameness that underlies the apparent differences in beings. He seeks that source of motivation, that source of human conduct, that is the same everywhere. At the first level he identified it as self-preservation, and at the next level he observed that this motive drives man straight into society. In that society they create governments, governments subject to certain rules,

4. Locke, para. 6.

62

certain limitations on power. This results from the initial impulse, driving men into government, which defines the limits of governmental power. No one would join this club if it meant sacrificing the right to life. Thus the government must be such that it cannot arbitrarily deprive one of life, liberty, or property. This fosters a relationship between contracting citizens and a government limited by the contract.

Of course this argument suffers the defect of jumping from the initial impulse to society (self-preservation) to the consummation of individual desires (happiness) without so much as pausing amidst the disorderly facts of human relationships and mutual dependencies. The Declaration of Independence's "pursuit of happiness" is perfectly Lockeian — and more succinctly so — in that regard. Human life lives itself out, and conduct is more determinative, not where ultimate motivations or enjoyments prevail, however. Rather, the messy state of classes and orders, ranks and positions, families and priests sets the measures that both inspire one's motives and set the limits to one's enjoyments. Hence, it matters to know whether a theory of individualism can provide prudent guidance through messiness.

*   *   *

To turn to our chroniclers, I want to focus ultimately on Tocqueville's personal reminiscences of revolutionary France in 1848, paving the way by revisiting his work on the revolution of 1789 (which he wrote in the same atmosphere in which he wrote his reminiscences). Afterwards I introduce reactions to the same events and from a slight distance by Karl Marx (who lived in London at the time of the troubles in France). It will be important to recall that the ferment in 1848 was not exclusive to France. Much if not all of Europe experienced radical ferment — Italy and Hungary prominently. Monarchy had been under pressure since the time of the first revolution in France, and democracy would undergo continual pressure after the revolutions of 1848. Tocqueville, then, provides a starting point for thinking about the issues involved in nineteenth-century radicalism.

We know Tocqueville as the author of *Democracy in America*, a great critic-analyst of democracy.[5] He was philosophically learned and also something of a historian to boot. Moreover he was a politician,

---

5. Alexis de Tocqueville, *Democracy in America* (New York: Modern Library, 1981).

WILLIAM B. ALLEN

who in 1848 was a participant-observer in the various assemblies and struggles of political parties as France underwent popular rebellion and reaction time after time. Tocqueville ended a minister in government under Louis Napoleon — that great non-democratic "voice of the people" of mid-nineteenth-century France.

Bearing in mind this history of Tocqueville, we can more readily comprehend his commentary on the original revolution, and there is no better place to begin our search than with the passage in his *Recollections* in which he discusses an episode with his manservant, Eugène [pp. 156-57]. Tocqueville retired to his room, exhausted from ongoing battles and deliberations in the city of Paris. He tried to fall asleep, when he heard a knock at his door. It was Eugène, who had looked in "to see if I had returned, and if I did not require his services." Eugène had left the bivouac that he had joined wearing a national guard uniform and carrying a good musket borrowed from Tocqueville.

> This man was no socialist, either by temperament or in theory. He was not even touched to a slight degree by that most usual sickness of the times, a restless mind, and one should have had trouble to find even in any other era than ours, one more quiet in his station and without any regrets whatsoever. Always very pleased with himself and tolerably pleased with others, he ordinarily desired only what was within his reach, and he pretty nearly got, believed he had gotten, everything he desired. In this manner all by himself he followed the precepts philosophers teach but seldom observe, and he enjoyed as a gift of nature that happy balance between powers and wants that alone brings the happiness promised by philosophy. Well, Eugène, I asked him, when he came in that morning, how are things going? "Very well, sir, perfectly well." "How do you mean very well, when I can still hear gunfire?" "Yes, they are still fighting. But everyone is saying that it will end very well." As he said that, he took off his uniform, cleaned my boots and brushed my clothes, and then, putting on his uniform again, said, "If you do not need anything else, sir, with your permission, I will go back to the battle."[6]

This is a particularly touching exchange between man — the aristocrat (Tocqueville was born an aristocrat, though in the politics of the

6. Alexis de Tocqueville, *Souvenirs* (Paris: Gallimard, 1964), edited by J. P. Mayer and B. M. Wicks Boisson, Pt. II, Ch. 10, pp. 240-41. [Translation by author]

day he was a republican) — and man — the servant. Both were then wrapped up in the great democratic turmoil of the insurgency of the people against their rulers and the bourgeoisie in May and June of 1848. The book opened in February amidst the first great overthrow, when the monarchy was overthrown directly by popular revolt. Tocqueville described this as the first time the people had actually rebelled and overthrown a government, as opposed to being led in that kind of activity by intellectuals or aristocrats or someone from the bourgeoisie.

To understand the significance of what happened in 1848, it is important to recapture a sense of what happened originally in France. The very first words in the first chapter of Tocqueville's book on the "old regime" are the words:

> Nothing more fitly reminds philosophers and statesmen to be modest than the history of our Revolution. For never were so great events, carried so far and better prepared, and so little foreseen.[7]

This presents what for Tocqueville constitutes the paradox of the French Revolution: that it was not in every decisive respect save one an innovation. All that had happened was in fact laid out in a chain of cause and effect stretching back several centuries. It was really the story of the undoing of the French monarchy or feudal monarchy (since it happened all over Europe save England). The undoing of the feudal monarchy was at the hands of feudal monarchs.

The *Old Regime* tells the story of how the monarchs set about to destroy for purposes of political order what, in a Burkean sense, is best called the social order. There had existed a society of balanced classes — peasants, lords, noblemen, kings, councilors — with everything in its place, the clergy naturally playing a major role. Over time, through internecine struggles at the level of the ruling class, they discovered the art of playing the people off against one another. And through the course of time they completely undid that balanced constitution for the sake of expediency.

That is the story of the old regime. Tocqueville is French, though, and he did not write about France in the manner that he wrote about America. He visited America in the early 1830s, and many describe the writings that resulted as more about France than America. The year

7. Alexis de Tocqueville, *L'ancien régime et la révolution* (Paris: Gallimard, 1967), edited by J. P. Mayer, Ch. 1, p. 57.

1832 marked the beginning of the French monarchy that was over-thrown in 1848. In 1832 the French enjoyed a breathing space, having undergone since 1789 several revolutions — a constitutional revolution replaced by a radical state, replaced by Robespierre and a Directory, replaced by Bonaparte, replaced by a constitutional monarchy, replaced by another constitutional monarchy, replaced by another despotism, and finally replaced by the constitutional monarchy of 1832. The aristocrat in America provided a natural connection between the two events. Thus, he traveled to the United States to inquire why they had not undergone the same turmoil the French had undergone. What in the way of France's enjoying democracy distinguishes it?

Tocqueville's writing about the events of 1848 and 1789 not only described what happened in France but from the point of view of someone seeking a useful perspective on those events. Nonetheless the details of the stories he told focus largely on speculation, the part speculation plays in driving political events. He identified the role of eighteenth-century enlightenment in shaping all the political events which occurred at the end of that century, meaning the American and French revolutions, and which proceeded to reshape the human moral and political landscape. We may throw in the economic landscape as well, for we see very shortly thereafter that notions derived from economists — particularly those of the Scottish philosophers — became completely wound up in the broader notions of enlightenment and liberal democracy.

We may divide enlightenment philosophy into two lines of thought. Tocqueville observed that:

> We rightly judge eighteenth-century philosophy as one of the main causes of the Revolution, and it is moreover true that that philosophy is profoundly irreligious. But one should pay careful attention to two parts of it, which are at once distinct and separable.
>
> In one gathered all the new or renovated opinions concerning the condition of societies and the principles of civil and political law — such, for example, as the natural equality of men, the abolition of all privileges of caste, class, and of professions — that are a consequence of it — i.e., the sovereignty of the people, the omnipotence of the social power, the uniformity of rules. . . . All these doctrines are not only the cause of the French Revolution, but constitute thus its substance, so to speak. They are what is most fundamental, most lasting, and most true throughout time in the work of the Revolution.

In the second part of their doctrines eighteenth-century philosophers attacked the church with a kind of fury. They attacked its clergy,
its hierarchy, its institutions, and its dogmas; and in order to be able
to overthrow them, they sought to tear out even the fundamentals of
Christianity.[8]

The two lines of development are clearly stated. One is the general
argument about humanity and the rights of man (and it is important here
to use the French Revolution language — "rights of man" — as opposed
to the language which still echoes the classical world, "natural rights" —
because a transformation has taken place. There is no longer from this
vantage point natural law or natural rights. The single, most important
dimension of human relations becomes power. Further, the principle
used to organize and guide power is the principle of the rights of man as
enunciated in the French *Declaration of the Rights of Man* in 1789.

The 1789 Declaration is a different tool than the *Declaration of
Independence* in the United States; where it remains possible to speak of
natural law; where it is still possible to speak of God as somehow the
Creator of human rights; and where God is somehow the Creator of
principles of association that are discerned to be inalienable as they
apply to human beings. There is a gulf between that kind of reasoning
and the claims that prevailed through the French Revolution. The gulf
forms in the various responses to the question: What are the activities
human beings can ordinarily pursue and from which they cannot reasonably desist?

The profoundest implication of this change is that efforts directed
toward self-preservation come to be seen in another light. Men derived
certain notions from this proposition that came increasingly to focus
on the more material aspects of humanity, those things having to do
with the immediate care and succor of our bodies. That came to be
addressed as the rights of man, where the rights defined a certain kind
of power. This led ultimately to a view that the failures of human beings
to do the things they try to do constitute deprivations rather than
failures relating to any intrinsic talents or abilities. The language of
Rousseau rose to the fore: "Man is born free, but everywhere we see
him in chains."[9] All inequalities began to be seen, not as the con-

8. Ibid., p. 63.
9. Jean-Jacques Rousseau, *Contrat social; ou principes du droit politique* (Geneva:
Chez Marc-Michel Bosquet, 1766), I, i.

sequences of any individual conduct but as relationships of oppression. The assumption is that, if a human being cannot fail to act to acquire what is good for himself, to secure such material substance as will render him comfortable in this world, then the failure cannot lie to his account but must be attributed to some intrusion, some obstruction. It is a social disorder parallel to the individual disorder in the case of suicide. On these grounds men began to speak of poverty in a different way than they would when informed by previous conceptions.

Tocqueville claimed that this transition was part and parcel of an enlightenment philosophy that not only generated a general picture of humanity but also a ferocious attack on religion, which was rooted in an older language. The notion of the higher law, which we know to play a role in the American constitutional tradition, was completely cut off from this new line of analysis that gave birth to the French Revolution and rendered an entirely different kind of revolution than that in the United States. How do they differ? In the first place the French Revolution was a revolution against society far more fundamentally than it was a revolution against government. The *Old Regime* explained that, when the revolution was accomplished, the French returned to the old powers of government. They tossed the social order upside down; they beheaded queens and princes, and they putatively enthroned the people. But they still had an all-powerful, centralized state. The real objective was to overturn social relationships, the orders of society, insofar as men perceived in those orders the immediate cause of social disparity. Social disparity became the most direct evidence of denial of rights, with rights now interpreted as the power to acquire comfort in this world.

Tocqueville described politics as well as philosophy in the *Old Regime*. In fact, he argued that the philosophers (or the literary men, as he called them), who generated the ideas for the revolution (so much so that the revolution was carried out more in the language of literature than that of politics), had no political experience and little political judgment. The politicians, on the other hand, were totally oblivious to the consequences of their own choices and their own judgments. The kings themselves adopted the language of the rights of man. The power holders themselves insinuated the very ideas that would flower in the outburst of the revolution. He maintained that the rulers:

> strive within their realms to destroy immunities and abolish privileges. They confuse the orders of society, equalize social conditions, and replace the aristocracy with a bureaucracy, local regimes with

centralized or uniform regulations, and the multiplicity of diverse powers with a unity of government. They undertake this revolutionary work with constant industry; and if they encounter some obstacle they adopt the procedures and maxims of the Revolution. They frequently adopt the expedient of playing poor against rich, commoner against nobleman, peasant against lord.[10]

By contrast, *Federalist* number ten identified the most constant source of faction as the "various and unequal distribution of property," but as a prelude to an argument about managing rather than eradicating the difference.[11] James Madison's argument held that this was essential in political life, and that the point of political thinking is to generate arrangements to deal with rather than eradicate a phenomenon intrinsic to our humanity. Thus, when projects begin that seek to eradicate the causes of inequality, one of the consequences is to watch bold and frightening initiatives that have no capacity to improve human life but extraordinary potential to destroy the order of society. Tocqueville, by discovering that it was not the philosophers or revolutionaries but the rulers themselves who made the crucial contribution by adopting the defective mode of reasoning, describes an intersection of politics and philosophy that returns in 1848 with devastating clarity.

The Old Regime constitutes a model of historical sleuthing. In it Tocqueville returned to all the old documents from the regional governments and municipalities in order to demonstrate systematically how a society of aristocrats and peasants used to have an organic connection. They were co-dependent and could each call upon the other for support, in much the manner of the interaction of Tocqueville and Eugène. This order was disestablished because monarchs, starting with Louis XIV, had decided that they needed to increase their power over the aristocrats. The aristocrats were independent power centers in this era of the birth of the nation-state. They needed to be reduced, and one means of accomplishing that was to detach them from the peasants. By the time the monarchs consummated the work, however, what France had were millions of isolated peasants who had no one to turn to. Aristocrats and peasants became natural enemies to each other rather than people organically connected in a single society.

10. Tocqueville, *L'ancien régime et la révolution*, pp. 66-67.
11. Alexander Hamilton, James Madison, John Jay, *The Federalist* (New York: Mentor, 1961), essay number 10.

The philosophy of the era, then, holds that there are no justifications for the distinctions we see in the social order. Parallel to the philosophy we find a politics in the era, in which those who are charged with preserving the social order sacrifice it for their own immediate political advantage. A third factor enters in the third chapter: the observation that the French Revolution was "worldwide." The revolution was not carried out in the name of this tribe, the French, but in the name of humanity. The revolution in the United States, by contrast, had an impact that was worldwide (and, as Lincoln correctly observed, the example of the United States continues to do so), principally by structuring peoples' expectations of political decency. Although the *Declaration of Independence* appeals to the "candid" judgment of the world, and the first *Federalist* holds that the American founding settles a question for mankind and not just for the United States, this revolution was not directed outside the immediate political sphere of the United States. Americans required to justify themselves to the world, because their sstandard was the standard of reason, which in turn was attached to natural law. Thus, they created a particular society, although no longer determined by blood, in the context of a general conception of humanity. The French revolution lacked such modesty; it was projected to declare illegitimate every foundation of sociopolitical order except those mirroring the events that transpired in France and the principles that underlay those events.

This produced a harmful consequence. Where one refuses to identify the French nation as having a peculiar title to these revolutionary claims, and where one would, besides, urge the imminent necessity of all humans acting accordingly, one ends by separating human beings rather than uniting them. The reason is that on these terms a Frenchman is no longer a Frenchman, strictly speaking. A Frenchman is merely a human being, one who has no greater reason to find intimacy with someone next door than with someone a thousand leagues away. There is no intrinsic principle by which one can argue that neighbors ought to sustain an immediate relationship, apart from going through the task of establishing a social contract and constitution and committing themselves to a specific political (not social) order, whose laws are binding with all the strength that Rousseau's "general will" called for. That also means an exaggeration of homogeneity among men. The existing social order that came under attack was not merely illegitimate, but all those who held places within it became illegitimate — deserving punishment. Hence, attacks upon the church and churchmen followed in France.

Tocqueville's argument means that the political dynamic of the revolution in France is largely a question of political ideas without political judgment creating a movement that gets out of control. That creates in turn a situation in which the only control that can be established is despotic. This became the story of France for the sixty years between 1789 and 1848. He described a process that eventuated in a situation in which there was no longer an authority to which ordinary citizens would subordinate themselves, their urges, their desires, their inclinations — their rights. It had ceased to be a question of bringing the people into a common framework. A common framework could barely contain their appetites. In the *Recollections*, Tocqueville focused earliest and most powerfully on envy and resentment. These are the feelings that come to the fore in the aftermath of destructive revolution.

Arguably, there is no more powerful argument against liberal democracy than that it invariably leads to France — i.e., it sets in motion leveling influences that destroy the respect human beings have for particular excellences. Thus it leaves human beings with nothing more to motivate their conduct than their own self-concern, which expresses itself most powerfully in envy and resentment towards all superior endowments. It is a flattening of social distinction simultaneously with a heightening of "every the least difference" among men.[12] We learn in this form of society to hate those who are unlike ourselves, a result that paradoxically subtends most if not all of the conversation regarding diversity, racism, and multiculturalism in the late twentieth century. Nor does this imitate the ancient world, in which people saw themselves as belonging to an *ethnos* — a tribe, a family, a nation — and therefore unlike any outside. Those differences were important precisely because they were not individual differences. The differences that led some to call themselves civilized and others barbarians were differences those men ascribed to themselves in a corporate posture, as part of a collectivity. It was a question of belonging and cultivation. That is not the soul of the conversation in the modern world, where, instead, the true spirit is that "every the least difference" rankles. It becomes for us something we cannot tolerate in proportion as we are imbued with the democratic ethos, in proportion as we believe that nothing apart from equality is acceptable and insofar as we can make no distinction between moral inequality and other forms of inequality. Tocqueville has shown us how these ideas came to be rooted in the

12. Locke, para. 21.

mind of the modern west (from which they have spread largely throughout the world), and the process notably precedes the intrusion of organized socialism. These ideas reduce to an accentuated regard for equality coupled with a heightened intolerance for apparent difference (materially and morally).

Why did this happen? In the third book of *The Old Regime*, Tocqueville returned to the philosophers, to show how they introduced such chaos:

> They ceaselessly busied themselves with thoughts concerning government; basically, that was their vocation. Folk daily listened to them discoursing on the origins of societies and on their primitive forms, on the primordial rights of citizens and those in authority, on the natural and artificial relations among men, the error or legitimacy of custom, and even on the fundamental principles of the laws. Thus prying apart each day the very foundations of the constitution of their day, they examined its structure with curiosity and critiqued its overall design.[13]

We may assume that earlier thinkers were led to raise these questions for the same reasons that we raise them so naturally and that they are intrinsic to our idea of progress.

In fact, however, contemporary man acquired a taste for such inquiry. So far is ancient man from identifying an evolutionary necessity with regard to change in human nature or human conduct, that he required first, and before raising a moral question about conduct or the origins of fundamental principles, to observe that such questions presuppose that he does not know already the answers. Human beings, however, do not commence empty and then fill themselves up bit by bit. They improve on the efficiency of mechanisms to pursue instrumental means, to make axes, hatchets, and slingshots; they do not become progressively certain of convictions that they should defend their lives, defend their families, raise their children, and live at peace with their neighbors. The latter are not, I would say, natural questions for man. Rather, one must be taught to ask such questions. Else he never would, for it is unnatural to look for the roots of conduct.

To assume otherwise is to presuppose that human beings evolve morally. Tocqueville, however, asked precisely why one would take

13. Tocqueville, *L'ancien régime et la révolution*, Liv. III, ch. 1, p. 230.

apart the foundations of society. For to do so implies that one already expects to be able to do something to improve it. The precondition of such a question is already an inclination towards change. To ask what is the foundation of a given social order is to think that it might, or perhaps ought to, be different. That is the perspective that Tocqueville argues to be unnatural. The natural instinct is to defend what is one's own, to defend what one has and what is. One must learn to desire to be different from what one is; one must acquire a belief in evolution or progress.

Typically, human beings in the ancient world believed that what was old, what was accomplished, was better. In some distant golden age the forefathers were near-gods and the contemporary descendants but pale shadows of the distant gods. All that descendants do undermines their forefathers' greatness, and the most they can do is try very hard not to undermine it too much by securing themselves faithfully within piety to their fathers' memory.

Human society characteristically organized itself thus, but a different form of organization in the modern world has inverted the order. Now we say that everything old is inferior. We must evolve, for we will never be good enough unless we become better than they were. We prefer change to stability, for change is always for the better — never the worse. That is the modern attitude, and it is sponsored by the disposition that entered the French Revolution. There you do not find talk about the higher law, or a nice concern to separate natural law from positive law, customary law, or constitutional law. Everything reduces to positive law — the expression of contemporary will.

Since man drives the process of change, the single most important element is the contemporary expression of his will.[14] That becomes law, and all attempts to organize society are attempts to organize that expression of will — to make it as clear and resounding as possible. Viewing political debates from this perspective makes clear that the principal point of dispute is how one acts to bring people together in such a way as to silence discord and produce as near as possible a clear and coherent expression of will. Governments are deemed better as they approximate that and worse in proportion as they do not. For that reason, twentieth-century social scientists have frequently rejected as a system

14. "The earth belongs to the living," Thomas Jefferson exclaimed in a 1789 letter to James Madison. See *The Portable Thomas Jefferson*, edited by Merrill D. Peterson (New York: Viking Press, 1975).

of "deadlock," in the words of James MacGregor Burns, the elaborate mechanism described by James Madison.[15] The system is not designed to surface a single voice; its multiple interests and voices, variously checking and balancing, produce confusion. It does not satisfy the ambition to change man.

Whether and how we should change ourselves is a subject that generates a good many differences of view. The first thing that derives from the habit described by Tocqueville is the invention of political systems of all kinds — each now predicated on obtaining a certain goal, which is to turn the new political systems first identified as liberal democracies into the coherent expression of public will. But every new turn on that system becomes more and more eccentric, as if it were some wild trial-and-error experimentation. Moreover, frustration increases upon each iteration of the process; the inventors become more and more inventive and less intuitive. Their systems speak less directly to moral principles in a language that we would easily recognize and that we could easily adopt.

Tocqueville believed that what was wanted was to replace the complex of traditional customs governing the social order of the day by simple, elementary rules deriving from the exercise of human reason and the natural law. That was the starting point that, over time, became infinitely more complex. Looking closely into it, Tocqueville observed:

> . . . one sees that what may be called the political philosophy of the eighteenth century properly speaking consists in this single notion. Such a thought was not new: it ebbed and flowed ceaselessly through three thousand years without being able solidly to establish itself in human imagination. How on this occasion did it succeed in conquering the intelligences of every writer? Why, instead of expiring as it had so often done before in the brain of this or that philosopher, did it drop all the way to the mob and there acquire the consistency and heat of a political passion — so greatly that one might observe general and abstract theories on the nature of society becoming the topic of daily intercourse for the idle and even firing the imaginations of women and peasants?[16]

15. James MacGregor Burns, *The Deadlock of Democracy; four party politics in America* (Engelwood Cliffs, N.J.: Prentice-Hall, 1963).

16. Tocqueville, *L'ancien régime et la révolution*, Liv. III, ch. 1, p. 231.

The argument is quite straightforward. Ordinary people today talk as though they were philosophers. They use abstractions and handle terms like "rights" as if they knew what they meant. They do not speak in terms of intimate relationship and the easy identifications and distinctions that one makes through mere familiarity. That was a change in the world, according to Tocqueville.

Now, does the fact that everyone speaks like a philosopher make everyone a philosopher — including so-called professors of philosophy? Is that what enlightenment comes to, to invent new vocabulary that, as it is used more widely, structures our experience and brings everyone to live like philosophers? We do tend to say today that everyone has a philosophy, do we not? Is it sufficient to use the language of philosophy to be able to philosophize?

In the political context, the question — Tocqueville's question — is how these abstract theories and generalizations regarding the nature of government were able to produce confidence in ordinary citizens. Consider religion in contrast. If we observed that ordinary citizens came to believe and use the language of the synoptic gospels, would it be appropriate to consider them divines? We need to inquire why we do not grant the same kind of authority to the common language of Christianity and religion in general that we grant to philosophy. Interestingly, we can trace the progress of religious language. We find people learning from missionaries and proselytizers, learning in Sunday schools regularly and tirelessly, repeating and memorizing the language. That is how we get this language worked into the soul of the believers, and not merely speaking and writing some books. It was a long and serious enterprise that took considerable effort and a long time to work its way even into the illiterate classes.

The revolution in France was different. Without having special schools set up for the purpose, the language of rights and abstract generalization, humanity in place of nationality, became pervasive. Ordinary people came to use this language in the same way they used to quote gospel verses. How could it have happened?

Tocqueville does not answer the question phrased in that way. But he does suggest an answer. After noting that the literary people became bolder and bolder and contemptuous of the wisdom of the ages, he argued, "It was the [writers'] very ignorance [about politics] that won the ear and the heart of the mob."[17] People, he meant, had been isolated

17. Ibid., p. 233.

from one another, so that the discourse of community was no longer clearly structured. There remained the underlying discourse of religion, but there was no conscious and open discourse of community that defined their circumstances. They were vulnerable to the first argument that came along.

The first argument to come along was a powerful appeal to their emotion. To identify the emotion, Tocqueville pointed out that in the twenty years prior to 1789 France enjoyed enormous prosperity. Louis XVI had presided over a recovery from the great depression that characterized the reign of Louis XV. In the attitude and atmosphere of great prosperity much of the imprudent language of class division was used. The emotion that was appealed to was greed, and in a circumstance in which people had no particular reason to be ashamed of being greedy. The social bonds that otherwise would have restrained had already been dissolved. They were left ripe for the picking. Tocqueville called this the debacle of freedom. In it the one freedom that overshadowed all others was "philosophizing without limit on the origins of societies, the essential nature of government, and the primordial rights of humankind . . . and the writers, assuming control of public opinion, also assumed momentarily the place that party leaders ordinarily occupy in free countries."[18]

France was not free but there was free discussion among people isolated from one another. They were alienated — not in the sense modern sociology employs but in a kind of political disarticulation. Tocqueville contrasts the American Revolution with the French Revolution:

[The American Revolution] effectively had great influence on the French Revolution, but owed it less to what was done at the time in the United States than to what folk were thinking at the same time in France. While for the rest of Europe the American Revolution was still nothing but a singular and novel fact, in France it reinforced more strikingly and palpably what folk already knew. Elsewhere it was surprising; in France it was convincing proof. The Americans seemed only to perform what our writers had conceived; they gave the reality of substance to things we were dreaming about.[19]

18. Ibid., pp. 233-34.
19. Ibid., p. 234.

76

Thus, French thinkers were bolstered first by getting ordinary people to adopt their opinions, and then they were bolstered by the view that history was on their side. Things were moving their way.

Again, the problem is to know what it takes to make people want to change a political system. The key is to believe that making a change does not expose one to much peril or what is the same, not believing that it is better to remain the same than to risk a change. People gain that confidence, it seems, especially from resentment, deep resentment. In place of the hope of something better one can install a powerful hatred of what is. That plays a large role in modern revolutions. Tocqueville noted that, in America, there was a resistance to such a development, in the form of its religion.

> Every American I meet, whether in his country or elsewhere, I ask whether he believes religion is useful for the stability of the laws and the good order of society. Without hesitating he responds that a civilized society, and above all a free society, cannot survive without religion. Respect for religion, in his eyes, is the greatest guarantee of the state's stability and the safety of individuals. The person least instructed in the science of government knows that much. Yet, there is in the world no country where the boldest political doctrines of eighteenth-century philosophers could be more rigorously instituted than America. Their anti-religious doctrines exclusively have never been able to see the light of day in America, even on behalf of the unlimited liberty of the press.[20]

The statement is extraordinary. Tocqueville described the origins of liberal democracy and how it operates in different arenas. Liberal democracy, which comes from the boldest theories of eighteenth-century philosophers, is effectively put into practice in the United States, but with a condition attached. The condition is the expression of confidence in religion in addition to those theories to produce stability. But the philosophers attacked religion ferociously. Thus, Tocqueville means that the Americans adopted these theories up to a point but stopped, whereas the French did not stop.

While religion is the topic here, the underlying subject is the need for principles of relationship independent of politics in order to make a liberal democracy work. It is a conversation about the reason one

20. Ibid., p. 248.

requires social principles beyond political principles in order to make liberal democracy work. The idea is that if one tries to make politics the totality of the human experience and organizes politics on the grounds of liberal democracy, one will produce moral chaos. One will leave people who require social and moral guidance without any restraint or guidance. They will see politics as the only instrument suited to the pursuit of desire or ambition. They will turn all of their relationships and their differences into moments of political contest and struggle. Every political judgment will become a judgment of persons, positions, and status. Therefore, unless one can give people beyond politics all of those elements of person, position, and status, and at the same time preserve some moral leverage over them, one cannot prevent the harmful effects of the regime of equality — liberal democracy — from destroying the society.

Tocqueville observed in his *Recollections* that he had "sometimes thought that, though the mores of different societies varied, the morality of the politicians in charge of affairs was the same everywhere." He added in this context that "I often glide between good and evil with a soft indulgence that borders on weakness, and my quickness to forget grievances seems more like a lack of spirit than an inability to suffer the memory of an affront rather than any virtuous effort to efface such an impression." These statements show Tocqueville's struggle with the spirit of revolution in France. The real question in all of his writings — one that he addresses directly only in *Democracy in America,* so far as I know — is to know why we cannot have in modern times someone who can exert an authority like the authority of founders in ancient times. Why cannot we have a Moses or a Lycurgus? That question contains the further question whether there is any way out of chaos, once the march of liberal democracy has begun and has spun into the disorder manifested in 1848. The answer seems to be no. Although he commends ways in which men may mitigate the disorders with which they live, he does not seem to believe it is possible to turn back modern principles. Tocqueville the critic thus poses the most powerful intellectual challenge to liberal democracy. He sees no way that it can be made safe for human beings, which is a far more important question than whether the world can be made safe for it.

The principle threat to liberal democracy, and for human beings, is its consistent tendency to surrender to radical challengers, the most potent political example of which has been socialism. Tocqueville correctly identified this as the underlying question of 1848 (as did Marx, though with different affection), and for more than a hundred years thereafter it grew in significance to become the overriding question. Little wonder, then, that as the world seemed finally to defeat socialism, many *imagined* that it had defeated the arguments against liberal democracy. When we look more closely at 1848 through the eyes of Tocqueville and Marx, however, we discover reasons to doubt the wisdom of the prevailing view.

Tocqueville (in the *Recollections*) and Marx (in the *Eighteenth Brumaire*) discuss the same issues. First, does society originate in justice or injustice? Second, do the institutions of society operate in such a way as to improve human life? Third, is there any prospect to realize the ambition referred to as universal suffrage when we talk only in institutional terms but which, morally and culturally, means something richer than just voting? The proposition of universal suffrage must be based on the idea that human beings can come to be altogether capable of reasoning together about the things of human life and the common good. Human beings altogether (or to so wide an extent that the omissions are trivial) must come to be capable of moderation, self-government, and moral sense in order to justify confidence in universal suffrage.

Anyone who thought that people only acted out of callous self-interest should have trouble defending universal suffrage. This, then, was the question of revolution in France — the oscillation between centralized power and revolts of the people. After February 1848, and the great popular rebellion in the name of universal suffrage, one finds in 1849 universal suffrage itself taken away by the republican government, under the fear that the people will abuse the power.

Is it true that the people will abuse power in general; ought power to be reserved only to those who have moral strength and understanding sufficient to exercise it? Or is there yet another basis for political life? One wants more to know how Tocqueville stands on this question than on the mere question of political affections.

Tocqueville is no simple democrat. He is skeptical about democracy. He does regard it as the irresistible wave of the future, but he does not think it a very good idea. For it delivers power to people who do not know what to do with it — people who will act out of envy rather than wisdom, who will be more concerned to level from their passion for equality than concerned to establish their particular city or country safely. Such a people will override a range of questions that statesmen need to handle, driven by their relative status vis-à-vis others in the community. The first volume of *Democracy in America* had already signaled this [p. 178]. Tocqueville described the disappearance of aristocracy in the United States, where even natural aristocrats go into hiding:

> Nowadays, one may say that the wealthy social classes in the United States are almost entirely outside the political arena. Moreover, wealth — far from being a right — there is a real cause of disfavor and an obstacle to reaching power. . . .
>
> The rich surrender to this state of affairs as an irremediable evil, while he avoids with exquisite care showing how hurt he is. . . . One hears him boast publicly of the benefits of republican government and the advantages of democratic forms. After all, what is more natural in men, after hating their enemies, than to flatter them?[21]

He suggests that real human distinction is an obstacle to gaining power in democracy. The death of aristocracy tells us something about the character of liberal democracy. We ask, "How we can originate the society without a principle of sociality, and how can we expect it to function if people are motivated solely by self-interest?" The answer usually presented as a responding miracle is the supposed discovery that we do not need moral principles, and we can make society work by orchestrating the interactions of self-interest so as to create a social equilibrium from everyone pursing his own goals and not caring about anyone else's.

Critics have denied the miracle. The Antifederalists, for example, favored some sense of community, some homogeneity, something social to hold things together sufficiently to foster mutual reliance in order to make democratic politics work. The argument from rights (understood as mere interest), however, says nothing about participation in politics and political responsibility. It ultimately assumes an almost utopian balance of forces in which all of the classical historical problems of human life have disappeared. Men have become consumed with pursuing their own interests and satiating their own passions.

Tocqueville urged that no such balance emerged in the revolution, for people were so bent on satiating their passions that they were almost resistless. One could not turn them back any time they had the idea that they could lay hands on someone else's goods. He described them:

21. Tocqueville, *Democracy in America*, Vol. I, p. 262.

Folk had assured these poor people that the property of the wealthy were somehow obtained by theft from them. Folk assured them that the inequality of fortunes was as contrary to morality and society as to nature. Many poor people believed it, assisted by needs and passions. That obscure and erroneous conception of right, which mated with brute force, imparted to this concept an energy, tenacity, and power that it never should have acquired singly.[22]

This is a portrait of the popular insurrection in June 1848. The "theories of socialism" held by the insurrectionists led them to believe they had a right to goods stolen from them on account of society's originating in injustice. They think the only way to recover their goods is to reach out and take them, because the inequalities they suffer are not only historically wrong but also a continuing moral injury to them.

The implication is that what began as an argument about individual rights veered off track, because it did not take into account the motivations of human beings. Men would see their own poverty, insofar as they experienced it, not as something momentary that they would overcome in due course as they enjoyed more and more of these rights, but as an injustice they had suffered. The only way to change those circumstances is to overthrow the regime and to take from others property wrongly owned. Tocqueville argues that a spirit of envy will undermine the supposed smooth operation of a system of entrepreneurial energy based on individual liberty.

Socialist theories in the shape of greedy, envious desires continued to spread among the people sowing the seeds of future revolutions, but the socialist party itself remained beaten and impotent. The Montagnards, who did not belong to that party, seemed to have been struck down beyond recall by the same blow that felled it. Even the moderate republicans were not slow to see that the victory that had saved them had left them on a slope sliding beyond a republic. They immediately made an effort to pull back but in vain.[23]

Naturally enough, Marx thinks very differently about these events than does Tocqueville. Nonetheless, in light of the foregoing Tocqueville passage, the following passage from Marx is instructive:

22. Tocqueville, *Souvenirs*, Part II, ch. IX, p. 213.
23. Ibid., ch. X, pp. 252-53.

81

If the overthrow of the parliamentary republic contains within itself the germ of the triumph of the proletarian revolution, its immediate and palpable result was *the victory of Bonaparte over Parliament, of the executive power over the legislative power, of force without phrases over the force of phrases.*[24]

In other words, Marx describes Bonaparte's coming to be the representative of the people, after continuing internecine struggles among the various classes intermediate between the people and the dictator. Thus, the popular will was to become the law of the nation not through the people ruling directly but through the force of the dictator. Marx continued:

In Parliament the nation made its general will the law; that is, it made the law of the ruling class its general will. Before the executive power it renounces all will of its own and submits to the superior commands of an alien will — to authority. The executive power in contrast to the legislative power expresses the heteronomy[25] of a nation in contrast to its autonomy. France, therefore, seems to have escaped the despotism of a class only to fall back beneath the despotism of an individual.[26]

Now, Tocqueville agrees with Marx. He also sees the emergence of Napoleon Bonaparte as fulfilling the popular revolution rather than a reaction to the revolution. Nonetheless, what Marx is saying, and what is important about it, is that what Tocqueville calls the people's "envy" has driven this process less than the self-interested behavior of the various classes (as he has identified them). In an earlier passage he even questioned whether we can regard those who are called the petty peasants a class. They have lost the sense of class; they are no longer in contact with one another; they are no longer in community; and yet they are the people who drive the popular uprising and bring Bonaparte to power in an alliance with the urban proletariat.

Thus, these isolated individuals — whether inspired by envy or

24. Karl Marx, *The Eighteenth Brumaire of Louis Bonaparte* (New York: International Publishers, 1963), p. 120. Italics in translation.

25. Today, this is called multiculturalism or diversity, and it contrasts with autonomy.

26. Marx, p. 121.

political submission — drive the nation relentlessly toward a concentration of power in the pursuit of their goal, which is to strike down the differences between themselves and the classes they see but do not acknowledge as their superiors. Both Tocqueville and Marx make this argument.

In context, we ask what the rhetoric of republicanism is all about? If liberal democracy is the rhetoric of republicanism, what is it all about? Why do not people simply talk politics, in the way they used to do in the old world? Why do not the French speak of the Italians, the Germans, and the Belgians in terms of their lack of civilization and the reason they ought to be destroyed? Why does politics become a language primarily about domestic concerns, which is true all over the earth today, including here in the United States? People who declaim that this is the greatest country in the world seem not to be talking politics but to be living in la-la land. Of course, though, politics classically and traditionally distinguished one people from another. While for us politics is what distinguishes one interest from another. In these writers, also, politics distinguishes one interest from another.

The question is: how did communities come to be disintegrated such that nothing important could be said about politics other than fellow citizens' mutual hatreds and struggles? Is it ever possible in terms of this discourse to refer to communities again? May we refer to the French as a community? If we read Marx's account of their struggles — struggles that always end in some degree of bloodshed — we find a people who kill over theories. They do not kill outsiders; they kill one another over theories.

Marx and Tocqueville wrote after the revolutionary struggles of 1848 to 1851 (and Tocqueville actually participated in them). In fact, though, many of those same conversations continued to resonate — first in many countries in Europe, then in Latin America, Asia, and Africa. Ultimately it became a world conversation that came to be known as the "cold war," in which people debated perhaps the merits of their civilizations but always under the guise of debating the relative merits of socialism and liberal democracy.

Is socialism really an alternative to liberal democracy?[27] If so,

---

27. There were many early nineteenth-century examples of state socialism, including within the United States. One of the more dramatic, however, occurred during the succession of constitutional struggles in Paraguay between 1816 and 1840.

what is its chief argument against liberal democracy? Far ahead of the development of explicit theories that fueled political revolutions, there was a notion that one had to do more than talk about the prospects of material progress or comfort. One also had to convert the discussion of material progress into a discussion of social cohesion. Socialists seem to have argued that liberal democracy does not permit social cohesion.

Marx provided the explanation for this conclusion, namely that liberal democracy is predicated on the conflict of classes. This is the form of life in which by definition they fight and kill one another by historical necessity — because of material conditions. Rousseau's discovery that society originates in the accidental discovery of property leads to Marx's discovery that the influence of this accident does not end with the social contract and a legislator, but sets in motion a historical train of events.

*   *   *

While Tocqueville has the concluding word, Marx has special relevance in this inquiry, because his methodological materialism lies at the foundation of much modern opinion regarding the relationship of economics and freedom. We have returned to the *Eighteenth Brumaire* because it is one of the first and clearest elaborations of the theory of historical materialism, and almost the only work in which Marx accomplishes a full illustration of the theory. Readers have previously underemphasized Marx's starting point as opposed to the end he envisioned, and in doing so they have obscured the implications of his teachings for all views of stratified, mediated, or complex communities.

Marx wrote clearly of the impossibility of community in general for all men who had lived until the time he wrote and for most if not all who would ever live. What makes community in general impossible, in Marx's view, is that what might be taken as the differentiated dynamics of a single community constitute in fact the inveterate antagonisms of true enemies and not potential friends. The theory runs thus:

> Upon the different forms of property, upon the social conditions of existence, rises an entire superstructure of distinct and peculiarly formed sentiments, illusions, modes of thought and views of life. The entire class creates and forms them out of its material foundations and out of the corresponding social relations. The single individual,

who derives them through tradition and upbringing, may imagine that they form the real motives and starting point of his activity.[28]

The beginning of the theory of Karl Marx — not the end, the utopianizing vision of a withering of the state — has the greatest relevance for continued theorizing about the state or society. That beginning is nothing less than a categorical refutation of the possibility of the *res publica* — that is, the reality of a true public and a common good in any of the arenas in which we traditionally observe politics.

The description of politics in Marx is a description of continuous warfare, where the terms "classes" or "social orders" replace the terms "armies" and "command and control." What this insight means for the present discussion is twofold. First, the denial of the possibility of a public good for or within a liberal democracy is the most radical challenge to that regime (hence, Tocqueville was right). Second, all discussion of a restoration or renaissance of a sense of civic culture must succeed first — before it can have an impact on the contemporary stage — to reclaim from Marx's devastating attack a legitimate role for differential cultural actors — individually and in groups.

Every modestly informed observer will forgive my not eliciting a list of examples to illustrate the ways in which contemporary commentary echoes Marx in assumptions of interested behavior and inveterate oppositions of interests among social strata as the basis of society. Besides, it would be far simpler to enumerate the rare cases in which the socialist presumption does not contribute the starting point of inquiry.

If it is true, however, and as I maintain, that the socialist presumption (that is, there is no common good under forms of the political organization of society) thoroughly reigns as orthodoxy across the spectrum of contemporary political opinions, then it must surely follow that socialism has rather been disapproved in practice than disproved in theory. What would follow from that is recognition of the need to respond to the radical challenges to liberal democracy as a precondition for undertaking the cultural strengthening of liberal democracy.

Here, too, we may lean on Marx:

Men make their own history, but they do not make it just as they please; they do not make it under circumstances chosen by them-

28. Marx, p. 47.

selves, but under circumstances directly encountered, given and transmitted from the past. The tradition of all the dead generations weighs like a nightmare on the brain of the living.[29]

The pervasive circumstance constraining the makers of a new history today is the pervasive, deadly influence of socialism inherited from the past. Tocqueville recognized this process as it was just beginning. He saw in the revolutions of 1848 not just a reordering but a dissolution or fragmentation of society — one meant to be permanent.

> This time, it was not merely a matter of the triumph of one party; people aspired to launch a social science, a philosophy, I could almost say a single religion that they could teach to all men and cause them to follow. That was the truly great departure from the old picture.[30]

Tocqueville stood among those who resisted the reduction of all human society to an abstract order. Indeed, they initially succeeded in branding socialism a sclerosis.

Marx foresaw that growing influence would follow the early defeats. But it was Tocqueville who explained why. Initially he explained how "socialist theories" penetrated the minds of the people "in the form of greedy and envious passions," planting "seeds of future revolutions" despite the impotence of the socialist party.[31] More profoundly, though, he asked:

> Will socialism remain buried in the scorn that so justly covered the socialists of 1848? I raise the question without answering it. I am certain that the fundamental laws of our modern society might be sharply modified in the fullness of time; they have already been so altered in several of their main parts. But shall it ever occur that folk will destroy and install others in their place? That seems impracticable to me. That's all I can say, for to the extent that I study the ancient condition of the world more closely, and also see up close our own world today; whenever I weigh the immense diversity that one encounters between them, not only within the laws but within the principles of the laws and the different forms that the right to land-

29. Ibid., p. 15.
30. *Recollections*, p. 125.
31. Ibid., p. 252.

holding have taken and retain, to this very day, no matter what folk say, I am tempted to believe that what folk call necessary institutions are often nothing but the institutions folk are used to. Regarding a social constitution the realm of possibility is so much vaster than the people living in any one society might imagine.[32]

32. Ibid., p. 131.

6. What to Do While Awaiting the Apocalypse: The Role of Creative Minorities in a Time of Cultural Crisis

STEVEN J. TONSOR

O N the eve of the turn of the century and the advent of the new millennium there seems to be no joy in the land. The Enlightenment project has been abandoned even by those who are building a plywood bridge to the twenty-first century. Utopianism is out of fashion even in science fiction, and the great Marxist intellectual scam which promised secular redemption for mankind exists only in the universities of the Western World. In the gray world of theory and chronology there is little room for the green of life's golden tree.

The popular *mentalité* of the very late twentieth century is again filled with apocalyptic expectations. Even Christians no longer express the confidence and hopefulness of Lord Acton a century ago who wrote "Christ is risen on the world and fails not," and then went on to enumerate the historical fruits of the Incarnation. The transforming character of God's grace expressed in the providential course of history has been pushed aside by the nihilists, the postmodernists, and the cultural "nervous Nellies" who are so busy ringing out the old that they have no ear for the sound of the advent of ". . . one far-off Divine event, to which the whole creation moves." Christians as a group confronting the millennium seem to be a dispirited group filled with eschatological hand-wringing and primitive, childish, fears. Far from anticipating the *Parousia* with joy, far from shouting with St. John, "Come

Lord Jesus, Come!" they join the uneducated ranks of those who live in fear and trembling. The new heaven and the new earth have no appeal to them.

It is well to observe here that these attitudes are not new. The fear of the consequences of "time's erosion," and the unwinding of the ages is an extremely old one. Our most fundamental human perception is that everything wears out, runs down, rusts, gets sick, and dies. Physicists say that energy moves from a less probable to a more probable distribution in the universe. The classical world sought various methods of regeneration through which a weary world might be reenergized and regenerated.[1] The mythic liturgical reenactment of the divine creative gesture through which all things came to be is the primary form of pagan religious expression. Judaism and Christianity denied the pagan myths and rites of temporal regeneration. God's actions in history are once and for all. History is a one-way street. There can be no doubling back to the beginning. The course of history is the story of fulfillment rather than the story of periodic decline and regeneration.

The mood of the present is in substantial measure determined by the confusion of the eschatological moment with the moment of cultural crisis. These are two quite different historical moments, though their conflation has been a commonplace in western history. Such indeed was the case with Adrian Leverkühn the composer, protagonist of Thomas Mann's great novel *Dr. Faustus*.[2] One might forgive Adrian Leverkühn his confusion. He was, after all, living in the last days of the Third Reich, bombs were raining down everywhere, the cities had become gigantic funeral pyres, thought was confused and intellectual and artistic endeavor polluted, and finally, Adrian himself was suffering from syphilis. No wonder it was appropriate that Adrian's greatest work was a great symphonic composition, Apocalypse, paraphrasing Beethoven's ninth in the style of Arnold Schoenberg. It was easy for those who lived through the final days of National Socialism to confuse cultural crisis with the apocalypse.

This confusion of cultural crisis with apocalypse was deepened

1. Mircea Eliade, *Cosmos and History, The Myth of the Eternal Return*, translated from the French by Willard R. Trask (New York: Harper Torchbooks, 1959).
2. Thomas Mann, *Doctor Faustus*, The Life of the German composer Adrian Leverkühn as told by a friend, translated from the German by H. I. Lowe-Porter (New York: Alfred A. Knopf, 1948).

in the twentieth century by the cult of Oswald Spengler, whose *Decline of the West*[3] sold hundreds of thousands of copies. For Spengler the *Untergang des Abendlandes* was an inevitable development inherent in the biological cycle through which all cultures pass. Spengler counseled that the attitude of westerners should be that of the soldier guards at Pompeii who stood at their posts and let the lava of Vesuvius flow over them.[4]

The apocalyptic note is struck repeatedly in the 50th Anniversary Issue of *Commentary Magazine*, in which 72 contributors discuss "the national prospect." They present us with a cultural lunar landscape that resembles an earth ravaged by an intellectual asteroid impact.[5] The *Commentary* writers, with a few exceptions, fail to realize the cultural context of the human condition. There has not been a "golden age" in the recent past from which there has been such a wrenching declension. Those of us who lived through the 1920s, 30s, and 40s know that these depressed and conflicted decades were far from a "golden age" in which the national purpose ran clear and pure. Nor, looking back upon the historic past, the American past in particular, can one identify a golden age during which morality, learning, and order were commonplace. One recalls that when John Quincy Adams traveled he carried a sword cane and a brace of pistols.

The past two thousand years have been a succession of great crises. One recalls in particular the great crisis of the Renaissance-Reformation era. No doubt there have been cases of stability. No wonder, then, that mankind, half out of yearning and half out of fear, has been filled with apocalyptic expectations. These expectations have been constant in western history. When the Millerites put on their judgment robes and climbed the nearest hill to await the rapture in the mid nineteenth century they were doing nothing unusual. Anticipating the apocalypse is almost a commonplace in the history of Western religiosity. It is to be noted that these anxieties become particularly acute in millennial years.[6]

All of which is not to say there is no crisis of this age and that it

3. Oswald Spengler, *Der Untergang des Abendlandes*, Umrisse eines Morphologie des Weltgeschichte, 2 vols. (München: Oscar Beck, 1924).

4. Oswald Spengler, *Man and Technies, A Contribution to a Philosophy of Life* (New York: Alfred A. Knopf, 1932), p. 104.

5. "The National Prospect," A Symposium, in *Commentary*, 50th Anniversary Issue, November, 1995, vol. 100, no. 5.

6. Henri Focillon, *The Year 1000* (New York: Harper Torchbooks, 1971).

is not particularly acute. A cultural crisis however is not necessarily a sign of the approaching last days. Cultural crisis is the natural condition of all human cultures.[7] Cultural crisis is as natural a social fact as water running downhill is a physical fact. One is reminded of the *jeu d'esprit* of Oscar Wilde who said when touring Niagara Falls, "It would be more impressive if it went up."

Because this is the case, one is driven to enquire into the causes of cultural failure; the roots of intellectual and social disorder. One need not be a radical Calvinist in the style of Karl Barth or Jacques Ellul to recognize the impact of man's creatureliness and sinfulness on human culture. One need not denounce Aristotle, St. Thomas, and the natural law in order to discern that high culture and the Church itself, in the course of history, have fallen into decadence and corruption. The Augustinian tradition has spoken eloquently and perennially on the subject. In spite of this recognition of man's sinfulness, his overreaching, his inadequacy, his lack of vision and discernment, there have been other and countervailing forces in the shaping and reshaping of culture.[8] The history of the world is indeed the story of man's repeated failure but it is also and more importantly, the story of God's creative and ordering purpose and his providential agency. Men participate with God in this cultural creativity. God's purpose and man's empowerment culminate in the Incarnation. With Lord Acton we can proclaim, "Christ is risen on the World and fails not." Cultural crisis becomes man's opportunity to participate in the order of creation and preservation.

That participation in reform, renewal, and new and creative ordering is not the work at its inception, of the "masses" and the "elites." Rather it is the imaginative work of small creative minorities, groups who stand aside from the dominant culture and propose a new solution to some of the perennial problems posed by the human condition.

Arnold Toynbee, half a century ago, in his massive and now neglected *A Study of History*, argued that determinative in the development of "civilizations" was the role of "creative minorities." These creative minorities are not fortuitous assemblages of dissident groups, cults, and nay sayers but, on the contrary a self-conscious movement of individuals and groups toward a new and purified cultural ideal. It

7. Pitirim A. Sorokin, *The Crisis of Our Age, The Social and Cultural Outlook* (New York: E. P. Dutton and Co., Inc., 1957).
8. H. Richard Niebuhr, *Christ and Culture* (New York: Harper & Row, 1951).

is they who provide both the prophetic critique of the present and a vision of a new and ideal culture. They are always at odds with the dominant minority, (read "elite"), and often suffer social ostracism or persecution. The dominant minority, incapable of producing necessary change, seeks, even while the structures of the culture are decaying, to impose changelessness by increasingly resorting to power. As Arnold Toynbee writes:

> The defensiveness which it substitutes for creativity, may be either indolent or recalcitrant; but, whether it is insanely defying the lightning or inertly resting on its oars, in either posture the dominant minority is refusing to hand over to other aspirants the protagonist's role which it has already proved itself incompetent to play.[9]

The invention of a culture by a creative minority is rarely the work of a dominant minority employing the mechanisms of power. There are, however, exceptions, and the most interesting of these exceptions was the work of Charlemagne in the creation of Europe in the ninth century. Those who have read Gregory of Tours' *History of the Franks*[10] are well aware of the precarious state of Christianity and culture north of the Alps on the eve of the advent of the Carolingians. "Europe" remained to be invented and "Italy" and the Papacy were in constant danger from the semi-barbarians and Islam. The idea that the baptism of Clovis was a turning pont in the history of France and Europe is something of an exaggeration even though Pope John Paul seemed to give it his *imprimatur*. By the time the Carolingians had displaced the Merovingians both Christianity and culture north of the Alps were drifting into chaos. The economic decline of Western Europe and the conquest of the Mediterranean by Islam had become a reality by the time Charlemagne appeared on the scene.[11] Worse still, there was no notion of the uses of power, the acquisition of legitimacy through the direction of power to an overriding ideal and the transformation of tribal warrior chieftain into *Sacerdos et imperator*. Nor was this trans-

9. Arnold Toynbee, *A Study of History,* a new edition revised and abridged by the author and Jane Caplan (London: Oxford U. Press and Thames and Hudson, 1972), p. 288.
10. Gregory of Tours, *The History of the Franks,* translated with an introduction by Lewis Thorpe (Harmondsworth, Middlesex: Penguin Books, 1974).
11. Richard Hodges and David Whitehouse, *Mohammed, Charlemagne and the Origins of Europe* (Ithaca, N.Y.: Cornell University Press, 1983).

forming vision solely that of Charlemagne. Surely Pope Leo III and the Frankish episcopacy played a major role in preparing for the events in Rome in 800. Even so, it must be remembered that the coronation of Charlemagne was the result of achieved status and of a vision already fulfilled. The road from Aachen to Rome was a long one and without a new and compelling vision on the part of Charlemagne would not have become reality.

That Karl der Grosse should have been proclaimed a saint by popular acclamation may seem strange to us. We have come to view power as demonic and the examples of those who have wielded power in the last century and at the present time do not seem to have been cut from the cloth of sanctity. True, in his personal life the morals of a ninth-century warrior chieftain do not seem to qualify him for saint-hood. Nor were his forcible conversion of the Saxons and the genocide he practiced against them the actions of a Christian. Alcuin, cleric, abbot, counselor, and friend, was firmly opposed to forcible conver-sions. (Another descendant of Saxons may be forgiven if he observes that perhaps Luther was the Saxon revenge for the policy of Char-lemagne.) Saints, however, are made of the knotty, cross-gained wood of humanity and Providential purpose is sometimes achieved by work-ing in a mysterious way.

The restoration of order, the extension of safety and Empire into the barbarian East, the legitimation of power, the use of power to secure the Christianization of Central Europe, and above all the establishment of the vision of Christian Empire, a vision later to be echoed by Dante — these were the work of a great visionary who worked at cross-purposes with the tendencies of his time.

Changes as momentous as the changes introduced by Char-lemagne are not and cannot be the work of one man. The architects of change at the court of Charlemagne were numerous and though they shared a common vision they were not simply Franks but were drawn from the Germanic peoples of proto Europe; Angilbert the Frank, the Lombard, Paul the Deacon, Alcuin the Anglo Saxon, Theodulf the Vis-igoth. It strikes the historian that "Europe" from its inception was cosmopolitan or better said, Christian.[12]

The work of renovation and restoration was not simply an effort to return to the Roman past. To be sure, there was a nostalgia for the

---

12. Jacques Boussard, *The Civilization of Charlemagne,* translated from the French by Frances Partridge (New York: McGraw-Hill, 1968).

order and unity of Rome, but order and unity had to be recast using the base metals of the Germanic tribes and inventing forms appropriate to the new era. As Toynbee observed, one of the evidences of the decadence of a dominant minority is its retreat into archaism. The temptation to archaism is always present in conservative and tradition-alist movements. One might characterize it as the Williamsburg resto-ration mentality. The recasting of art and architecture in new and in-novative forms is one of the great achievements of the Carolingian impetus, derivative, to be sure from the Roman past but new in detail and intention that prepares the groundwork for the emerging style of the Medieval era.[13] It is this blending of tradition and innovation which always characterizes the best in the work of creative minorities. Fulda is a long way from Ravenna and yet by way of Charlemagne's chapel at Aachen, St. Michael's Church at Fulda (in the ninth century on the edge of the Carolingian Empire) echoes San Vitale in Ravenna and the whole course of Roman and Byzantine architecture. Echoes and yet shapes into a new and most beautiful form, for St. Michael's is one of the great achievements of the human spirit. It has too often been argued that Carolingian intellectuality, politics, theology, art, and architecture are a simple replication of the past. Those who invented "Europe," that creative minority of the ninth century, made a new world in all its dimensions.

The most subtle and important characteristics of any culture are those habits of the mind, patterns of discourse, theological and liturgical usages and attitudes of reverence, the alchemy of education, and the making of books, through which a culture is ordered and given unity and diffused throughout a society. The pictures given to us by Einhard and Notker[14] of Charlemagne and his circle engaged in the construction of the European mind are extremely moving. Charlemagne, with an innocence and naivete which is characteristic of saints was himself the first scholar of the land. He began the restoration of literacy. His monas-teries invented and employed a script, the Carolingian minuscule, which made possible the clear, rapid, and beautiful reproduction of texts. It was an invention on a level of importance with the invention of movable type. The assembling of libraries was a matter on a level

13. Roger Hinks, *Carolingian Art, A Study of Early Medieval Painting and Sculp-ture in Western Europe* (Ann Arbor: The University of Michigan Press, 1962).
14. Einhard and Notker the Stammerer, *Two Lives of Charlemagne,* translated with an introduction by Lewis Thorpe (Harmondsworth: Penguin Books, 1969).

with the construction of military defenses, for libraries were to serve as a "bulwark against ignorance." We have a catalogue of the monastic library of Lorsch which contained 375 books. The monastery of St. Emmeram in Regensburg counted 500 volumes and Richenau numbered 400. At Lorsch the beautiful Carolingian building once thought to be a gatehouse and sometimes called the "Königshalle," we now have good evidence served as the monastic library. Education made a civilized society possible, but without laws and rational procedures, without theological clarity and liturgical uniformity, the order and unity necessary for a functioning society would have been impossible.

Charlemagne and his circle did not have the energy or time necessary for the transformation of society. At his death in 814 the inertia of the past and consequences of sin eroded the extraordinary achievements of this creative minority. However, the power of the past is never adequate to completely undo the positive creations of any social order. In the nineteenth century, millenarian thinkers saw the period from the Coronation of Charlemagne in 800 to the Reichsdeputations Hauptschluss in 1806, that one thousand years of the Holy Roman Empire of the German Nation, a second Rome and harbinger of the Third Reich, "third and last Rome." These millennial dreams were a fatuous historical notion. One cannot help, however, seeing that the "Europe" with the increasing unity of France, Italy, and Germany which emerged at the end of World War II, was as much the creation of Charlemagne as the creation of Jean Monnet and Konrad Adenauer.

If Charlemagne and his companions were a creative minority who transformed history for all time, standing at the edge of the abyss Claus Schenk Graf von Stauffenberg gave his life in a cause which must have seemed futile and without historic consequence. Like the heroic pagan, Siegfried, in the *Nibelungenlied*,[15] Claus Schenk Graf von Stauffenberg and his co-conspirators went to their terrible deaths without hope or assurance of any achievement. It must have seemed to them the end of hope, and their mean and tortured deaths the vestibule of Götterdämmerung. That was more than fifty years ago and today their redemptive act appears to us in a wholly different light. Those who act in the drama of history can never foresee with any certainty the consequences of their actions.

The von Stauffenberg name reveals that the reference to Siegfried

15. *Das Nibelungenlied,* Nach der Ausgabe von Karl Bartsch, Heraus gegeben von Helmut de Boor (Wiesbaden: F. A. Brockhaus, 1961).

and the *Nibelungenlied* was a part of the Hohenstaufen thirteenth-century artistic and literary heritage of modern Germany. The von Stauffenbergs were quintessential members of the Imperial nobility.[16] In the twentieth century, however, the scions of this noble house were born into a corrupt era characterized by the most extreme social and cultural crisis. The crisis of German society and culture in the first half of the twentieth century was not simply a German crisis, it was the crisis of cultural and social modernity, for "German was," as Erich Heller once remarked, "the mother tongue of modernity."

Claus and his brothers, Bertold and Alexander, confronted the crisis head on. For Claus, Roman Catholicism was a major and enduring influence. The day before he placed the bomb in the Führerbunker, July 20, 1944, he spent some time in meditation in church. The Church in Weimar Germany was remarkably vibrant and creative. The liturgical and theological revival directly influenced and formed the daily lives of Catholics. Romano Guardini, one of the leading literary critics and moralists of that terrible time, did much to invent the Catholic youth movement, Quickborn, and place the liturgical revival at the center of youth activities. The youth movement, both secular and confessional, developed out of the widespread perception of cultural crisis and their belief that cultural renewal must be the work of a youth which distinguished itself from an older and decadent society.

The von Stauffenberg brothers shared this perception, though in their case it took an unusual turn. Membership in youth groups was not the consequence of simply joining. Membership was through recruitment, and election and leadership in the groups fell to older, charismatic individuals. These groups saw themselves as the regenerative force in a new society, a creative minority who would through their distinctive lifestyle and mystical idealism shape a new society. The model of that society was frequently medieval, the medievalism of the Hohenstauffen empire. Charismatic leadership was the prevailing leadership form, even in, or perhaps, especially in intellectual circles. The "guru" of the cultural world of the 1960s was but a pale reflection of the *magister*, the "master" of the first three decades of the twentieth century. It is well to remember that the circles who surrounded Leo Strauss and Eric Voegelin were in this tradition.

One of the most important and impressive of the *Magistern* of

16. Peter Hoffman, *Stauffenberg, A Family History, 1905-1944* (Cambridge: Cambridge University Press, 1995).

these decades, the leader of a circle into which the von Stauffenberg brothers were recruited, was the poet Stefan George.[17] George believed that European culture, and particularly German culture, was in collapse and that its regeneration could be accomplished through the work of a creative minority of poets. They, guided by the inspired vision of the "master," would create the new and enduring cultural forms. They would create a new nobility of the soul and though their example the materialism, positivism, and democratic mediocrity would be swept away. The circle surrounding George was at first a circle of companions, but due to the dynamics of charisma soon became a circle of followers. They were young men of great genius who distinguished themselves in the German-speaking world by a new style of scholarship and a lifestyle that invited *mimesis*. To it belonged the great literary critic, Friedrich Gundolf; Hugo von Hofmannsthal, the dramatist; the poet Karl Wolfskehl; Edgar Salin, who later recorded his first-hand impressions of George; and Ernst Kantorowich, the biographer of Friederich II, Hohenstauffen. It was into this exclusive circle that the von Stauffenberg brothers were recruited.[18]

Their intention, to change the world, was thwarted by the rise of National Socialism to power and the assumption of absolute power by Adolf Hitler. Claus Schenk Graf von Stauffenberg opted for the army as a career, where he became a brilliant staff officer. His brother Berthold entered the diplomatic service, and Alexander, the third brother, became a professor of classics. Claus married happily but at each step along their courses in adult life, they were confronted by the tragedy of German civic and intellectual life. The war made it clear that it would be difficult for Germany to survive National Socialism. As Germany lurched toward defeat, Stefan George lay dying. The dreams of a new and noble Germany based on the vision of the "Master" now seemed vain and empty. It became clear to Claus Schenk Graf von Stauffenberg that Hitler must die if Germany was to be saved and that he, Claus, would have to do the deed. Siegfried was impelled to slay the dragon.

To that end he organized a conspiracy that would seize power and put in place the vision of a new Germany. Fate or Providence

17. *Stefan George in Selbstzeugnissen und Bilddokumenten*, Dargestellt von Franz Schonauer (Hamburg: Rowoht Verlag, 1960), *Stefan George* by E. K. Bennett (New Haven: Yale University Press, 1954).

18. Michael Winkler, "Der Jugendbegriff im George-Kreis" in *"Mit uns Zieht die Neue Zeit" Der Mythos Jugend*, eds. Thomas Koebner, Rolf-Peter Janz and Frank Trommler (Frankfurt a. M.: Suhrkamp Verlag, 1986).

decreed otherwise and instead of becoming the tyrant slayer, Claus and his confederates became martyrs.[19]

History seems to turn on the hinge of fate and the door slams shut on dreams, movements, and individuals. No one, at this remove, can quite account for the total lack of success. Perhaps it was the weather; the day in July was unusually warm and the windows of the Führer Bunker were open, thus dissipating the force of the blast. Perhaps the table filled with maps over which Hitler was leaning flew up and protected him from the full force of the blast. Perhaps God in his providence saw that, for legitimation and cleansing, Germany needed martyrs who would call out over the ruins of a nobler past to those who would create the new Germany. These are questions the historian must ask but is never able to answer.

It is profitable to compare the actions of Colonel von Stauffenberg to the career and death of a German General who was more famous but less distinguished than von Stauffenberg; General Ernst Udet depicted by his friend the dramatist Carl Zuchtmayer as *Des Teufels General* (The Devil's General). Zuchtmayer and Udet were old friends. Udet had been the great Luftwaffe hero of World War I, daredevil adventurer. Udet and Zuchtmayer attended the same parties in Berlin in the "Golden Twenties," when it seemed that rules were made to be broken and that the pleasure of the moment was the most important objective in life. Udet was courted and flattered by the Nazis and became a Luftwaffe General. Having a not entirely uncritical turn of mind he eventually came to see the disaster that yawned before Germany. Zuchtmayer had departed for America. Udet remained behind doing the Devil's bidding. Finally, when his disgust became too great, Udet committed suicide. Superficial inspection might lead one to assume that the defiant gestures of Udet and von Stauffenberg were equally vain and unimportant. Von Stauffenberg and his confederates set their stamp upon the future. Udet died by being drawn into the suction of the absurd.

It is important to try to account for this difference. There were many and diverse groups seeking to resist National Socialism.[20] None

19. Joachim Fest, *Plotting Hitler's Death, The Story of the German Resistance*, translated by Bruce Little (New York: Metropolitan Books, Henry Holt and Co., 1996).

20. Peter Hoffman, *The History of the German Resistance, 1933-1945*, translated from the German by Richard Barry (Cambridge, Mass.: The MIT Press, 1977).

of these efforts had quite the clarity, forward-looking purpose or dedication of that of the July 20th plotters. The reasons for this are complicated but go to the heart of the discussion of creative minorities in a time of crisis. These men and women were conservatives drawn from the nobility and the army. They were for the most part intensely religious, they were deeply aware of the noble German past, that had often been associated with or influenced by the youth movement, and finally they belonged to groups which had a coherent vision of a new and better Germany. It is easy now to dismiss this vision as a conservative fantasy world but it is just possible that much of the political and social architecture of present-day Germany bears a strange resemblance to the vision of the plotters.

Enduring institutions are not shaped by the so-called "creative masses" of Marxist historical mythology, nor are they shaped through the exercise of naked power, thought recently to reside in power elites of one kind and another. The work of culture and the creation of enduring institutions are the realization of visions and dreams of relatively small creative elites who by inspiration project a future worthy of imitation (mimesis). The immediate consequence of their actions may appear to be failure. It is easy to imagine that the garden falls into ruin with the death of the gardener. But that is never the case. The large scheme in its practical details may disintegrate and institutions once in power may, and probably will, become corrupt. Cultural crisis is the normal condition of human societies. And yet after every major crisis and as a consequence of every creative minority there is a step forward, an enduring reshaping of the cultural landscape. It is astonishing how much of the material past survives. Our museums, archives, and libraries are filled with the artifacts of a past which we find difficult to understand at this remove in time. Even more of the intellectual and spiritual experience of mankind has survived. Layer on layer of the habituated patterns of thought unconsciously shape our actions and color our dreams. Can it be a matter of doubt that the work of creative minorities will endure beyond the brief lifetimes of the men who proposed a new and more adequate culture?

We live at a time when the cultural creations of modernity have exhibited fully their flawed character and are everywhere falling into desuetude. This time of the breaking of nations and cultures is not, however, a time in which creative minorities have faltered. Many of these groups — religious, social, political, intellectual, and artistic — are busy recreating the cultural horizon. In Europe one thinks of the inspired work of Konrad Adenauer and Jean Monnet which laid the basis for the European Union. In the United States the conservative revolution, made at its inception by a few intellectuals in the immediate postwar years, is a prime example of the impact of creative minorities. Perhaps no less important in the reshaping of contemporary society has been the work of the Chicago School of economists. That Central and Eastern Europe have moved steadily towards freedom is in no small measure the work of a few academicians. The unraveling of "the evil empire" is in no small measure the work of a spiritual genius, Pope John Paul II. Throughout Catholicism and Evangelical Protestantism, groups are deeply engaged in the process of reformation and renewal within the tradition of orthodoxy. Opus Dei and the Taizé community are examples of initiatives which recast traditional patterns in forms consonant with the realities of the twentieth century.

Creative minorities must not hold on to the decaying culture of modernism. It is over, if not yet completely a matter of the past. That is conservatism in the worst sense. Successful creative minorities in the past have always taken from tradition that which is truest, that which is noblest, that which is best, and conformed it to an overriding vision of a better and more holy future. It is this prophetic vision of the world made new drawing its sustenance from the orthodoxy of tradition that will meet the challenge of perennial cultural crisis.

7. Women in a Changing World: The Consequences and the Implications

ELIZABETH FOX-GENOVESE

Today, we expect things to change fast, and when they do not change fast enough, we are likely to get impatient. In fact, we are coming to accept breathless change as the one constant in modern life. Six months after you buy a computer, it is obsolescent, but the new, superior model costs less than the old one cost when you bought it six months ago. Now that is the kind of change we want! Technologies become more powerful and more sophisticated, and at the same time cheaper. How many of us stop to think that within the last fifty years the technology we now take for granted was the stuff of science fiction? Robots, talking computers, picture-flashing telephones, flight to the moon, whatever. It is all here, or will be tomorrow or the next day. I am not the only one here who is old enough to remember a world without saran wrap. But then, who would have thought that 1996's blockbuster equivalent of science fiction would be *Twister?* Apparently someone in Hollywood has figured out that the truly devastating, ungovernable power comes not from the machine of a malevolent genius but from nature.

Yet, nature is not a popular idea these days, at least not among the university professors and radical feminists who shape so much of our culture. And if nature is not popular, the power of nature is positively anathema. And when someone dares to link nature and human beings the fireworks really begin. Should someone have the bad taste

101

to suggest that some attributes might be naturally more common to women than to men, or the reverse, the battle lines are drawn. The very idea that there might be a core female nature that women, or most women, share is taken to insult the intelligence and stifle the ambition of any self-respecting modern woman. Whatever we are, we assuredly are not what our mothers and grandmothers were before us, for we are the pioneers of the new world of gender equality in which men will have their turn at bearing babies, and women their turn at leading armies.

The possibilities opened by cloning and even the new technologies feed the illusion that human nature itself has become like putty in our hands. And the more ambitious the possibilities, the more likely people are to assume that all natural limitations to human dreams and desires have melted away or may readily be destroyed. Sex-change operations permit those who do not feel at home in the sex in which they were born to switch. And so the utopian vistas of living — not merely the life we choose but a multiplicity of lives in a single body — stretch alluringly before us. The enthusiasts for these possibilities have no interest in considering their price, much less the dangerous unintended consequences they may unleash. Yet even they live amidst an abundance of evidence that some core aspects of human nature — notably sexual identity — have remained inexplicably resistant to the brave new world of social and sexual engineering. Political agendas to accelerate change abound, but have yet to sweep most people's sense of themselves aside. Years ago, Lionel Trilling, in a defense of Freud, wrote that the biological foundation of human identity provides us with a valuable defense against others' attempts to coerce us into one or another belief. Trilling was defending Freud against charges of biological determinism, and, in stressing the importance of biology in grounding our independence, he was thinking of the scares about "brainwashing" that were so prevalent during the years after World War II. Without such a grounding, he reminded us, we put ourselves at high risk to become mere playthings in the hands of whatever sinister forces predominate at the moment.

For the postmodern sensibility that currently dominates much feminist thought and, indeed, intellectual life in general, the social construction of knowledge, gender, and identity constitutes the first rule of human life. In this universe, the very notion of a human nature betrays the reactionary "essentialism" of the person who advances the notion. Committed postmodernists rarely stop to think that their embrace of the infinite plasticity of human beings may transform human society into a gigantic kaleidoscope in which no one is what he or she (temporarily) appears to be. And if, at first blush, this idea appears to offer the ultimate in liberation, it takes little thought to recognize that it actually betokens not merely the death of God, but the death of the human being. Much in postmodernism commands serious attention, not least because it faithfully captures many aspects of the world in which we live, but here I shall argue that many of its premises have infiltrated areas of our national life and public policies in disastrously inappropriate ways. Changes in technology have indisputably transformed countless commodities and practices. They have arguably transformed (as in the ability to send a fax) our perception of time and space. And they have leveled many of the physical impediments to women's ability to perform a variety of occupations and professions as successfully as men. What they have not transformed is the core — or "essential" in contrast to accidental or contingent — difference between women and men.

Women stand at the center of the dizzying changes that are engulfing us. Today, women enjoy opportunities that their grandmothers and even their mothers could barely have dreamed of. From Wall Street to Congress to the Air Force to construction crews and spaceships, women now claim places alongside men. Women practice surgery, sit on the Supreme Court, and attend The Citadel. Less dramatically, but, in the long run more significantly, countless women go out to work for some or all of their lives. Nationally, women outnumber men in college and are close to matching them in graduate and professional schools. Thirty years ago, women earned fifty-nine cents on the male dollar; today, women who do the same work as men start out earning the same pay. And if, over time, some women do earn less than men for the same work, it is overwhelmingly because they have chosen to take time out along the way to raise a family.

The numbers are worth a moment's attention, especially since they so readily lend themselves to distortion. Take undergraduate education. According to many feminists, undergraduate women are dramatically disadvantaged relative to men. Yet today, young women account for something in the order of 53 or 54 percent of undergraduate students, and, at some small liberal arts colleges, they account for as much as 60 percent. Even in professional and graduate schools, which, even recently, few women attended at all, the gap between women and men is closing rapidly: by 1994, women were receiving almost half of all doctorates awarded, more than a third of all MBAs, a third of all medical and dentistry degrees, and close to 45 percent of all law degrees. And since these changes have occurred within roughly a twenty-year period, one may safely say that the rate of improvement has been extraordinary. The picture for women's earnings is even more optimistic, provided one looks at figures that are genuinely comparable, namely, the same work and the same amount of time devoted to it.[1]

Yes, we all know that women do not always do the same work as men, although in this regard, too, the changes of the last twenty years have been impressive. But, above all, most women do not work as uninterruptedly as men, which is to say, they do tend to give more time to family, especially to children. And, as one feminist report after another angrily points out, girls are less likely than boys to pursue careers in Math and Science — and likely to score lower on SATs. We do not fully understand the reasons for the differences between women and men, even when experience and common sense tell us that there are some. During the past three decades, we have watched differences that previous generations believed immutable melt away. Yet the more radical feminists continue to rail against discrimination, presumably because they believe that all of the remaining differences between women and men should be leveled. In the battle for perfect equality, they deploy the argument that difference between women and men can only be explained by the harmful effect of stereotypes, and they eagerly muster evidence that one woman may differ more from another woman than women as a group differ from men as a group. The point of this reasoning is to discredit the last vestiges of nature by destroying sex — or "gender" — as a respectable category: supposedly there are no natural differences between women and men that justify different treatment for them.

Throughout most of history, most people have taken for granted that the biological differences between women and men did justify some kind of sexual division of labor. For example, societies have typically been less ready to risk in warfare the lives of women, who bear children, than those of men, who do not. And typically, the more advanced — or civilized — the society, the more likely it has been to

1. A fuller discussion and statistical justification of these arguments and many of those that follow may be found in Elizabeth Fox-Genovese, *"Feminism Is Not the Story of My Life": How Today's Feminist Elite Has Lost Touch With the Real Concerns of Women* (New York: Doubleday/Nan Talese, 1996).

elaborate a complex system of roles that were taken to derive from basic biological differences between the sexes. At the extreme, these systems forcefully excluded women from many activities and occupations in which they could easily have performed well. During the nineteenth century, for example, some American doctors seriously argued that menstruation obviously made women too delicate to pursue a college education. Other societies have held that the biological differences between women and men justified women's complete subordination to their male kin — father, husband, brothers. The patterns have varied widely, but all have in common a tendency to relate women's roles and opportunities to their sexuality and, especially, their ability to bear children.

The sexual revolution of the last thirty years or so has stripped such rationales of most of their plausible justification. In what seems like the twinkling of an eye, artificial contraception, especially the pill, and abortion have "liberated" women to engage in the kind of sexual freedom normally associated with adolescent men. Initially, most people seem to have thought that the sexual revolution would simply free "nice" girls to have sex before marriage without ruining their reputations or risking their father's wrath. One may suspect that many fathers have not changed as rapidly as their daughters have in this regard, but that is another story, and, since growing numbers of daughters do not live with their biological fathers, it may be irrelevant. What is clear is that once the fabric of sexual decorum started to unravel, there was apparently no stopping it.

Today, the words adultery and illegitimacy have virtually disappeared from our vocabulary, presumably because they invoke unacceptably censorious and discriminatory attitudes. Many feminists now take single motherhood as a proud badge of women's sexual freedom, just as they insist that abortion on demand is that freedom's necessary guarantee. The bottom line in these arguments is that women will never be equal to men until they are liberated from the consequences of their sexuality. How dare nature burden women with children just because they seek equal access to individual pleasure? Thus are children reduced to an unfortunate byproduct of or limitation on the sexual freedom of women. Not for nothing did Senator Moynihan characterize partial-birth abortion as a form of infanticide. But then, many of you may not know that Lawrence Tribe, the legal genius who has plotted so much of the Supreme Court's recent strategy, has argued that a woman's right to abortion requires that a fetus who survives the abortion be killed on the grounds that the woman is entitled to a successful abortion. Please hear this: we are not here talking about the killing of a fetus, but about the killing of a baby out of its mother's womb.

If the sexual revolution has liberated women, we should remember that it has even more dramatically liberated men. From one perspective, we might reasonably regard the whole of human history as a sustained attempt to bind men to the women they impregnate and the children they father. It has been an uphill struggle. Now, with the snap of the fingers, we have turned them loose to pursue their pleasure where they wish without regard to the consequences. Elite women may feel that their own freedom is well worth the price. Less affluent women often see the trade-off differently, especially since so few of them can support children on their own. But then, if we take feminist rhetoric seriously, it is permissible to suspect that feminists believe that the true liberation of women above all requires their liberation from children. The trouble with that agenda, as a matter of social policy, is that it makes a mockery of the truth that many women regard the rearing of children as one of their primary joys and satisfactions, and for them liberation may well mean the freedom to stay home at least while the children are young.

Technological change has indeed brought us a brave new world of apparently limitless possibilities. But limits remain, and nature will not just lie down and die. If today we women can delight in possibilities that our mothers could barely imagine, if we can indeed do most things as well or better than men and earn as much or more money by doing them, we also remain our mothers' daughters. Like them, we are women whose bodies may always betray us just as they may reward us with the gift of new life and the responsibility for its nurture.

Feminism's determination to liberate women from children is all the more disappointing since, notwithstanding various excesses, the women's movement has made real contributions to our debates on public policy and social justice. Briefly, few women or men would today oppose equal pay for equal work, a woman's right to get credit in her own name, or zero tolerance for sexual harassment. Yet official feminism as represented by NOW, NARAL, the Fund for the Feminist Majority, and the MS Foundation continues to show little interest in families and children except in the case of single mothers and same-sex marriage. And, in the measure that feminists show any interest in women's relation to children, that interest normally focuses on assuring women's ability to support children without the assistance or cooperation of a resident father. Thus, feminists implicitly measure the improvement in women's economic circumstances by the standard of women's ability to make it on their own rather than as the member of an interdependent marriage and family.

The improvement in women's economic position has, in some measure, assured such independence to more women than ever before, but it has also unfolded in tandem with a host of other changes that have had disastrous consequences for families and children. The most dramatic include the massive entry of married women, especially mothers of young children, into the labor force; the increase in divorce, and the proliferation of single motherhood. Most of us are familiar with the numbers. As many as half of all marriages will end in divorce. As many as a third of all children are born to single mothers and as many as 70 percent of African-American children. Today, the typical working woman is a mother and the typical mother is a working woman. Feminist rhetoric often plays upon the special problems of the working mother, but feminists almost invariably insist that the woman above all needs greater freedom from her children and more unencumbered time for her work. Feminist solutions, accordingly, emphasize the need — women's right to — more affordable (publicly funded) day-care and more assistance from fathers. They have thus shown a distressing tendency to measure women's needs either by the yardstick of sexual freedom, which they defend as a woman's fundamental right, or by the standard of absolute equality with men, which they also regard as a woman's fundamental right. Neither of these measures, however, promises much good for women's relations with families, especially children, and they have, as Maggie Gallagher argues in her new book, *The Abolition of Marriage*, proved disastrous for marriage.[2]

Sexual liberation and individual self-realization, aided and abetted by the transformation of our economy, have powerfully conspired to destroy marriage as it has been known throughout world history. Our culture's obsession with individual freedom has blinded us to the mounting evidence of the havoc wrought by divorce, cohabitation, single motherhood, child abuse (including sexual), and violence perpetrated by children, not to mention children's suicide, alcoholism, and substance abuse. And those who have at least acknowledged the

2. Maggie Gallagher, *The Abolition of Marriage: How We Destroy Lasting Love* (Washington: Regnery Publishing Inc, 1996).

signs have invariably found a specific villain to blame: conservatives charge women with neglecting their responsibilities; feminists charge men with brutality; everyone deplores deadbeat dads. As with the allocation of blame, so with the prescription of remedies: some preach a restoration of family values, others preach sexual equality and joint parenting, and some increasingly look to a rejuvenation of fatherhood. In fairness, all of the charges, like most of the panaceas, have some merit. But they all avoid the real problem: marriage as the essential social unit — the glue that binds men and women to one another and, from infancy, binds children to society — has disintegrated.

The mounting evidence leaves no doubt of the magnitude of the disaster. The myth of the "good divorce" is precisely a myth. Short of pathological abuse and brutality, divorce is not good for children and, however surprising it may seem, not much better for the adults who seek it. Professional caretakers or the "village" cannot adequately substitute for the family, which must be a living organism — not some sociological model of a congeries of roles and functions that any number of interchangeable professional caregivers can fill. The very idea that marriage and family may appropriately be desegregated into a panoply of roles, relations, partnerships, and all the rest have drained marriage of its significance, meaning, and, yes, sanctity.

Remarriages following a divorce solve none of the problems and frequently exacerbate them. Stepfathers rarely invest as much time and love in children as biological fathers and are much more likely to abuse them. Sexual abuse is overwhelmingly perpetrated by stepfathers and mothers' live-in boyfriends. Meanwhile, divorced biological fathers rapidly lose their sense of responsibility for and engagement with children with whom they do not live. Cohabitation before marriage does not improve the marriage's chances for success: it weakens them. Divorced mothers can rarely provide children with the attention, resources, and opportunities they need and to which they are entitled, and the children of mothers who have never married fare even worse than those of divorced mothers. Nothing serves children as well as the presence and commitment of their biological father. And, should you doubt the importance of the commitment, please consider that the children of widows do not manifest the same problems as the children of divorced or never-married mothers.

The delusion that divorce and single-motherhood do not harm children presumably originated in adults' need for comfort and reassurance for themselves. No matter how selfishly we behave our children and we will be okay. With respect to the needs of children, that wisdom amounts to nonsense. But then, it is serving adults no better. Thinking to have liberated ourselves from the bondage of undying promises and their attendant responsibilities, we have condemned ourselves to a wasteland of anomie, loneliness, and despair. We are beginning to acknowledge the burdens that sole responsibility for children imposes upon women, especially if they are poor. We have been slow to acknowledge the tremendous cost that men's freedom to leave or never engage in marriage imposes upon us all, beginning with men themselves. The men who father children outside of marriage disproportionately end in jail, addiction, or premature death. And they are demonstrably wreaking havoc not merely with their own lives, but with the quality of life in countless impoverished communities.

Within the past few decades, the centuries-long attempt to bind men to women and children — literally to domesticate their propensity for aggression and sexual irresponsibility — has unraveled. Fatherhood — good fatherhood — grounds children's well-being; its absence painfully cripples them and all of us. It is clear that fatherhood remains essential to the health and prosperity of any society. Whatever we may like to believe, neither mothers alone nor the "village" can substitute, and the personal failings of individual men inescapably result in "a major public crisis." To be sure, "traditional" marriages and fatherhood frequently fell short of the ideal. But one need not posthumously romanticize them to understand that today's collapse is of an entirely different and more ominous order.[3]

It seems increasingly clear that no-fault divorce has caused more harm than good, yet even the most well-meaning feminists and liberal policymakers refuse to credit the evidence. Instead of focusing upon parents' responsibilities to children, they focus upon what both parents and children need from society. Thus, they insist that both children and parents depend on wider nets of social ties, on communities, and, predictably, remind us of the liberals' favorite slogan — "the popular African proverb," according to which, "It takes a village to raise a child." As it happens, many across the political spectrum would agree that the disintegration of schools or the infestation of neighborhoods

---

3. David Popenoe, *Life Without Father: Compelling New Evidence that Fatherhood and Marriage are Indispensable for the Good of Children and Society* (New York: Free Press, 1996); David Blankenhorn, *Fatherless America: Confronting Our Most Urgent Social Problem* (New York: Basic Books, 1995).

by drug dealers, among other crying evils, jeopardizes children.[4] But what of the collapse of two-parent families?

Growing numbers of policy analysts, especially the more liberal among them, appear to have thrown up their hands on the question of family cohesion and stability. A decade ago, William Julius Wilson argued forcefully that the disappearance of fathers and the proliferation of single motherhood were disastrously impairing the chances of inner-city youth to make something of their lives. In his most recent book, however, the pleas for a restoration of families have virtually disappeared. There can be no doubt that the disappearance of work from inner-city neighborhoods has indeed had devastating consequences. Nor can there be any doubt that the causes of that disappearance frequently transcend the behavior and attitudes of individuals in the affected communities. It nonetheless remains indisputable, as morally committed organizers on the ground will be the first to tell you, that no improvement is conceivable without a change in the behavior and attitudes of the individuals in those communities.[5] If we concede that sexual promiscuity and attendant out-of-wedlock births represent normative (even desirable) behavior and reflect worthy attitudes, we are most unlikely to see those communities begin to reconstitute themselves.

Feminists and liberal policymakers who do not see the stable two-parent family as a high priority typically argue that a generous infusion of social services can ensure the well-being of children. Some even argue that those who place too much emphasis upon the importance of a resident father to a child's prosperity and productivity add stigmatization to the troubles that already shadow children of divorced or never-married mothers. And many decry any mention of women's responsibility to spend as much time as possible with their children,

4. Hillary Rodham Clinton, *It Takes a Village and Other Lessons Children Teach Us* (New York: Simon and Schuster, 1996). On social welfare problems, see, for example, Valerie Polakow, *Lives on the Edge: Single Mothers and Their Children* (Chicago: Univ. of Chicago Press, 1993); William Julius Wilson, *The Truly Disadvantaged: The Inner City, the Under Class, and Public Policy* (Chicago: Univ. of Chicago Press, 1987); William Julius Wilson, *When Work Disappears: The World of the New Urban Poor* (New York: Alfred A. Knopf, 1996).

5. Thus the Reverend Mr. Eugene Rivers, the Pentecostal minister of the Asuza Christian Community in Dorchester, Massachusetts, and his gifted and dedicated coworkers focus much of their effort upon the reconstitution of families, church attendance, and the acquisition of education.

especially when the children are very young. The arguments about women's need for personal development and independence as well as those about the value of "quality time" spent with children are too familiar to require rehearsal here. What all of these positions have in common is the determination to encourage people to "feel good about themselves" no matter what they are doing. If this is the revolt against the ghost of Victorian sexual and personal "repression," it has been successful beyond anyone's wildest dreams.

As it happens, few would disagree about our responsibility to help all children feel respect for themselves and for others regardless of family circumstances. But it is a big — and disingenuous — reach from the respect children deserve as individuals to the claim that we should not deplore the proliferation of single-parent families and do everything in our power to strengthen two-parent families. The point is not that the strengthening of marriages will alone improve the prospects of children, but it seems foolhardy indeed not to place strong marriages high on the list of what children need. The more one reads even the most thoughtful and sympathetic pro-village proposals for the improvement of children's lives, the more one suspects that their main goal is to train teachers, social workers, law enforcement officers, and community leaders to replace parents. In other words, they want all these figures to cultivate the sensitivity of parents to the needs of the individual child. And even the most telling criticisms of bureaucratic rigidity ultimately point toward a transformation of institutions into informal networks that, like families, can respond appropriately to a myriad of different individual needs.[6]

The goal of flexibility and understanding can hardly be faulted, but, even if it were attained, it could not adequately substitute for the people with whom children live. Any child's first need lies in feeling himself or herself the most important thing in the world to someone, and that is a need which even the best trained, most caring, and most enlightened professions are unlikely to fill. Furthermore, there is good reason to be cautious about the responses we may reasonably expect from the public sector. There are, for example, a number of responsible and innovative public schools scattered around the country, but even the most generous estimate would only argue that they account for a

---

6. Richard Weissbourd, *The Vulnerable Child: What Really Hurts America's Children and What We Can Do About It* (Boston: Addison Wesley, 1996) offers an especially thoughtful version of these attitudes and assumptions.

mere few hundred among the total number of 83,000 public schools. Similarly, here and there one finds of flexible and responsible social service agencies or dedicated law enforcement officers who really know and serve their clients. But they, too, remain a distressingly small minority, and it is impossible to be sure they will have successors.

It is impossible to exaggerate the importance of schools, social services, and police forces. In our world, no family can reasonably count upon going it alone. But those who insist upon the need for a village to raise a child invariably begin by trying to teach the agents of the village to provide what the psychiatrist D. W. Winnicott called "good enough" mothering and fathering.[7] If all we need is for the agents of the village to behave like good enough parents then why do we not begin by encouraging the parents who know the child best to do the job themselves? Then, when they need help, as most parents do, we can encourage the agents of the village to behave like good enough public servants. For, if we cannot do this much, we may just as well give up on our ability to provide any kind of decent future for American children.

The feminists and pro-village advocates have yet to offer an adequate reply to those "traditionalists" who insist upon policies that give priority to the two-parent family and who certainly do not advocate the stigmatization of children raised by a single parent. All children, regardless of background, need a judicious mixture of adequate resources and attentive, demanding love. Up to a point, the village does play a role in the provision of resources for lack of which too many children still falter, but it can never provide that selfless, tough love without which no child can thrive. Only when we appreciate the unique value of two-parent families can we begin to talk intelligently about how to provide them with the support that they indisputably need.

But the two-parent family returns us to where we began. For many feminists, that family constitutes the primary site of women's oppression — although some rank "patriarchal" religion even higher — which they take to mean that if women are ever to be liberated, the two-parent family must go. That it is, in front of our eyes, going may not be solely attributed to feminist agitation. The dual sexual and economic revolution of the past thirty years or so has done the real work. But feminism

7. D. W. Winnicott, *The Maturational Process and the Facilitating Environment: Studies in the Theory of Emotional Development* (London: Hogarth Press, 1972; orig. ed., 1965).

has led the way in instructing us on how to interpret the changes that engulf us and, more ominously, in constantly pressuring us to further them. Above all, in a painful irony, the same feminism that has fought such a relentless fight for "liberation" has led the way in demanding new social and political constraints, albeit of a different kind. Feminists, that is, have discovered that for women truly to move freely and "equally" in the public sphere, some agent of authority must safeguard them and, having abolished the role of husbands and fathers as protectors, they have had to turn to the government. In this respect, women's need for public authorities to replace private authorities in defending their interests has reinforced the tendency to expect those same public authorities to substitute for parents in the lives of children.

Having been reasonably critical of feminism's influence upon the expectations of children and the cohesion of families, let me conclude with a reminder that feminism has also made important positive contributions not merely to women's lives, but to our society in general. The vast majority of women have no desire to return to the days in which they could not get credit in their own name, could not expect equal pay for equal work, could not expect fair treatment in — or even admission to — graduate and professional programs, or could not have some confidence that their talent and diligence at work would be rewarded by pay increases and promotion. If anything, more importantly, it is no longer possible to go back. Nostalgia and reaction are no more appropriate to the problems that confront us than utopian or nihilistic radicalism. Our times call for virtues of an entirely different order, namely those of balance and moderation. Above all, they call for a modicum of humility and good will in our continuing attempts to renegotiate the relations between those things which change and those which do not.

8. Marriage and the Illusion of Moral Neutrality

ROBERT P. GEORGE

FREQUENTLY I hear students (and others) say: "I believe that marriage is a union of one man and one woman. But I think that it is wrong for the state to base its law of marriage on a controversial moral judgment, even if I happen to believe that judgment to be true. Therefore, I support proposals to revise our law to authorize same-sex 'marriages.'" The thought here is that the state ought to be neutral as between competing understandings of the nature and value of marriage.

Of course, the claim that the law ought to be morally neutral about marriage or anything else is itself a moral claim. As such, *it* is not morally neutral, nor can it rest on an appeal to moral neutrality. People who believe that the law of marriage (and/or other areas of the law) ought to be morally neutral do not assert, nor does their position presuppose, that the law ought to be neutral as between the view that the law ought to be neutral and competing moral views. It is obvious that neutrality between neutrality and unneutrality is logically impossible. Sophisticated proponents of moral neutrality therefore acknowledge that theirs is a controversial moral position whose truth, soundness, correctness, or, at least, reasonableness, they are prepared to defend against competing moral positions. They assert, in other words, that the best understanding of political morality, at least for societies such as ours, is one that includes a requirement that the law be morally neutral with respect to marriage. Alternative understandings of political morality, insofar as they fail to recognize the principle of moral neutrality, are, they say, mistaken and ought, as such, to be rejected.

Now, to recognize that any justification offered for the requirement of moral neutrality cannot itself be morally neutral is by no means to establish the falsity of the alleged requirement of moral neutrality. My purpose in calling attention to it is not to propose a retorsive argument purporting to identify self-referential inconsistency in arguments for moral neutrality. Although I shall argue that the moral neutrality of marriage law is neither desirable nor, strictly speaking, possible, I do not propose to show that there is a logical or performative inconsistency in saying that "the law (of marriage) ought to be neutral as between competing moral ideas." It is not like saying "No statement is true." Nor is it like singing "I am not singing." At the same time, the putative requirement of moral neutrality is neither self-evident nor self-justifying. If it is to be vindicated as a true (correct, sound, and so on) proposition of political morality, it needs to be shown to be true (and so on) by a valid argument.

It is certainly the case that implicit in our matrimonial law is a (now controversial) moral judgment: namely, the judgment that marriage is inherently heterosexual — a union of one man and one woman. (Later in this chapter, I will discuss the deeper grounds of that judgment.) Of course, this is not the only possible moral judgment. In some cultures, polygyny or (far less frequently) polyandry is legally sanctioned. Some historians claim that "marriages" (or their equivalent) between two men or two women have been recognized by certain cultures in the past.[1] However that may be, influential voices in our own culture today demand the revision of matrimonial law to authorize such "marriages." Indeed, the Supreme Court of the State of Hawaii has for some time been on the verge of requiring officials of that State to issue marriage licenses to otherwise qualified same-sex couples under the Equal Rights Amendment to the Hawaii Constitution. Unless the people of Hawaii are able to amend their state constitution to

1. The late John Boswell, for example, claimed that brother/sister-making rituals found in certain early medieval Christian manuscripts were meant to give ecclesiastical recognition and approval to homosexual relationships. See *Same-Sex Unions in Premodern Europe* (New York: Villard Books, 1994). However, as Robin Darling Young has observed, "the reviews [of Boswell's work] after the early burst of hopeful publicity, have been notably skeptical — even from sources one would expect to be favorable." "Gay Marriage: Reimagining Church History," *First Things*, 47 (November, 1994): 48. Darling Young herself concludes that Boswell's "painfully strained effort to recruit Christian history in support of the homosexual cause that he favors is not only a failure, but an embarrassing one." Id.

prevent the imposition of "same-sex marriage," it will then fall to the federal courts, and, ultimately, to the Supreme Court of the United States, to decide whether the "full faith and credit" clause of the Constitution of the United States requires every state in the Union to recognize such "marriages" contracted in Hawaii.

Anticipating the Hawaii Supreme Court's action, Congress passed the Defense of Marriage Act which guarantees the right of states to refuse to recognize same-sex "marriages." The Act went to the President to sign or veto in the course of the 1996 presidential campaign. After denouncing the Act as both mean-spirited and unnecessary, Clinton quietly signed it into law literally in the middle of the night. Of course, a second opportunity for a veto effectively rests with any five justices of the Supreme Court of the United States. Although it is impossible to say with confidence how the Supreme Court will ultimately rule on the inevitable constitutional challenge to the Defense of Marriage Act, the stated ground of the Court's decision in the 1996 case of *Romer* v. *Evans* (the so-called Colorado Amendment 2 Case) will surely inspire hope among those whom Clinton disappointed by failing to veto the Act. In *Romer*, the Court invalidated an amendment to the Constitution of the State of Colorado by which the people of that State sought to prevent its municipalities from enacting ordinances granting protected status or preferences based on homosexual or bisexual orientation. Six justices joined in an opinion written by Associate Justice Anthony Kennedy holding that Amendment 2 could only have been motivated by constitutionally impermissible "animus" against a politically vulnerable minority group.

There are two ways to argue for the proposition that it is unjust for government to refuse to authorize same-sex (and, for that matter, polygamous) "marriages." The first is to deny the reasonableness, soundness, or truth of the moral judgment implicit in the proposition that marriage is a union of one man and one woman. The second is to argue that this moral judgment cannot justly serve as the basis for the public law of matrimony irrespective of its reasonableness, soundness, or even its truth.

In the analysis that follows, I shall mainly be concerned with the second of these ways of arguing. The task I have set for myself is to persuade you that the moral neutrality to which this way of arguing appeals is, and cannot but be, illusory. To that end, however, it will be necessary for me to explain the philosophical grounds of the moral judgment that marriage is a union of one man and one woman, and to discuss the arguments advanced by certain critics of traditional matrimonial law in their efforts to undermine this judgment.

Here is the core of the traditional understanding: Marriage is a two-in-one-flesh communion of persons that is consummated and actualized by acts which are reproductive in type, whether or not they are reproductive in effect (or are motivated, even in part, by a desire to reproduce). The bodily union of spouses in marital acts is the biological matrix of their marriage as a multi-level relationship: that is, a relationship which unites persons at the bodily, emotional, dispositional, and spiritual levels of their being. Marriage, precisely as such a relationship, is naturally ordered to the good of procreation (and to the nurturing and education of children) as well as to the good of spousal unity, and these goods are tightly bound together. The distinctive unity of spouses is possible *because* human (like other mammalian) males and females, by mating, become a single reproductive principle. Although reproduction is a single act, in humans (and other mammals) the reproductive act is performed not by individual members of the species, but by a mated pair as an organic unit. The point has been explained by Germain Grisez:

> Though a male and a female are complete individuals with respect to other functions — for example, nutrition, sensation, and locomotion — with respect to reproduction they are only potential parts of a mated pair, which is the complete organism capable of reproducing sexually. Even if the mated pair is sterile, intercourse, provided it is the reproductive behavior characteristic of the species, makes the copulating male and female one organism.[2]

Although not all reproductive-type acts are marital,[3] there can be no marital act that is not reproductive in type. Masturbatory, sodomitical, or other sexual acts which are not reproductive in type cannot unite persons organically: that is, as a single reproductive principle.[4] There-

2. Germain Grisez, "The Christian Family as Fulfillment of Sacramental Marriage," paper delivered to the Society of Christian Ethics Annual Conference, September 9, 1995.

3. Adulterous acts, for example, may be reproductive in type (and even in effect) but are intrinsically nonmarital.

4. Securely grasping this point, and noticing its significance, Hadley Arkes has remarked that " 'sexuality' refers to that part of our nature that has as its end the purpose of begetting. In comparison, the other forms of 'sexuality' may be taken

fore, such acts cannot be intelligibly engaged in for the sake of marital (that is, one-flesh, bodily) unity as such. They cannot be marital acts. Rather, persons who perform such acts must be doing so for the sake of ends or goals which are *extrinsic* to themselves as bodily persons: sexual satisfaction, or (perhaps) mutual sexual satisfaction, is sought as a means of releasing tension, or obtaining (and, sometimes, sharing) pleasure, either as an end in itself, or as a means to some other end, such as expressing affection, esteem, friendliness, and so on. In any case, where one-flesh union cannot (or cannot rightly) be sought as an end-in-itself, sexual activity necessarily involves the instrumentalization of the bodies of those participating in such activity to extrinsic ends.

In marital acts, by contrast, the bodies of persons who unite biologically are not reduced to the status of extrinsic instruments. Rather, the end, goal, and intelligible point of sexual union is the good of marriage itself. On this understanding, such union is not a merely instrumental good, that is, a reason for action whose intelligibility as a reason depends on other ends to which it is a means, but is, rather, an intrinsic good, that is, a reason for action whose intelligibility as a reason depends on no such other end. The central and justifying point of sex is not pleasure (or even the sharing of pleasure) *per se*, however much sexual pleasure is rightly sought as an aspect of the perfection of marital union; the point of sex, rather, is *marriage itself,* considered as a bodily ("one-flesh") union of persons consummated and actualized by acts which are reproductive in type. Because in marital acts sex is not instrumentalized,[5] such acts are free of the self-alienating and dis-integrating qualities of masturbatory and sodomitical sex. Unlike these and other nonmarital sex acts, marital acts effect no practical dualism which

---

as minor burlesques or even mockeries of the true thing." Now, Professor Arkes is not here suggesting that sexual acts, in what he calls "the strict sense of 'sexuality,'" must be *motivated* by a desire to reproduce; rather, his point is that such acts, even where motivated by a desire for bodily union, must be reproductive in type if such union is to be achieved. This, I believe, makes sense of what Stephen Macedo and other liberal critics of Arkes's writings on marriage and sexual morality find to be the puzzling statement that "[e]very act of genital stimulation simply cannot count as a sexual act." See Hadley Arkes, "Questions of Principle, Not Predictions: A Reply to Stephen Macedo," *Georgetown Law Journal*, 84 (1995), pp. 321-27, at 323.

5. This is by no means to suggest that married couples cannot instrumentalize and thus degrade their sexual relationship. See Robert P. George and Gerard V. Bradley, "Marriage and the Liberal Imagination," *Georgetown Law Journal*, vol. 84, 301-20 (1995), esp. p. 303, n. 9.

volitionally and, thus, existentially (though, of course, not metaphysically) separates the body from the conscious and desiring aspect of the self which is understood and treated by the acting person as the true self which inhabits and uses the body as its instrument. As John Finnis has observed, marital acts are truly unitive, and in no way self-alienating, because the bodily or biological aspect of human beings is "part of, and not merely an instrument of, their *personal* reality."[6]

But, one may ask, what about procreation? On the traditional view, is not the sexual union of spouses instrumentalized to the goal of having children? It is true that St. Augustine was an influential proponent of such a view. The strict Augustinian position was rejected, however, by the mainstream of philosophical and theological reflection from the late middle ages forward, and the understanding of sex and marriage that came to be embodied in both the canon law of the Church and the civil law of matrimony does not treat marriage as a merely instrumental good. Matrimonial law has traditionally treated marriage as consummated by, and only by, the reproductive-type acts of spouses; by contrast, the sterility of spouses — so long as they are capable of consummating their marriage by a reproductive-type act (and, thus, of achieving bodily, organic unity) — has never been treated as an impediment to marriage, even where sterility is certain and even certain to be permanent (as in the case of the marriage of a woman who has been through menopause or has undergone a hysterectomy).[7]

According to the traditional understanding of marriage, then, it is the nature of marital acts as reproductive in type that makes it possible for such acts to be unitive in the distinctively marital way. And this type of unity has intrinsic, and not merely instrumental value. Thus, the unitive good of marriage provides a noninstrumental (and thus sufficient) reason for spouses to perform sexual acts of a type which consummates and actualizes their marriage. In performing marital acts, the spouses do not reduce themselves as bodily persons (or their marriage) to the status of means or extrinsic instruments.

At the same time, where marriage is understood as a one-flesh union of persons, children who may be conceived in marital acts are

6. John Finnis, "Law, Morality, and Sexual Orientation," in John Corvino, ed., *Same Sex: Debating the Ethics, Science, and Culture of Homosexuality* (Lanham, Md.: Rowman and Littlefield, 1997), sec. III.

7. See George and Bradley, "Marriage and the Liberal Imagination," pp. 307-9.

understood, not as ends which are extrinsic to marriage (either in the Augustinian sense, or the modern liberal one), but, rather, as gifts which supervene on acts whose central justifying point is precisely the marital unity of the spouses.[8] Such acts have unique meaning, value, and significance, as I have already suggested, because they belong to the class of acts by which children come into being — what I have called "reproductive-type acts." More precisely, these acts have their unique meaning, value, and significance because they belong to the *only* class of acts by which children can come into being, not as "products" which their parents choose to "make," but, rather, as perfective participants in the organic community (that is, the family) that is established by their parents' marriage. It is thus that children are properly understood and treated — even in their conception — not as means to their parents' ends, but as ends-in-themselves; not as *objects* of the desire[9] or will of their parents, but as *subjects* of justice (and inviolable human rights); not as *property*, but as *persons*. It goes without saying that not all cultures have fully grasped these truths about the moral status of children. What is less frequently noticed is that our culture's grasp of these truths is connected to a basic understanding of sex and marriage which is not only fast eroding, but is now under severe assault from people who have no conscious desire to reduce children to the status of mere means, or objects, or property.

It is sometimes thought that defenders of traditional marriage law deny the possibility of something whose possibility critics of the law affirm. "Love," these critics say, "makes a family." And it is committed love that justifies homosexual sex as much as it justifies heterosexual sex. If marriage is the proper, or best, context for sexual love, the argument goes, then marriage should be made available to loving, committed same-sex as well as opposite-sex partners on terms of strict

8. Ibid., p. 304.

9. I am not here suggesting that traditional ethics denies that it is legitimate for people to "desire" or "want" children. I am merely explicating the sense in which children may be desired or wanted by prospective parents under a description which, consistently with the norms of traditional ethics, does not reduce them to the status of "products" to be brought into existence at their parents' will and for their ends, but rather treats them as "persons" who are to be welcomed by them as perfective participants in the organic community established by their marriage. See George and Bradley, "Marriage and the Liberal Imagination," p. 306, n. 21. Also see Leon Kass, "The Wisdom of Repugnance: Why We Should Ban the Cloning of Humans," *The New Republic* (June 2, 1997), pp. 17-26, esp. 23-24.

equality. To think otherwise is to suppose that same-sex partners cannot really love each other, or love each other in a committed way, or that the orgasmic "sexual expression" of their love is somehow inferior to the orgasmic "sexual expression" of couples who "arrange the plumbing differently."

In fact, however, at the bottom of the debate is a possibility that defenders of traditional marriage law affirm and its critics deny, namely, the possibility of marriage as a one-flesh communion of persons. The denial of this possibility is central to any argument designed to show that the moral judgment at the heart of the traditional understanding of marriage as inherently heterosexual is unreasonable, unsound, or untrue. If reproductive-type acts in fact unite spouses interpersonally, as traditional sexual morality and marriage law suppose, then such acts differ fundamentally in meaning, value, and significance from the only types of sexual acts that can be performed by same-sex partners.

Liberal sexual morality which denies that marriage is inherently heterosexual necessarily supposes that the value of sex must be instrumental *either* to procreation *or* to pleasure, considered, in turn, as an end-in-itself or as a means of expressing affection, tender feelings, and so on. Thus, proponents of the liberal view suppose that homosexual sex acts are indistinguishable from heterosexual acts whenever the motivation for such acts is something other than procreation. The sexual acts of homosexual partners, that is to say, are indistinguishable in motivation, meaning, value, and significance from the marital acts of spouses who know that at least one spouse is temporarily or permanently infertile. Thus, the liberal argument goes, traditional matrimonial law is guilty of unfairness in treating sterile heterosexuals as capable of marrying while treating homosexual partners as ineligible to marry.

Stephen Macedo has accused the traditional view and its defenders of precisely this alleged "double standard." He asks:

> What is the point of sex in an infertile marriage? Not procreation: the partners (let us assume) know that they are infertile. If they have sex, it is for pleasure and to express their love, or friendship, or some other shared good. It will be for precisely the same reason that committed, loving gay couples have sex.[10]

10. Stephen Macedo, "Homosexuality and the Conservative Mind," *Georgetown Law Journal* 84 (1995): 261-300, at 278.

ROBERT P. GEORGE

But Macedo's criticism fails to tell against the traditional view because it presupposes as true precisely what the traditional view denies, namely, that the value (and, thus, the point) of sex in marriage can only be instrumental. On the contrary, it is a central tenet of the traditional view that the value (and point) of sex is the *intrinsic* good of marriage itself which is actualized in sexual acts that unite spouses biologically and, thus, interpersonally. The traditional view rejects the instrumentalization of sex (and, thus, of the bodies of sexual partners) to any extrinsic end. This does not mean that procreation and pleasure are not rightly sought in marital acts; it means merely that they are rightly sought when they are integrated with the basic good and justifying point of marital sex, namely, the one-flesh union of marriage itself.

It is necessary, therefore, for critics of traditional matrimonial law to argue that the apparent one-flesh unity that distinguishes marital acts from sodomitical acts is illusory, and, thus, that the apparent bodily communion of spouses in reproductive-type acts which, according to the traditional view, form the biological matrix of their marital relationship is not really possible. And so Macedo claims that "the 'one-flesh communion' of sterile couples would appear . . . to be more a matter of appearance than reality." Because of their sterility such couples cannot really unite biologically: "their bodies, like those of homosexuals, can form no 'single reproductive principle,' no real unity."[11] Indeed, Macedo goes so far as to argue that even fertile couples who conceive children in acts of sexual intercourse do not truly unite biologically, because, he asserts, "penises and vaginas do not unite biologically, sperm and eggs do."[12]

John Finnis has aptly replied that:

in this reductivist, word-legislating mood, one might declare that sperm and egg unite only physically and only their pronuclei are biologically united. But it would be more realistic to acknowledge that the whole process of copulation, involving as it does the brains of the man and woman, their nerves, blood, vaginal and other secretions, and coordinated activity is biological through and through.[13]

11. Ibid., p. 278.
12. Ibid., p. 280.
13. Finnis, "Law, Morality, and 'Sexual Orientation,' " sec. V.

Moreover, as Finnis points out,

> the organic unity which is instantiated in an act of the reproductive kind is not, as Macedo . . . reductively imagine[s], the unity of penis and vagina. It is the unity of the persons in the intentional, consensual *act* of seminal emission/reception in the woman's reproductive tract.[14]

The unity to which Finnis refers — unity of body, sense, emotion, reason, and will — is, in my view, central to our understanding of humanness itself. Yet it is a unity of which Macedo and others who deny the possibility of true marital communion can give no account. For this denial presupposes a dualism of "person" (as conscious and desiring self), on the one hand, and "body" (as instrument of the conscious and desiring self), on the other, which is flatly incompatible with this unity. Dualism is implicit in the idea, central to Macedo's denial of the possibility of one-flesh marital union, that sodomitical acts differ from what I have described as acts of the reproductive type only as a matter of the arrangement of the "plumbing." According to this idea, the genital organs of an infertile woman (and, of course, all women are infertile most of the time) or of an infertile man are not really "reproductive organs" — anymore than, say, mouths, rectums, tongues, or fingers are reproductive organs. Thus, the intercourse of a man and a woman where at least one partner is temporarily or permanently sterile cannot really be an act of the reproductive type.

But the plain fact is that the genitals of men and women are reproductive organs all of the time — even during periods of infertility. And acts which fulfill the behavioral conditions of reproduction are acts of the reproductive-type even where the nonbehavioral conditions of reproduction do not happen to obtain. Insofar as the object of sexual intercourse is marital union, the partners achieve the desired unity (that is, become "two-in-one-flesh") precisely insofar as they mate, that is, fulfill the behavioral conditions of reproduction, or, if you will, perform the type of act — the only type of act — upon which the gift of a child may supervene.[15]

14. Ibid., sec. V.
15. John Finnis has carefully explained the point:

> Sexual acts which are marital are "of the reproductive kind" because in willing such an act one wills sexual behaviour which is (a) the very same as causes generation (intended or unintended) in every case of human *sexual* reproduc-

The dualistic presuppositions of the liberal position are fully on display in the frequent references of Macedo and other proponents of the position to sexual organs as "equipment." Neither sperm nor eggs, neither penises nor vaginas, are properly conceived in such impersonal terms. Nor are they "used" by persons considered as somehow standing over and apart from these and other aspects of their biological reality. The biological reality of persons is, rather, part of their personal reality. (Hence, where a person treats his body as a subpersonal object, the practical dualism he thereby effects brings with it a certain self-aliena-tion, a damaging of the intrinsic good of personal self-integration.) In any event, the biological union of persons — which is effected in repro-ductive-type acts but not in sodomitical ones — really is an interper-sonal ("one-flesh") communion.

Now, Macedo considers the possibility that defenders of the tradi-tional understanding are right about all this: that marriage truly is a "one-flesh union" consummated and actualized by marital acts; that sodomitical and other intrinsically nonmarital sexual acts really are self-alienating and, as such, immoral; that the true conception of marriage is one according to which it is an intrinsically heterosexual (and, one might here add, monogamous) relationship. But even if the traditional understanding of marriage is the morally correct one — even if it is true — he argues, the state cannot justly recognize it as such. For, if disagreements about the nature of marriage "lie in . . . difficult philo-sophical quarrels, about which reasonable people have long disagreed, then our differences lie in precisely the territory that John Rawls rightly marks off as inappropriate to the fashioning of our basic rights and liberties."[16] And from this it follows that government must remain

---

tion, and (b) the very same as one would will if one were intending precisely sexual reproduction as a goal of a particular marital sexual act. This kind of act is a "natural kind," in the morally relevant sense of "natural," not . . . if and only if one is intending or attempting to produce an *outcome*, viz. repro-duction or procreation. Rather it is a distinct rational kind — and therefore in the morally relevant sense a natural kind — because (i) in engaging in it one is intending a *marital* act, (ii) its being of the reproductive kind is a necessary though not sufficient condition of its being marital, and (iii) marriage is a rational and natural kind of institution. One's reason for action — one's ra-tional motive — is precisely the complex good of marriage.

Finnis, "Law, Morality, and 'Sexual Orientation,'" sec. V.
16. Stephen Macedo, "Reply to Critics," *Georgetown Law Journal* 84 (1995): 329-37, at 335.

neutral as between conceptions of marriage as intrinsically heterosexual (and monogamous), and conceptions according to which "marriages" may be contracted not only between a man and a woman, but also between two men, two women (and, presumably, a man or a woman and multiple male and/or female "spouses"). Otherwise, according to Macedo, the state would "inappropriately" be "deny[ing] people fundamental aspects of equality based on reasons and arguments whose force can only be appreciated by those who accept difficult to assess [metaphysical and moral] claims."[17]

It seems to me, however, that something very much like the contrary is true. Because the true meaning, value, and significance of marriage are fairly easily grasped (even if people sometimes have difficulty living up to its moral demands) where a culture — including, critically, a legal culture — promotes and supports a sound understanding of marriage, both formally and informally, and because ideologies and practices which are hostile to a sound understanding and practice of marriage in a culture tend to undermine the institution of marriage in that culture, thus making it difficult for large numbers of people to grasp the true meaning, value, and significance of marriage, it is extremely important that government eschew attempts to be "neutral" with regard to competing conceptions of marriage and try hard to embody in its law and policy the soundest, most nearly correct conception. Moreover, any effort to achieve neutrality will inevitably prove to be self-defeating. For the law is a teacher. And it will teach *either* that marriage is a reality that people can choose to participate in, but whose contours people cannot make and remake at will (for example, a one-flesh communion of persons consummated and actualized by acts which are reproductive in type and perfected, where all goes well, in the generation, education, and nurturing of children in a context — the family — which is uniquely suitable to their well-being), *or* the law will teach that marriage is a mere convention which is malleable in such a way that individuals, couples, or, indeed, groups, can choose to make it whatever suits their desires, interests, subjective goals, and so on. The result, given the biases of human sexual psychology, will be the development of practices and ideologies which truly do tend to undermine the sound understanding and practice of marriage, together with the pathologies that tend to reinforce the very practices and ideologies that cause them.

17. Ibid., p. 335.

Joseph Raz, though himself a liberal who does not share my views regarding homosexuality or sexual morality generally, is rightly critical of forms of liberalism, including Rawlsianism, which suppose that law and government can and should be neutral with respect to competing conceptions of morality. In this regard, he has noted that

> monogamy, assuming that it is the only valuable form of marriage, cannot be practised by an individual. It requires a culture which recognizes it, and which supports it through the public's attitude and through its formal institutions.[18]

Now, Raz does not suppose that, in a culture whose law and public morality do not support monogamy, someone who happens to believe in it somehow will be unable to restrict himself to having one wife or will be required to take additional wives. His point, rather, is that even if monogamy is a key element of a sound understanding of marriage, large numbers of people will fail to understand that or why that is the case — and will therefore fail to grasp the value of monogamy and the intelligible point of practicing it — unless they are assisted by a culture which supports, formally and informally, monogamous marriage. And what is true of monogamy is equally true of the other marks or aspects of a morally sound understanding of marriage. In other words, marriage is the type of good which can be participated in, or fully participated in, only by people who properly understand it and choose it with a proper understanding in mind; yet people's ability properly to understand it, and thus to choose it, depends upon institutions and cultural understandings that transcend individual choice.

But what about Macedo's claim that, when matrimonial law deviates from neutrality by embodying the moral judgment that marriage is inherently heterosexual, it denies same-sex partners who wish to marry "fundamental aspects of equality?" Does a due regard for equality require moral neutrality? I think that the appeal to neutrality actually does not work here. If the moral judgment that marriage is between a man and a woman is false, then the reason for recognizing same-sex marriages is that such unions are as a matter of moral fact indistinguishable from marriages of the traditional type. If, however, the moral judgment that marriage is between a man and a woman is true, then Macedo's claim that the recognition of this truth by government "denies

18. Joseph Raz, *The Morality of Freedom* (Oxford: Clarendon Press, 1986), p. 162.

fundamental aspects of equality" simply cannot be sustained. If, in other words, the marital acts of spouses consummate and actualize marriage as a one-flesh communion, and serve thereby as the biological matrix of the relationship of marriage at all its levels, then the embodiment in law and policy of an understanding of marriage as inherently heterosexual denies no one fundamental aspects of equality. True, many persons who are homosexually oriented lack a psychological prerequisite to enter into marital relationships. But this is no fault of the law. Indeed, the law would embody a lie (and a damaging one insofar as it truly would contribute to the undermining of the sound understanding and practice of marriage in a culture) if it were to pretend that a marital relationship could be formed on the basis of, and integrated around, sodomitical or other intrinsically nonmarital (and, as such, self-alienating) sex acts.

It is certainly unjust arbitrarily to deny legal marriage to persons who are capable of performing marital acts and entering into the marital relationship. So, for example, laws forbidding interracial marriages truly were violations of equality. Contrary to the claims of Andrew Koppelman, Andrew Sullivan, and others, however, laws which embody the judgment that marriage is intrinsically heterosexual are in no way analogous to laws against miscegenation. Laws forbidding whites to marry blacks were unjust, not because they embodied a particular moral view and thus violated the alleged requirement of moral neutrality; rather, they were unjust because they embodied an unsound (indeed a grotesquely false) moral view — one that was racist and, as such, immoral.

9. *The Law and the Loss of Urbanity*

HADLEY ARKES

A BOUT eighteen years ago, in the spring of 1979, my small college community in Amherst, Massachusetts, was affected by a wave of shame and embarrassment: crosses had been burned outside the Charles Drew House, a hall that had become reserved, in effect, for black students. Classes were suspended as the community broke up into different groups to undertake deep forays of introspection and group therapy. But these rigors of self-flagellation came to an abrupt end when it was discovered that the crosses had been fashioned and burned by residents of the Drew House. An officer on the campus police, a fellow of modest background who had not been to college, apparently knew something that fell outside the education even of these students from Amherst: he knew that lumber was often sold in numbered lots, and he found, in the basement of the Drew House, the boards that were adjacent, in number, to the boards that had been used to form the crosses.

At other times and other places, with a moral sensibility different from the sensibility we find these days in college towns, this exercise in fraud and hokum might have been expected to ignite a sense of outrage. In part it did, but it also elicited a further round of contrived excuses and justifications. The tone of the day will be marked for me evermore by the line attributed to one student, a young woman who had grown up in one of the comfortable suburbs of New York. She said, "Do you see what *we made* them do?" That is, so powerless were these black students, so desperate in their plight at Amherst, that they had to strike out to dramatize racism even when the racists did not have the nerve to make their presence known themselves.

128

The situation seemed to confirm, at once, Herman Kahn's observation that higher education in America was now rendering students imbecilic. It used to be understood, as G. K. Chesterton remarked, that the purpose of education was to render young people old, or to save them, as Chesterton said, from the degrading slavery of being children of their own age. The liberal arts were not meant to be vocational, but even so, it used to be understood that education was supposed to make us more worldly, more anchored, more aware of moral up and down. It was at that moment that I decided to embark upon a series of pieces I would later write in the style of Damon Runyon — pieces in which I would try to call back those characters of Runyon's Broadway, and imagine their reactions to the politics of our own day. For the remark of that girl from the suburbs drew me back, as a contrast, to a time when this country managed to produce a more urbane population, even — or perhaps because — our people were not burdened with a college education. We had to wonder: how would the denizens of Runyon's Broadway have reacted to the view of the world offered by this young Amherst student, sprung from the suburbs? What if we had come to Nathan Detroit or Sam the Gonoph and said, "Nathan, Sam, do you see what *we* made them do?" How much credulity could we have counted on there?

A colleague of mine used to say that one purpose of education was to produce students who could not be bought and not be fooled — and we liked to think that we brought them closer to a condition in which they could not be bought if we brought them into a condition in which they could not easily be fooled. Our aim then was to produce people who would not be credulous in the presence of overtures or arguments that should not claim, even for a moment, the credulity of the urbane. And in fact, when I tried to sum up this combination of worldliness and wit, it did seem to come together in the notion of urbanity. That is the ingredient that seems to be vanishing from our universities, and therefore, from those enclaves that are shaping the sensibilities of judges and shaping the character of our law.

It seemed to me also that urbanity usually makes itself known to us, in a flash, through wit. And the connection is hardly casual. Some of my friends here have heard me suggest on other occasions that there is a critical connection between comedy and philosophy. Comedians and philosophers make their livings in the same way, by playing off the shades of meaning contained in our language. Henny Youngman would say, "My wife will buy anything that's marked down. She

129

brought home an escalator." I used to say that my favorite epistemol-
ogist was Lou Costello, because in one of his skits, when his partner,
Bud Abbott, came up with an apt idea, Costello remarked, "That's an
excellent thought — I was just going to think of it myself."

At times, the laughs mark contradictions that run to the core of
what some people affect to regard as the anchoring principles of their
lives. And so we recall, in this vein, Bertrand Russell's joke about
Christine Franklyn-Ladd, who was a "solipsist." That is, she earnestly
professed that she could not know for sure that there was anyone in
the world apart from herself — though she lamented, at the same time,
that she could not find other solipsists, to come to meetings. If we took
the time, I think I could show you that we would find a remarkably
precise moral anthropology of this country, and a fairly accurate reflection of what people in this country could be counted on as knowing
about "natural law," if we merely take the tapes from the old Jack Benny
programs, and notice the laugh-lines. Comedy provides an unambigu-
ous test here: there is a laugh only if the audience "gets it," and at
times, the point they need to "get" is a point in logic or natural law.
One of Mr. Richard Lederer's students wrote, "Bach was the most
famous composer of his age — and so was Handel." The laughs come
instantly, and yet what had to be grasped here, in an instant, was the
logic of saying that Bach was "the most famous" — than whom no one
else was more famous — and that so, too, was Handel! In the case of
Jack Benny, the reflections of natural law were threaded through the
jokes. In one episode, Jack establishes that he is, with a bow and arrow,
a lethal threat. Phil Harris bets him that he cannot hit an apple on the
head of Jack's announcer, Don Wilson. Harris bets him a dime — and
Jack sees the bet. Don Wilson protests — he wants none of this — and
Jack responds, "Why are you getting so upset? It's *our* money." Once
again, the interval between the line and the laugh could be measured
in milliseconds, and yet I submit that there is no laugh, no joke, unless
people grasp at once the sense of disproportion that comes through
natural law: in this case, that life is too important to be hazarded, in a
jest, for a stake of ten cents. The understanding behind the laugh is the
same understanding that comes into play when I read to my students
a list of defenses that were heard in a courtroom in Chicago in response
to the question, Why did you kill him? One answer was: "He ate the
last piece of pizza."

Jack Benny's writers had to assume that they could count on the
presence of this understanding, as a kind of natural understanding,

even in a mass audience, even among people who were not very educated. Mr. Mel Brooks is not an especially subtle man, and he does not count on refined subtlety in his audience. And that may be why we can take it as a measure of the moral sensibility of the public — or on the moral understanding that Brooks thinks he can count on in the public — when he includes a scene of this kind in his "History of the World, Part I": the King of France, out skeet-shooting, shouts "pull," and one of his minions triggers the spring, hurling into the air, not a clay pigeon, but a *peasant* to be shot. Once again, there is no joke unless it is understood that life is not to be taken as a kind of plaything, or as something to be destroyed for such a casual reason.

It may serve a useful point to try a similar exercise with some of our judges, past and present, and it may be more illuminating to reverse the sequence for a moment, to offer the sardonic line first in order to prepare people for the lines spoken by the judge. Imagine, then, that we heard a proprietor in midtown Manhattan saying, "It is important that we have more police on Madison Avenue; we've had a rash of murders, and it is important to protect people against murder on Madison Avenue, because, if we didn't, it would be bad for business." The laugh will often precede the recognition of just what made the line funny. There is a sense that something is off, something askew. In this case, it was the lowering of the importance of life, as something not good in itself, but subordinate to the truly overriding good of doing business, making money. But if that much is evident at once to the person who responds to the line with a laugh, does it not put into place everything that would make laughable these recent lines from Justice Breyer, in his dissenting opinion in *United States* v. *Lopez*:

> [W]e must ask whether Congress could have had a *rational basis* for finding a significant (or substantial) connection between gun-related school violence and interstate commerce. . . . Could congress rationally have found that 'violent crime in school zones,' through its effect on the 'quality of education,' significantly (or substantially) affects 'interstate' or 'foreign commerce'? . . . Congress could . . . have found a substantial educational problem — teachers unable to teach, students unable to learn — and conclude that guns near schools contribute substantially to the size and scope of the problem.
>
> Having found that guns in schools significantly undermine the quality of education . . . , Congress could also have found, given the effect of education upon interstate and foreign commerce, that gun-

related violence in and around schools is a commercial, as well as a human, problem.[1]

This exertion was offered, of course, in an attempt to justify the use of federal power to ban the use of guns in or around schools. We must presume that Justice Breyer, an accomplished man, does not ordinarily hold conversations, in his own circles, offering arguments as banal as the one he is willing to set down so earnestly here. The danger of gun play presumably inhibits learning, the shortfalls of education will hamper youngsters in their lives and work, and those youngsters will not contribute in the future the kinds of efforts that will make for a more vibrant commerce. No one suspects for a moment that Justice Breyer would wish to save lives *for the sake* of raising reading scores, or helping people make more money. He himself would no doubt tell us that he cast his argument in this way only because he thought that it was necessary to fit the cast of the Commerce Clause, and the Commerce Clause seemed to be the only possible device that would allow the federal government to legislate on guns near schools. And yet, there should be a jural principle here that would be grasped at once by the urbane even if they never had a course in law: something is askew — something is seriously in disarray — when the legal justification for the law is so radically at odds with the real wrong of the case, or the moral reasons that animated the legislators in passing the act. Clearly, Congress was not worried about commerce so much as the killing and terrorizing of students, and members of Congress thought that there might be a more pronounced effect, on the part of law enforcement, if the weight of the federal government were brought into this situation. That is a plausible interest, and it cannot be beyond the concern of the federal government. But when there is such an inversion in the argument that it becomes nearly comic, that comic effect should be taken as a signal or a warning: if this is the best one could do under the Commerce Clause, then the Commerce Clause is being stretched beyond its coherence when it produces reasoning of this kind.

But of course we have seen this kind of artificial reasoning before, many times, most notably with the litigation over the Civil Rights Act of 1964, and some of the landmark decisions on the Commerce Clause running back to the 1930s. It became easier for Justice Breyer to engage in an argument that he should have trouble saying with a straight face,

1. See *United States* v. *Lopez*, 131 L Ed 2d 626, at 675-76 (1995).

precisely because other earnest lawyers, such as Archibald Cox, were willing to engage in the same ritual, if those were the words that were needed under the Commerce Clause. When he was Solicitor General of the United States, Mr. Cox was willing to lead the Supreme Court along the same path when it came to the problem of explaining how the federal government could bar discriminations based on race in private inns and restaurants open to the public. In order to fit the case within the frame of the Commerce Clause, the Court did not seek to explain the nature of the wrong in principle in the case, and indeed it had to shift its focus away from the wrongs done to black people. For the sake of sustaining the law, the Court had to argue in this fashion: the prospect of discrimination may be enough to discourage black people from travelling in interstate commerce. We do not know that they do, or in what numbers they might hold back, but we simply postulate that they do hold back; and in that event, there will be fewer people on the road stopping for meals and rooms. There will be, in turn, fewer orders for meat, silverware, linens. And as the ingenious calculus was run through in this way, what was the wrong involved in discriminating against black people?: It would interfere in the interstate flow of meat! As a friend of mine once put it, if that is the problem, it could be offset simply by having the racists in the country eat more meat.[2]

In the recent Lopez case, there was a comparable answer on the part of Justice Rehnquist: if we accept Justice Breyer's mode of reasoning, then the schools themselves could depress interstate commerce if they turned out to teach poorly — and in that case, the federal government could bypass the States and govern the schools more directly. But beyond that, children may be affected adversely in their performance in schools if there is, in their homes, no respect or encouragement for schooling. The breakup of families may have a further, unsettling effect on children in their work at schools. And so, what might Congress reasonably conclude from all of this, with the generous license offered by Justice Breyer?: that the federal government may take custody of the children? Or that federal law may now supplant the laws of the State on marriage and the family?[3]

Chief Justice Rehnquist has not exactly been a comic type, but

---

2. See *Katzenbach* v. *McClung*, 379 U.S. 294 (1964) and my commentary on the problem in "Segregation, Busing, and the Idea of Law," in *The Philosopher in the City* (Princeton: Princeton University Press, 1981), pp. 223-55.

3. See *United States* v. *Lopez, supra,* note 1, at 658.

when his opinion is set against the reasoning of Justice Breyer, his lines may sound like something struck off from Rodney Dangerfield. The late, and rather unlamented Justice James McReynolds, had to be counted as a notably unfunny man, but the same kinds of reasoning under the Commerce Clause moved him, in the 1930s, to a similar flexing of imagination and caustic commentary. Once again, it was a contrast manufactured by a government straining, earnestly, in offering up the most implausible arguments. The comedy was precipitated when the implausible arguments met a curmudgeon who simply exposed their emptiness. Justice McReynolds merely spoke the lines that were invited by the situation, and he could suddenly appear as a mild version of Oscar Wilde.

McReynolds came to display that rarely used wit during those critical cases in 1937, in which the Court began to uphold legislation from the New Deal. At the same time, the Court would throw over understandings that had long been settled to restrict the reach and the powers of the federal government under the Commerce Clause. These were the so-called Labor Board cases, in 1937, and one of them involved a firm in Richmond that manufactured men's clothing. The company produced less than one half of one percent of the men's clothing produced in the United States. There was no evidence that the alleged discrimination against members of the union had brought the company to the threshold of a strike or the stoppage of production. If the reach of the law was to be measured in proportion to the "effect" on interstate commerce, then the "effect" in this case had to be reckoned as trivial or null.[4]

But the law was cast in a form that was virtually indifferent to questions of scale. It could apply to the Jones & Laughlin Corporation, to a clothing factory, or even to a cattle ranch. Justice McReynolds raised, then, the questions that were still apt to be raised, the questions that had not been dissolved by anything in the opinion written for the majority by Chief Justice Hughes. McReynolds wrote:

> If a man raises cattle and regularly delivers them to a carrier for interstate shipment, may Congress prescribe the conditions under which he may employ or discharge helpers on the ranch? . . . May a mill owner be prohibited from closing his factory or discontinuing

4. See *National Labor Relations Board* v. *Jones & Laughlin Steel Corp.*, 301 U.S. 1, at 87, and see also 88-93, for more details of the case.

his business because so to do would stop the flow of products to and from his plant in interstate commerce? May employees in a factory be restrained from quitting work in a body because this will close the factory and thereby stop the flow of commerce? May arson of a factory be made a Federal offense whenever this would interfere with such flow? If the business cannot continue with the existing wage scale, may Congress command a reduction?[5]

McReynolds is not remembered for a nimble wit, and yet the empty formulas put forth, in this case, as surrogates for jural reasoning, were targets perfectly framed. The whole, elaborate construction of the law was built, after all, on this predicate: that the absence of unions posed a danger to interstate commerce through the threats of strikes and violence. The onset of a strike, and its attendant disruptions, was the "evil" for which this legislation would be justified as a "remedy."

But the refutation fell precisely into place as soon as the framers earnestly contended that it was *the avoidance of strikes* that was the object of the policy. If that were the end of the legislation, there was no need to address that end in the most indirect way by dealing with all of the remote contingencies that *might* lead to a strike. As McReynolds remarked, that end could be addressed most directly by barring the strike itself. And the case for this position could only be deepened if the judges accepted the theory of a "continuous stream of commerce," for in that event, as McReynolds pointed out, the government could be warranted in suppressing *any* strike that could act, even in a tangential way, to affect the stream of commerce.

From every angle, the rationale served up here under the Commerce Clause could justify the extension of the federal power to the smallest, most prosaic enterprises. That point was confirmed with a dramatic finality — and to our enduring disbelief — five years later in the improbable case of *Wickard* v. *Filburn*. On that notable occasion, the government was sustained when it sought to punish Mr. Roscoe Filburn, a farmer in Ohio, for the misdemeanor of setting aside a portion of his wheat for the consumption of his own family. In a line that would resound over the years in the law reports, Justice Robert Jackson would "explain":

5. Ibid., pp. 97-98.

That appellee's own contribution to the demand for wheat may be trivial by itself is not enough to remove him from the scope of federal regulation where, as here, his contribution, taken together with that of many others similarly situated, is far from trivial.[6]

That passage would be cited by the Supreme Court when it had to explain how the Civil Rights Act of 1964 would reach Ollie's Barbecue in Birmingham, Alabama. Drawing on the same doctrines established in these cases, Professor Lawrence Tribe would later testify before a committee of Senate in 1992 and argue that the Congress could legislate, under the Commerce Clause, to guarantee the right to an abortion. Once again, the Commerce Clause was capacious enough to cover all. It was previously thought that States violated the Commerce Clause when they *impeded* the flow of traffic; but now it was alleged that the laws of the State could offend the Constitution if they might *encourage* movement on the highways. Tribe could speak darkly then of a "highway of anguish," as women were forced to drive for the sake of travelling to a State with less restrictive regulations:

[L]ocal or statewide restrictions on reproductive freedom would likely force many women to travel from States that have chosen to erect legal barriers to contraception or to abortion, to States or foreign nations where safe and legal procedures are available. Indeed, the years preceding Roe and Doe saw precisely such a massive interstate migration, as hundreds of thousands of women travelled from restrictive States to those where abortions were more freely performed. In 1972, for example, almost 80 percent of all legal abortions in this country took place in just two States: New York and California.[7]

Of course, it never seemed to occur to the partisans of the Freedom of Choice Act that the formulas of the Commerce Clause would work in a strikingly different direction if one came to the problem with a set of assumptions, quite different from theirs, about the "persons" who were the victims in these cases and the bearers of rights. If one supposed for just a moment that the victim might be the child who was dismem-

6. *Wickard* v. *Filburn*, 317 U.S. 111, at 128 (1942).
7. See Tribe's statement in, "The Freedom of Choice Act of 1991," Hearings of the Committee on Labor and Human Resources, U.S. Senate (May 13, 1992), pp. 31-36, at 31.

bered or poisoned in these surgeries, the Commerce Clause could even be used more persuasively on the side of the unborn child. Even if we stick to the non-moral formulas of the Commerce Clause, it could be contended, after all, that an abortion threatens to interfere most emphatically with the right of the fetus to travel in interstate commerce! But with the arguments that became familiar in the Civil Rights cases, the engagement of the Commerce Clause would become even deeper: it was postulated, as mentioned earlier in this paper, that discrimination against black people would discourage blacks from travelling between the States, and from that point the inference was drawn that the shortfall in traffic would diminish the orders for meat, linens, silverware — in short, that it would have a vast, depressing effect on commerce. Professor Tribe would later make much of the fact that, in the judgment of the Court, there had been no need to prove any of these points, taken as predicates for the Civil Rights Act. It had been enough for the Congress simply to postulate them, as possibilities that seemed highly plausible. In contrast, we need not depend so wholly on speculation when it comes to abortion, for we know fairly precisely the number of abortions that are performed each year. And by the application of the same form of reasoning, the argument would flow here even more powerfully: with about 1.3–1.5 million abortions each year, it is manifestly the case that the current volume of abortions is having a vast, depressing effect on the demand for bassinets, baby food, toys, first cars, college educations, weddings. And that says nothing of the production and revenue lost from a cohort of over a million new taxpayers who would start to come on the scene, in waves, eighteen years hence.

Even liberal commentators on the law have treated with a certain mirth the reigning fictions of the Commerce Clause. Conservative critics have railed against these doctrines, but without much effect so far (except for the recent decision in *United States* v. *Lopez*). And yet, the experience of our jurisprudence lately suggests that even doctrines long settled for judges may be overturned in a fortnight when they suddenly seem to collide with the "right to an abortion," which seems to be regarded more and more as a touchstone. We might find ourselves producing then the most pronounced turnabout on this matter, not by summoning moral arguments against the use of the Commerce Clause, but by showing how the reigning doctrines of the Commerce Clause would work even more powerfully to curb, or even deny, the right to an abortion. With only the slightest alterations — indeed, with only the filling in of the blanks — Justice Jackson's argument would have a rather unsettling application to that woman, in the isolation of her privacy, who is contemplating an abortion. Jackson's argument then could unfold itself in this way:

> That your own abortion by itself seems to affect only you, is not enough to remove you from the scope of the federal regulation. For when your own abortion is joined with those of others, and when those others begin to number over a million each year, it becomes evident that you are contributing to a stream of activity, and to a pattern that becomes unmistakable in the large: the destruction of life on a sobering scale; the removal, from the population, of a massive cohort that would add each year, in the future, one and a half million new taxpayers, new workers, new people to fuel the economy and support our social services.

What seems to come as a surprise for Professor Tribe and for most lawyers these days is that the Commerce Clause offers no formula for excluding the unborn child as a possible bearer of rights under the Commerce Clause and the Constitution. That is something that Tribe and his friends hope that they have settled through *Roe* v. *Wade* and its sequelae. But in order to establish a constitutional right to an abortion, they had to persuade themselves that the fetus has no standing as a being, or as a person, to receive the protections of the law. They know that whales and snail darters may receive the protections of the law, but unborn children are not even placed on the same plane as protected animals.

Yet, nothing in this construction of rights flowed out of the logic of the Constitution; and if anything, the Constitution pointed in a strikingly different direction. The Constitution was founded, after all, on an understanding of "natural rights" and the critical distinction in nature between humans and other animals. In the original understanding, we do not govern human beings, beings who can give and understand reasons, in the way that humans may rightly rule dogs and horses. Even in this age of animal rights, we do not sign labor contracts with dogs and horses, and we do not seek the informed consent of our household pets before we authorize surgery for them. But human beings, by their nature, deserve to be ruled or committed only with their consent, by a government that can offer reasons or justifications for the measures it would impose as law.

138

James Wilson, one of the most learned and philosophically acute of the Founders, took the matter to the root in his lectures on jurisprudence in 1790-91. As Wilson understood, the very purpose of the government was not to create new rights, but to secure and enlarge the rights we already possessed by nature. Even in the State of Nature people did not have the right to rape and murder, and the laws that now restrained them from raping and murdering did not deprive them of anything they ever had a "right" to do. But if we have "natural rights," when do they begin? The answer, tendered by Wilson, was at once simple and clear: they begin as soon as we begin to be.

> In the contemplation of law, [wrote Wilson] life begins when the infant is first able to stir in the womb. By the law, life is protected not only from immediate destruction, but from every degree of actual violence, and, in some cases, from every degree of danger.[8]

Wilson recalled the practice, running back to ancient Greece, of exposing newborn infants, or confirming to their fathers the power of life or death. But the common law, he said, marked off a radically different tradition: "With consistency, beautiful and undeviating, human life, from its commencement to its close, is protected by the common law." Yet, in our own day, we have found even conservative judges who think this question of the beginning of human life can be treated, under our institutions, as an open question — as though the regime itself did not presuppose an answer to that question. And so, Justice Scalia of all people could remark in *Planned Parenthood* v. *Casey* (1992),[9] that the question of when human life begins must be a "value judgment." But when he says that the question of human life forms the subject of a "value judgment," he would seem to imply that this is a question to which there is no objective answer, or no answer that reason can supply. As a "value judgment," it must depend on the "values" of the society that frames and measures this question. For that reason, Scalia regards the matter as a distinctly political question. And as a political judgment, it belongs in the hands of legislators, who are elected, and responsible to the people who are governed with their

8. James Wilson, "Of the Natural Rights of Individuals," in *The Works of James Wilson* (Cambridge, Mass.: Harvard University Press, 1967; originally published in 1804), vol. 2, pp. 585-610, at 597.

9. *Planned Parenthood* v. *Casey*, 505 U.S. 833 (1992).

consent. In this reading, offered by Scalia, the question of abortion is conspicuously not a judicial question: it does not raise a question that finds a clear answer in the text of the Constitution. Nor can an answer be supplied by anything within the arts and the discipline of the judges. Scalia remarked in the Cruzan case, in 1990, that the point at which life becomes worthless or open to protection is not "set forth in the Constitution"; nor is it "known to the nine Justices of this Court any better than . . . [to] nine people picked at random from the Kansas City telephone directory."[10]

But as Harry Jaffa aptly pointed out in another context, in the discussion of slavery, the question of just who is a human being, and the bearer of rights, cannot be a "value judgment." We cannot say at the same time that there are rights arising out of the nature of human beings, rights that do not depend on the votes of a majority — but then turn around and say that it falls within the proper discretion of the majority to detach a whole class of beings from their natural rights, and from the protections of the law, by the simple expedient of declaring that they do not happen to be human beings and the bearers of rights. As Lincoln remarked, the question is whether the Negro is, or is not, a man, a human being. "If the negro is a man, then my ancient faith teaches me that 'all men are created equal'; and that there can be no moral right in one man's making a slave of another."[11] But that primary question of whether a black man, or any other man, is a man, and not an animal, cannot depend on the vote of a majority. That question had to be answered in principle before we could settle on the nature of the majority, or the "legislature," that would vote upon the question. After all, how was it decided just which creatures in the animal kingdom would be qualified to sit in a legislature voting on this question? Did someone determine that it would have to be a biped — that cattle and horses could not vote — but that a man who had lost one leg still might? In other words, when Justice Scalia speaks about putting back into the political process the question of when human life begins, he seems to forget what most of our Founders already knew: that *our institutions already presupposed an answer to that question.* And if there was any doubt

10. *Cruzan* v. *Director,* Missouri Health Department, 111 L Ed 2d 224 (1990), at 251.

11. Speech in Peoria [on the Kansas-Nebraska Act] (October 16, 1854), in *The Collected Works of Abraham Lincoln,* ed. Roy P. Basler (New Brunswick, N.J.: Rutgers University Press, 1953), vol. 2, p. 266.

on the matter, those institutions also implied some rather clear modes of reasoning about the problem in a principled way.

We might consider, in that respect, a minor thought experiment. Through a series of constitutional amendments we forbade slavery or involuntary servitude. The amendments said nothing about blacks, but they provided that people should not be barred, on the basis of race, from "the equal protection of the laws." Let us imagine for a moment that a State was allowing some black people to be kept in slavery, or that it was withdrawing the protections of the law, and allowing black people to be lynched. Imagine that a question is raised, but that the State insists that race has nothing to do with the matter: the State argued that certain people of a deep color are not even human, and so the normal protections of the law simply do not apply to them. In support of this position, the State produces an authoritative "color chart," to measure gradations in shading, and we are told, with the voice of authority, that these shadings mark degrees of "humanness."

Is it really conceivable that the commitments of the law could be subverted in this way? What is more likely to happen, of course, is that a suit would be brought on these terms: the authorities would be compelled to show that there was some ground of principle, or scientific evidence, to support the proposition they had stipulated in legislation. They would be pressed, that is, to prove that the steps along the color chart truly marked off degrees of humanity, or discontinuities in nature, so that as soon as we exceeded, say, Shade 11, and moved to 12, we were no longer dealing with a human being. There is hardly a mystery, in our own day, as to how a court is likely to respond to an argument of that kind: the court is likely to say that the law was passed in a manner that was formally legal, but that it lacked the substance of justice; that it deprived people of their freedom; that it withdrew the protection of their lives, on the strength of criteria that were finally arbitrary.

Justice Scalia is a deeply thoughtful man, but he seems to have overlooked the point that this question about the beginning of human life can be subject to the same discipline of principled reasoning. After all, if a legislature allowed abortions up to the third trimester, or if it permitted abortions in the case of children who were likely to be infirm or retarded, why would not the same style of reasoning come into play? Why would it not be quite as plausible for us to ask, What separates the child in the womb at six months from the child at six months and a day? How could that child have crossed a barrier between the non-

141

human and the human? What attributes, necessary to her standing as a human being, did she not have the day before, when she was twenty-four weeks old?

The conclusion of the judges should be the same: in all of these instances, the law is based on distinctions, or classifications, that are finally arbitrary. And on the basis of these arbitrary distinctions, the law is declaring a whole class of beings outside the protections of the law. In effect, the law is creating a license to destroy these people at will without the need to render a justification.

If I am right, there is no inscrutable, or even unusual, question presented to the courts by this problem of abortion or the need to settle on an understanding about the beginning of human life. The question requires no canons of reasoning different from the principles that the judges are well practiced in applying to the run of cases that come before them. In that event, the judges have, well within their means, the principles of reasoning that would allow them to judge any policy that would withdraw the protections of the law, for the most arbitrary reasons, from a whole class of people. The more interesting question is, How have the judges managed to talk themselves into the notion that this is such an inscrutable question, or that they do not possess, as judges, sufficient arts of principled reasoning to address it? And the answer, I think, is that it has taken a steady dose of legal theory, and bad philosophy, in order to bring judges to the point where they cannot see any longer with a clear juridical lens. In order to put themselves into this state of mind, judges virtually had to talk themselves into academic versions of skepticism, the kind of skepticism that wars with common sense. How much distance is there, after all, between the solipsism of Mrs. Christine Franklyn-Ladd, and the notorious "mystery passage" in *Planned Parenthood* v. *Casey*, in which Justices O'Connor, Kennedy, and Souter intoned that, "At the heart of liberty is the right to define one's own concept of existence, of meaning, of the universe, and of the mystery of human life."[12]

The fatuity of that passage may not have been detected so easily in a Court that had built up a whole branch of our law on that aphorism of Mr. Justice Harlan, that "one man's vulgarity is another man's lyric." That line, dashed off in *Cohen* v. *California* in 1971, was meant to establish the point that there were no principled grounds for distinguishing between the kinds of speech that were assaulting or innocent, just as

12. *Planned Parenthood* v. *Casey*, 505 U.S. 833 at 851 (1992).

there was no way of distinguishing, on rational grounds, among the contending ends or interests in political life. Justice Harlan managed to gain a reputation here for innovation through the simple device of discovering anew the logical positivism that reigned in the schools of philosophy forty years earlier when he was a student. What apparently passed his understanding was that this teaching — that moral terms were mainly emotive, without rational content — had long been refuted in the schools of philosophy. But with this decision, in *Cohen* v. *California,* Harlan launched a new doctrine in our law, and by 1993, the result was that even conservative jurists, like Justice Scalia, professed that they had no means of judging the content of speech. It was hard to imagine that Scalia could not in fact tell the difference between the expressive act of burning a cross and the expressive act of burning a shoe box. But as a judge, apparently, he must proclaim the inability of the law to understand the difference, and to make these distinctions. Only a generation ago, that notion would have struck even judges as bizarre, but in our own time, the bizarre has been incorporated as part of the settled understandings of the law, and that inversion we owe to Mr. Justice Harlan in *Cohen* v. *California.*

There is no body of precedents, built up by the Court, that has done more to undermine the possibilities for an urban life in America, apart from the decision in the famous Miranda case. The decision in *Cohen* v. *California* undermined the moral framework for an urban life. Urbanists are constantly urging us to create urban forms that encourage strangers to meet, or encounter one another in public places. They prefer, in this vein, collective transport over the isolating privacy of automobiles. And yet, this whole construction depends on the prospect that people can depend on the protections of civility when they enter public places. But with *Cohen* v. *California* the Court undercut this framework of civility and restraint. The understanding once planted in the law was that people had an obligation to restrain themselves in public places out of a respect for the sensibilities of others. Yet, with *Cohen* v. *California,* the presumptions were turned around. Robert Paul Cohen walked through the courthouse in Los Angeles with a jacket bearing the message, "F--- the Draft." By the time the Court was through with this case, Cohen and other people became possessed of a presumptive right to express themselves in public, and the burden of avoidance would fall on any passerby who might take offense. It was apparently thought unreasonable now to put the burdens of restraint and civility on citizens in a republic.

In the construal of the Court, the Constitution itself seemed to award a certain preeminence to the person who wished to express himself, no matter how vulgar or assaulting that expression might be. It was as though the regime itself came forth with this instruction: that it was altogether preferable to leave people unconstrained in their freedom, while their victims simply declined to enter, on these terms, onto the streets of the city or its public spaces. With these doctrines, the police became timid in ejecting from airports rather aggressive religious hawkers, or from the streets of the city the rather menacing panhandlers. People affecting to be "homeless" could virtually appropriate to themselves some of the choicest locations in the downtown sections of our cities, and the laws on loitering became dead letters overnight. I could not make a catalogue here of the good restaurants that finally had to go out of business on Connecticut Avenue in Washington, near DuPont Circle, because patrons became simply unwilling to move through the gauntlet of panhandlers and aggressive, demented characters who lined the paths to these restaurants every night. The Court had withdrawn the protections of civility that supported an urban life, and it accomplished that notable move on the strength of theories that would not make sense for a moment to most dwellers in the city.

Again, it was not a matter of formal education, but a loss of that common sense that we associate with people anchored in the world. And we know that the flight from this common sense has taken place among the educated, even on matters that run to the meaning of "persons," personal identity, and the axioms of understanding. Bertrand Russell might have made a joke of Mrs. Christine Franklyn-Ladd, but her type can now be found all through the academy, backed up by colleagues of like mind who no longer find anything particularly funny or odd in her perspective. Tom Stoppard has characters in one of his plays lamenting the untimely, tragic death of a young philosopher, removed from the scene by a murder, just before a conference at which he was scheduled to speak. One colleague, in a surge of sentiment, says, "Poor Duncan . . . I like to think he'll be there in spirit." And the other adds — yes, "if only to make sure the materialistic argument is properly represented." In this age of deconstruction, anti-foundationalism, and fifty-seven varieties of relativism, it is no longer even surprising to find undergraduates, or even their professors, floating in the same, benign haze. I recall a late colleague of mine, who professed at times not to know that he himself existed — though he was bitterly certain that the check from Blue Cross was late.

Daniel Robinson has remarked in this vein that the amnesiac suffers doubt as to *who* he is, but he suffers no trace of doubt *that he is.* In that respect, he grasps, without much self-consciousness, the axiom that eluded even the redoubtable Descartes. Descartes' curious oversight here was pointed up, in his characteristic, penetrating, and witty way, by Thomas Reid. As Reid remarked, "A man that disbelieves his own existence, is surely as unfit to be reasoned with as a man that believes he is made of glass":

> There may be disorders in the human frame that may produce such extravagancies, but they will never be cured by reasoning. Descartes, indeed, would make us believe that he got out of this delirium by this logical argument, 'Cogito ergo sum,' but it is evident he was in his senses all the time, and never seriously doubted of his existence; for he takes it for granted in this argument, and proves nothing at all. I am thinking, says he — therefore I am. And is it not as good reasoning to say, I am sleeping — therefore, I am? or, I am doing nothing — therefore, I am? If a body moves, it must exist, no doubt; but, if it is at rest, it must exist likewise.[13]

Just a few years ago, we found a minor flexing of genius on the part of some Jesuits, armed with degrees in biochemistry, who wished to persuade their readers that the human embryo does not retain the same identity in all of its phases. The contention was that the zygote is still wanting in the attributes that are necessary to its completion as a human being. Those attributes needed to be supplied by molecules from the mother, conveyed to the zygote only after it is implanted in the uterine wall.[14] Up to this point, we find a progressive division of cells,

13. Thomas Reid, "Inquiry into the Human Mind," collected in *The Works of Thomas Reid* (Edinburgh: MacLachlan, Stewart, 1896), p. 100.
14. Professors Carlos Bedate and Robert Cefalo have stood among the doctors of biology and obstetrics who have offered this argument:

> The information used for the development of a human embryo involves more than the zygote's chromosomal genetic information, namely, the genetic material from maternal mitochondria, and the maternal or paternal genetic messages in the form of messenger RNA or proteins. In terms of molecular biology, it is incorrect to say that the zygote possesses all the informing molecules for embryo development; rather, at most, the zygote possesses the molecules that have the potential to acquire informing capacity. That potential informing capacity is given in time through interaction with other molecules.... [W]hen

with changes so marked that it becomes hard to say that the first cell is really the "same being" as that complex cluster of cells. The notable break comes when that colony of cells is suddenly transformed into one, ontologically distinct human being. But according to this argument, the zygote is not the same being, or the same person, and it is nearly laughable to suggest that it claims the same moral or ontological standing as the being who fills out its features after it is implanted on the wall of the uterus.

This was the argument over so-called "delayed hominization," and the purpose behind this lunge toward originality seemed quite evident: the object was to detach people from the temptation to protect the being in the womb from its earliest moments. And when the argument was pressed by Jesuits, the design seemed to be to encourage the Church to temper its opposition to abortion, which seemed to be so unseasonably adamant.

I remarked to a meeting of the Bishops a few years ago that this was a case of merging new biology with old fallacies.[15] The proponents of "delayed hominization" were utterly persuaded that those early clusters of cells could not be the same as that unique being who emerged at the end of the process. I suggested that we attach a name to that new being: we might call her Wendy Himmelstein. Some of these commentators are convinced that those ungainly cells are not Wendy Himmelstein. And yet the people who wish to forego the advent of Wendy Himmelstein seem to know precisely just which cluster of cells they must strike at if they would prevent the emergence of Wendy Himmelstein. There would seem to be, then, a relation of identity between those cells and Wendy Himmelstein.

The argument, of course, becomes more refined, but as refined as it becomes, it can never get around the fact that we have here the ancient problem of "identity." Socrates sitting is the same as Socrates standing. The Brown who was caught embezzling tells us that he has undergone

the molecules interact, the result is . . . a completely new and different molecule. . . .

See Carles A. Bedate and Robert C. Cefalo, "The Zygote: To Be or Not Be a Person," *Journal of Medicine and Philosophy* 14 (Dec. 1989): 641-45, at 642-43.

15. My fuller argument was contained in the piece, subsequently published, "On 'Delayed Hominization': Some Thoughts on the Blending of New Science and Ancient Fallacies," in Russell E. Smith (ed.), *The Interaction of Catholic Bioethics and Secular Society* (Braintree, Mass.: Pope John Center, 1992), pp. 143-62.

a conversion, and he is now no longer the same as the one who had embezzled. If we punish him, we would be punishing the wrong man. His conversion may be welcome, and for all we know, some new, improved soul is inhabiting the body we identify with Brown. But we are in fact souls embodied, and we are obliged to treat Brown, in all of the phases of his life, as the same man, moving through different phases, some of them with a moral refurbishing. But the thing that connects, in all of these phases, is Brown himself, his continuing existence, as the repository of his lengthening record of experience. For many of us, the anchor of our own knowledge may come with the recognition of the child that he is, today, the same one he was yesterday; that the experience of the day before belongs to him. We deal here with one of the axioms of our understanding, and indeed, of our being. And so, the biochemists and philosophers who are straining their genius on the scheme of "delayed hominization" are elaborating arguments that cannot reach any matter of moral consequence, for they run up against axioms, which cannot be evaded or dislodged.

So, too, do our jurists who have followed along the path of Justice Harlan, leading out from *Cohen* v. *California,* and talked themselves into the notion that they cannot judge the content of speech. Justice Harlan declared that "one man's vulgarity is another man's lyric," and about twenty-five years later, Judge Sarokin in New Jersey thought that librarians could not eject from a public library an unbathed man who confronted other people with menacing stares. Following in the grooves of the Cohen case, Judge Sarokin found that Mr. Richard Kreimer had a presumptive right to express himself, even in an offensive way, and who was to judge?: as Sarokin put it, in an echo of Harlan's aphorism, "one man's ambrosia is another man's hay fever." And of course, by the time we arrived at youngsters burning a cross in St. Paul, outside the apartment of a black family, we found Justice Scalia writing for a unanimous Court, which could no longer find a discernible, assaulting meaning in a burning cross. When the cross-burning took place at Amherst in 1979, no one seemed to doubt that, if it were real, it was the symbol of an assault, an act animated by hatred, a gesture of hostility aimed at black people. And several years later, when swastikas were painted on the walls of a synagogue in Silver Spring, people seemed to have no trouble in decoding the significance of a swastika. No one suggested that the swastika was too subjective to have a meaning, or that it would be necessary to take evidence on whether members of the synagogue had suffered traumas or measurable injuries. The act of

147

defacing the walls could have been prosecuted under local laws as a defacement of property or as an act of trespass. Of course, the walls would have been defaced if the vandals had printed on the walls excerpts from the Declaration of Independence or pictures of Barbara Walters. This act of vandalism could be brought under the reach of the federal Civil Rights Acts only if they were affected by a racial animus. And the Supreme Court, in 1986, decided that this inference could plausibly be made: that is to say, there was nothing in the least subjective about a swastika; its meaning could be extracted, and it could be read for what it was: it could be read for the meaning that was plain to any man on the street, as a symbol of hostility and assault.[16]

But this recognition, planted in the common understanding, did not carry over to the burning of crosses, because the judges have not yet been dislodged from the inventiveness of Justice Harlan in *Cohen* v. *California*. His inventiveness, as I say, came in discovering the doctrines of logical positivism about thirty years after they had been rejected in the schools of philosophy. He had managed to persuade himself and most of his colleagues that the moral language of politics was largely emotive, without rational content. Cohen's jacket carried the words, "F--- the Draft," and Harlan could ask with earnestness, "How is one to distinguish this from any other offensive word?" In Harlan's estimate, there was "no readily ascertainable general principle" by which one could draw a distinction any longer between words or gestures that were insulting or assaulting, on the one hand, as opposed to terms that were innocent, neutral, or even complimentary, on the other.

I need not take up our time to review the ways in which even the proponents of logical positivism came to recede from their own doctrines. For our purposes it is quite sufficient to note that the problem expressed itself for Justice Harlan in this way: there was a notable contradiction between Harlan's insistence on the subjectivity of all political or contentious speech, and the ground of his surety that Cohen's expression was distinctly "political" and deserving of a constitutional protection. Harlan took it as evident that Cohen, with his jacket, was "asserting a position on the inutility or immorality of the draft."[17] But of course, if speech were entirely subjective, the expression "F--- the Draft" might mean nothing of the kind. Even treating the expression in the style of Harlan, it would be precious to claim that

16. See *Shaare Tefila Congregation* v. *Cobb*, 95 L Ed 2d 594 (1986).
17. *Cohen* v. *California*, 403 U.S. at 18.

"F--- the Draft" was a shorthand form of saying that the draft was "inutile." If speech were subjective, the "draft" could have been referring to the wind, or if it referred to conscription, perhaps Cohen meant that he wished to make love to the draft.

But no one half-way functional could have attributed such a meaning to Cohen's jacket. Harlan could treat Cohen's jacket as a political statement only because he could tell, as anyone else could tell, that Cohen was *condemning* the draft. On this point, there is a longer account to be filled in, and I have done some of the filling in myself.[18] But the heart of the problem is that we have, established in our language, the moral functions of condemning and commending, applauding and deriding. Those functions exist in our language, not as mere artifacts of our language, or the way in which we happen to use words. They exist because they reflect something in our nature. As Aristotle understood, we are the only being with a capacity for moral judgment, a capacity to give reasons over matters of right and wrong. The words that carry these functions in our language may alter from one period to the next, but if that moral function is to be present in our language, it must be possible, at any time, for ordinary persons to understand the words that are established right now, in common usage, as terms of condemnation or insult.

It turns out that juries of ordinary people are quite reliable as judges in these matters, for the problem is exactly measured to the question of what ordinary people understand about the way words and gestures are used all about them. The matter is not so esoteric that it requires a college education; indeed, it appears that truck drivers and construction workers have quite precise antennae when it comes to the matter of detecting gestures or words that are patronizing or insulting. Any observer could readily establish the point for himself by giving any panel of persons, selected at random, this rather elementary test. We may ask people to indicate just which words in this list are clearly established right now as terms of insult or defamation, just which words would be terms of compliment or approval, and which words might be on the borderline between derision and neutrality. We may also tell them that, when in doubt, do not raise their hands and indicate that the word is a term of insult. With these instructions, we may give people a list of this kind: Nigger, dentist, Kike, bastard, nurse, Polack, saint,

18. See my book *The Philosopher in the City* (Princeton, N.J.: Princeton University Press, 1981), pp. 69-74, 90-91.

Wop, meter maid, registrar. For people who have spent some time in Washington, the term "meter maid" may be charged with all kinds of adverse associations, but for the most part the trials will show a high degree of convergence in the responses. Most people will have no trouble in picking out the terms that are established right now in the language as terms of insult, just as most people would have no trouble in telling the difference between a burning shoe box or a burning cross, or the difference between a cross used for the purpose of religious devotion and a cross anchored in a vat of urine for the sake of deriding Christians.

These are not judgments that are especially inscrutable; they are judgments that fall readily within the competence of ordinary people, especially if they are anchored in the world. It has taken a rather hefty dose of refined, academic theory before our judges have been able to talk themselves into the notion that distinctions readily accessible to people of ordinary wit are too freighted with ambiguity for judges, and too imprecise to be woven into the judgments of the law. But in that respect, it must be said that there has been, on the part of judges and the legal profession, the most unaccountable flight from urbanity. And the result is to leave us with judges, saying in the courtrooms, and saying earnestly, things too silly for them to repeat in the circles of their friends.

G. K. Chesterton once remarked on the brand of cultivated obtuseness shown by Mr. H. G. Wells, when the latter asked, as the heading in one of his chapters, "Where is the Garden of Eden?" Wells seemed to think that he would do something to discount, or even dissolve, the story of the Fall if he could make a plausible case, say, that the Garden of Eden was somewhere in Mesopotamia. As Chesterton observed, "To come down to a thing like that, and to think it telling, when talking to an intelligent Catholic about the Fall, that *is* provinciality; proud and priceless provinciality."[19] But ordinary French peasants, who sense that the Fall is about something enduring in the human condition, would be puzzled by Wells's scheme of inquiry. In their simplicity, they would not see what bearing it had on the main question, and in that puzzlement they would reveal, as Chesterton said, that they were far less provincial than this great man of English letters. In the same way, our judges have drifted further from the core, or the grounding of jurispru-

19. G. K. Chesterton, "The Things: Why I Am a Catholic," in *Collected Works*, Vol. III (San Francisco: Ignatius Press, 1990), p. 310.

dence, as they have drifted into the academic theories of the day, and drifted further, then, from the language of ordinary men and women. For most men and women do not live in a deconstructed world, where meanings are endlessly open, as the saying goes, to negotiation; where nature and gender may be shaped anew to the limits of our imagination; where love and betrayal and respect can be undone, or turned around, simply by using words in a new way. To restore to the law the language of the urbane is to restore the sense that we can see the world as it is; a world that contains principles, and beings with a moral nature, as surely as it contains clouds and rocks and trees.

10. Immunity, Not Surgery: Why it is Better to Exert Cultural Authority Than to Impose Censorship

MARTHA BAYLES

I will start with a couple of definitions. Then, after staking out my position as a maverick critic, I will explain why, despite the ugliness coursing through every level of our culture, censorship of the traditional arts or of popular culture is not the solution. I will give my reasons for this, which are not those of a free-speech absolutist. And I will close by describing what to me is the better alternative — the wise and judicious use of old-fashioned cultural authority.

The word *culture* has two distinct meanings, which is confusing. The first and older meaning is the traditional one: *culture* as purposeful activity aimed at improving and perfecting its object. Derived from the Latin *cultivare*, meaning to till the soil, *culture* in this traditional sense denotes evaluation, especially of artistic and intellectual activity. Thus its synonyms include words like "development" and "refinement."

The second meaning dates only to the nineteenth century, when Sir Edward Burnett Tylor established *culture* as the core concept of anthropology. This anthropological meaning of *culture* refers to the whole way of life of a people. Not just intellectual and artistic activity (though this is not excluded) but behavior patterns, customs, beliefs, rituals, and the whole material apparatus of life, from tools to textiles, totems to sacred texts.

In the early days of anthropology, one of the chief obstacles facing Westerners studying non-Western societies was their own sense of cultural superiority. For the sake of scientific objectivity, they tried to bracket their own moral and aesthetic values. They did not always succeed, as we know. But they tried. And because of that, the anthropological meaning of *culture* denotes disinterested study, not evaluation.

It is easy to make an analytic distinction between these two meanings of *culture*. But it is hard to keep them separate in practice. For most commentators today, the so-called culture war is less about *culture* in the traditional sense than about *culture* in the anthropological sense. Family breakdown, addiction, unemployment, crime — these are problems with the way we live, not our artistic and intellectual activity. The two are linked through education, of course. But they are also linked through that peculiar amalgam known as *popular culture*.

Here I must make another definitional point. I do not use the word *popular* as the opposite of *high, serious,* or *good*. This usage is both illogical and a-historical: in every time and place, there have been works of art that possessed both popularity and artistic merit. And conversely, works that are low, unserious, and bad are not necessarily popular. If that were true, then every mouth-breather and lunatic in Hollywood would be a millionaire.

Ironic but true, the same usage can be found on the academic Left. In the hybrid discipline known as cultural studies, *popular* is routinely regarded as the opposite of *high, serious,* and *good*. The cultural theorist Frederic Jameson, for example, has stated explicitly that the rise of the electronic media and popular culture means "the necessary death of art and the aesthetic."[1]

I dispute this assumption, on both the Right and the Left. This is because I have spent several years thinking and writing about popular culture in a way that is intellectually serious but not, by current lights, academic. I have also spent quite a lot of time hanging around television, film, and recording studios. And I can tell you, the people who work in these places are not all mouth-breathers and lunatics. Yes, Virginia, there are some charlatans in this business. But the daily grind, the habitual shop talk, of the men and women who actually do the creative work is akin to that of artists everywhere.

Popular musicians think and talk about music. Film and TV scriptwriters wrestle with old-fashioned things like plot and dialogue. Production designers worry about color, texture, and line. Actors and directors act and direct. The language these people speak is a craft language,

1. Frederic Jameson, quoted in John Storey, *Cultural Theory and Popular Culture* (Athens, Ga.: University of Georgia Press, 1993), p. 169.

and it is directly descended from that of the traditional arts, especially the performing arts.

The electronic media have introduced new craft languages, of course. The language of cinematography, of recording, of editing, and more recently of digital processing are new. But here, too, traditional ideas of art and the aesthetic play a vital role. The finest practitioners, the ones who win the technical Oscars, Grammys, and Emmys, are not young whippersnappers but elders who have mastered both the technology of the future and the craft lore of the past.

My point is that these people do not use *popular* as the opposite of *good.* They understand the depredations of commerce. Indeed, they understand them better than most intellectuals do. But they also strive for that rare prize, the chart or ratings or box office success that is also a work of art. Such miracles do not happen every day, or even every year. But they do happen. And what is more, they last. They pass the most reliable test of artistic merit, the one laid down by Samuel Johnson: the test of time.

Coleman Hawkins's 1939 recording of *Body and Soul, The Philadelphia Story*, directed by George Cukor and starring Katherine Hepburn, the thirty-nine episodes of *The Honeymooners* that ran on CBS between 1955 and 1956 — decades later, we do not hesitate to call these classics. And if they can be preserved (by no means a foregone conclusion), they will still be classics many years from now.

For this to occur, there have got to be continuities between traditional and popular culture. I am hardly the only critic to have noticed these continuities. They are plainly visible to anyone whose background is in the traditional humanities and who does not wear ideological blinkers when looking at popular culture.

But the picture I am painting is not entirely a rosy one. The continuities I speak of are not always positive. Indeed, my whole critique of popular culture is based on the idea that some (not all) of its worst excesses are taken directly from a certain strain of modernism that I call *perverse.* I do not condemn all of modernism, by any means. But I do separate its genuine accomplishments from what Hilton Kramer calls its *revolté* impulses.

These impulses are not postmodernist, in the sense of having arisen in the 1960s. On the contrary, they date back to the middle of the last century. Perverse modernism arose with the dream of total social and political revolution. And, like that dream, it has decayed into arrogance and folly. Serious artists have long since abandoned what Isaiah

Berlin calls "the doctrine of art as free creation."[2] Serious artists no longer think of art as radically autonomous, liberated not only from its own tradition but also from moral considerations of any kind. But this idea still attracts the un-serious and the un-talented. And, as one of the continuities I speak of, it pervades popular culture.

This is not just a question of "sex and violence." In the abstract, sex and violence are the bottom line, the bedrock of civilized life. Demand their removal from art, and you look pretty silly. All your opponents need do is point out how much sex and violence there is in the world's great masterpieces, and you stand accused of wanting a culture made up entirely of Barney the purple dinosaur.

The real problem, which shows up most clearly at the so-called cutting edge of popular culture, is sex and violence turned into a nasty joke. Seduced by the *revolté* impulses of perverse modernism, certain writers, directors, and performers pride themselves on taking a deliberately obscene view of these primal experiences. That is, they portray sex and violence in a way that is unfeeling, indifferent, detached from the consequences of actions, and contemptuous of moral concerns.

The result is what I call the culture of transgression. Again, this problem exists on every level of our culture, from the galleries of Manhattan to the hills of Hollywood. It is not a function of public versus private funding of the arts. It is not a question of traditional versus electronic media. It is an all-pervasive phenomenon with deep historical roots. For artists of all kinds and degrees of sophistication, Beauty is Transgression, Transgression Beauty; that is all they know on earth, and all they need to know.

Consider gangsta rap, a crude entertainment that has evolved into a form of cultural toxin with the blessing, and elaborate justification, of countless academics and intellectuals. Or consider films such as *Natural Born Killers, Pulp Fiction, Kids,* and now *Crash.* Lest you think I am stretching the point, consider what David Cronenberg, the director of *Crash,* said about the scene in which his protagonist, a fellow who gets sexual thrills from automobile accidents, has intercourse with a gaping wound in a young woman's leg. Asked by the *New York Times* whether there is "any limit to what he would put in one of his movies," Cronenberg replied blandly, "in terms of concept, I don't think there's

2. Isaiah Berlin, "European Unity and Its Vicissitudes," *The Crooked Timber of Humanity* (New York: Vintage Books, 1992), p. 188.

anything that you cannot discuss."[3] The judges at the Cannes Film Festival were so taken with *Crash*, they devised a new category of award: "Audacity, originality, and daring."

Excuse me, but why is this a new category? Have not filmmakers always tried to be audacious, original, and daring? Or have these words become code for something else? At the heart of the moral ugliness pervading the arts is plain old hypocrisy. I for one would feel better if they would just come out and say that they are giving a prize for transgression.

We now arrive at the question of censorship. If we are sinking ever deeper into a culture of transgression, then what, if anything, can be done about it? Recently we have witnessed a revival of the classic argument in favor of censorship. Walter Berns, Irving Kristol, and Robert Bork are just three of the prominent figures urging that liberal democracy cannot survive unless its citizens have good moral character. If the citizens cannot govern themselves individually, this argument goes, they will never be able to govern themselves collectively. Therefore, liberal government has an overriding interest in curbing negative moral influences. Even if this means curbing free speech.[4]

The standard reply is that of the free speech absolutists. This side warns that all governments, even liberal governments, tend to trespass on the liberty of their citizens. It is better, therefore, to tolerate negative moral influences, even flagrant abuses of free speech and expression, than to give government the power to censor.[5]

These are powerful arguments. But neither one of them describes the regime under which we actually live. That regime has always steered a middle course between public morality on the one hand, free speech on the other. Actually, I should say *regimes*. For during this century America has had *two* regimes: one for the print media and the fine arts, and another for the electronic media and popular culture. Each grants a different degree of liberty.

3. Anthony DePalma, "A Director Collides with the Proprieties," *New York Times* (March 19, 1997), pp. B1, B5.

4. The classic American statement of this argument can be found in Alexander Meiklejohn, *Free Speech and Its Relation to Self-Government* (New York: Harper, 1948). For a more nuanced and up-to-date version, see the writings of Harry M. Clor, most recently *Public Morality and Liberal Society: Essays on Decency, Law, and Pornography* (Notre Dame: University of Notre Dame Press, 1996).

5. This argument is most fully expressed in the many dissenting opinions of U.S. Supreme Court Justices Hugo Black and William O. Douglas.

To begin with the first regime: we now live in an era of unprecedented liberty for both the print media and the fine arts. On both, the only legal restraint is the obscenity law, and that is exceedingly narrow. Indeed, it is much narrower than the original obscenity law, passed by British Parliament in 1857. That law, which became the model for similar laws in America, empowered any local official to seize any publication that was, in his opinion, obscene. Thus began a 100 years' war over the depiction of sex in literature.

In Britain, this 100 years' war ended with Obscene Publications Acts of 1959 and 1964, which defined a work as obscene only if "its effects . . . taken as a whole . . . tend to deprave and corrupt," and if it cannot be proven to be "in the interests of science, literature, art, or learning." In America, the 1973 Supreme Court decision *Miller* v. *California* defined obscenity as the depiction of "sexual conduct" in a "patently offensive way" that, "taken as a whole," lacks "serious literary, artistic, political, or scientific value."

By requiring that a work be judged as a whole, and by allowing the opinions of art critics and literary scholars to be submitted as evidence, modern obscenity law opens what I call the art loophole. To escape prosecution, all the writer or artist need do is stake a claim to "serious artistic value." The satirical songwriter Tom Lehrer captured this strategy in his immortal lyric: "As the judge said on the day that he acquitted my Aunt Hortense / To be smut it must be utterly without redeeming social importance."

With hindsight, we can see that the art loophole has been both blessing and curse. It has been a blessing because genuine artists may now include sexually explicit references in their work without being called pornographers. Were they writing today, James Joyce and D. H. Lawrence would not have to fight the same battles. Most people, and certainly most judges and juries, now make a distinction between serious art that deals with the erotic side of life, and mindless trash that pursues sexual thrills for their own sake.

But here is the rub: in the 1950s a certain kind of artist began deliberately to blur this distinction. If Tom Lehrer had looked at literature, he might have come up with this lyric: "As the judge said on the day that he acquitted Henry Miller / The whole point here is high-class smut, the rest is merely filler." To writers such as Miller, William S. Burroughs, and Allen Ginsberg, literature was largely a crusade against censorship. Since the last vestige of censorship was the obscenity law, obscenity became their battle cry. Works like *Tropic of Cancer, Naked*

157

MARTHA BAYLES

Lunch, and *Howl* have made their way into the modern literary canon. But that does not mean that they are not obscene.[6]

The danger of this artistic use of obscenity was that it would open the art loophole so wide, everything would be able to pass through. To a staggering degree, this is exactly what has occurred. In the domain of fine art (or rather, in the cultural space once occupied by fine art), hardcore pornography is now admired for its transgressive clout. To quote Robert Mapplethorpe: "There was a feeling I could get looking at pornographic imagery that . . . had never been apparent in art. And I thought if I could somehow retain that feeling . . . then I would be doing something that is uniquely my own."[7]

Does the art loophole give the same latitude to popular culture? To judge from the 1991 acquittal of the obscene rap group 2 Live Crew, it would seem to. Yet remember, popular culture is governed by a different regime. The electronic media have from their inception been subject to various forms of government control. In Britain and Europe, the government has until recently owned and monopolized the electronic media. The BBC is a perfect example.

In America, where free enterprise is the ideal, the government has limited itself to regulating and licensing media companies that are privately owned. Yet even this is more control than the government exerts over the print media and the fine arts. In the liberal tradition America shares with Britain, no citizen needs a government permit or license to publish a book, paper, or magazine. Or to mount an exhibition or stage a performance. These are unregulated activities subject only to the obscenity law. By contrast, the operation of a radio or television station requires a government license. In classic legal terms, this is called prior restraint.[8]

So we live under two regimes: near total liberty for the print media and the fine arts; prior restraint for the electronic media and popular culture. The question, in this age of the Internet, is which regime will

6. See Harry M. Clor, *Obscenity and Public Morality: Censorship in a Liberal Society* (Chicago: University of Chicago Press, 1985), ch. 7; and Home Office, *Report of the Committee on Obscenity and Film Censorship* (Bernard Williams, chairman) (London: Her Majesty's Stationery Office, 1979), ch. 8.

7. Quoted in Wendy Steiner, *The Scandal of Pleasure: Art in an Age of Fundamentalism* (Chicago: University of Chicago Press, 1995), p. 57.

8. See Thomas G. West, "The Twentieth-Century Decline of Freedom of Speech in America," paper presented to the August 1995 meeting of the American Political Science Association.

dominate the future? Are the electronic media becoming more free, like print? Or is the converse happening? The question is framed by the late Ithiel de Sola Pool, professor of communications theory at MIT:

> What is true for the United States is true . . . for all free nations. . . . All are moving into the era of electronic communications. So they face the same prospect of either freeing up their electronic media or else finding their major means of communications slipping back under political control.[9]

This is the issue at stake in the recent Supreme Court case, *Reno* v. *The ACLU*. Hearing oral arguments for and against the Communications Decency Act of 1996 (a bipartisan effort to control obscenity and indecency on the Internet), the nine justices were concerned less with the message than with the medium. To quote the *Washington Post*, "The real question isn't what's *on* the Net, but rather what *is* the Net."[10]

I do not claim to understand all the legal ins and outs, but let me sum up the problem this way: how exactly do we define a smut peddler in cyberspace? As a creep threatening children in a city playground, to be publicly shamed if not locked up? As a pornographic movie theater, to be zoned into a red-light district and required to keep out minors? As a broadcaster, to be placed under the watchful eye and raised eyebrow of the FCC? As a video store, to be subject to local ordinance and/or company policy when it comes to requiring proof of age before renting R- and X-rated videos? As an artist, exempt from prosecution under the existing obscenity law? Or as a citizen exercising his right to political speech in a public forum?

As you might imagine, the laws and regulations of our two regimes govern each of these scenarios differently. That is why the justices went home with a headache. The precedents, the legal arguments, presented by the various parties depend on the various scenarios they choose. And as if things were not complicated enough, the technology keeps changing. And every time it does, it throws up new scenarios. In the case of *Reno* v. *The ACLU*, the Supreme Court decided that the federal law against indecent material on the Internet violated the First

---

9. Ithiel de Sola Pool, *Technologies of Freedom: On Free Speech in an Electronic Age* (Cambridge, Mass.: Harvard University Press, 1983), p. 8.

10. John Schwartz, "Shouting Porn! on a Crowded Net," *Washington Post* "Outlook" section (30 March 1997), pp. C1, C4.

Amendment. But suffice it to say that the issue of censorship in cyber-space is not going away.

But while the courts and legislatures haggle, the rest of us should not lose sight of certain facts. First, the issue is not going to be resolved by social science. When it comes to the hot-button topic of sex and violence in popular culture, the most effective advocates of censorship have not been Berns, Kristol, and Bork, but Gore, Clinton, and Reno — well-meaning liberals pushing for a regulatory crackdown. These people are effective because instead of harping on soft subjects like public morality, they stick with the supposedly hard facts gathered by social science.

The trouble is, the impact of media on behavior is one of those areas where the hard facts are not all that hard. As James Q. Wilson has explained:

> It is unlikely that social science can either show harmful effects [of media violence] or prove that there are no harmful effects. . . . These are moral issues and ultimately all judgments about the acceptability of restrictions on various media will have to rest on political and philosophical considerations.[11]

This brings me to the second fact we must face. Even with all the political will in the world, it may not be possible to impose censorship in a world where all the separate media (television, radio, recordings, movies, computers, telephones, libraries, databases, and publishing) are converging in one vast system. On the bright side, this prospect could yield what Russell Neuman has called "the universal Alexandrian library."[12] A system by which every human being on the planet may be linked, via two-way fiber-optic cable, to every other human being and to all of the world's electronically stored information.

The trouble is, that electronically stored information includes the culture of transgression in all its ugly manifestations. Needless to say, this prospect is somewhat less bright. In the words of James Ferman, the director of the British Board of Film Classification (formerly known as the British Board of Film Censorship):

11. James Q. Wilson, "Violence, Pornography, and Social Science," *The Public Interest* 22 (Winter 1971): 58, 61.
12. W. Russell Neuman, *The Future of the Mass Audience* (New York: Cambridge University Press, 1991), p. 37.

It may well be that in the twenty-first century, that it simply becomes impossible to impose the kind of old-fashioned regulation that the Board exists to provide. . . . After all, what's the point of cutting a gang-rape scene in a British version of a film if that film is accessible down a telephone line from outside British territorial waters?[13]

Some governments think they can meet this challenge. In China, officials brag of having developed the capability to admit useful information via the Internet, while keeping out such Western poisons as rock music and political dissent.[14] Yet their claim to a Great Chinese Firewall may be overblown. To judge by recent events in Eastern Europe and the former Soviet Union, Big Brother cannot control CNN, much less the Internet. The cyberpunks have a point when they say, "The Internet interprets censorship as damage and routes around it."[15]

So what about America, land of the free and the V-chip? As mentioned earlier, our system has always been one of indirect government control. First, the government creates a level playing field, albeit one for a handful of giant media companies. Then it regulates lightly, hoping that the giants will play nicely. If they do not, the government huffs and puffs, threatening a crackdown. And the giants respond by setting up a self-policing operation. Such as the Hays Office, which monitored the movies between the 1930s and the 1960s; the network censors, which still keep tabs on mainstream television; or the ratings system of the MPAA, Motion Picture Association of America.

This is the system that has given us the V-chip. Despite all the rhetoric, in which words like *empowerment* buzz like horseflies, the V-chip is merely an effort to extend an MPAA-style ratings system into the home. It wins points as a political fig leaf. But not as an effective solution to the problem of raising children in a culture of transgression.

Let me try to explain. The V-chip is based on the concept of age grading. That is, classifying material according to how old someone must be to see it. Now, the age-graded ratings system of the MPAA made sense twenty years ago, when access to movies could be moni-

13. Tom D. Mathews, *Censored* (London: Chatto & Windus, 1994), p. 286.
14. Joseph Kahn, Kathy Chen, and Marcus W. Brauchli, "Beijing Seeks to Build Version of the Internet That Can Be Censored," *Wall Street Journal* (January 31, 1996), pp. A1, A4; and Seth Faison, "Chinese Tiptoe Into Internet, Wary of Watchdogs," *New York Times* (February 5, 1996).
15. John Gilmore, quoted in Peter H. Lewis, "Limiting a Medium Without Boundaries," *New York Times* (January 15, 1996), p. D4.

tored (more or less) by an adult selling tickets at the theater door. But with the advent of cable and the VCR, age-grading went the way of the dodo bird.

There is also the inconvenient fact that children of different ages tend to live in the same house. And that whatever older siblings know, they inevitably pass on to their juniors. The V-chip might work if every household were made up of loving, mature adults and tiny, vulnerable offspring. But what about those meddlesome creatures known as adolescents? As I say, the V-chip is a fig leaf. It covers the politicians' keisters long enough to get them elected, but it does not change anything. Between the state of the media and the state of the culture, government seems to be losing the capacity to protect either the liberty of artists or the innocence of children.

What is to be done? For answer, I borrow a metaphor from the realm of cyber-security. Since the Pentagon played a big role in creating the Internet, it is hardly surprising that the U.S. military is now studying ways to control it. Indeed, a team of researchers from the RAND Corporation has recently been pondering how to protect America's communications system from "logic bombs" and other forms of "information warfare." Their conclusion? That "erecting perfect barriers around public networks is not only impractical but also probably undesirable." The Chinese government can try surgery. But the RAND researchers prefer immunity. For them, the best defenses would be those that "mimic a biological immune system." They "are intrigued by the possibility of developing software agents that act like antibodies."[16]

Well, this may or may not work out for the good people at RAND. But I like the metaphor. It captures what I want to say about cultural authority. First of all, antibodies are active. They do not assume that just because something is circulating in the blood, it is therefore good. Here I draw a parallel with the libertarian faith in the free market. Too often, this faith translates into tacit approval, on populist grounds, of the worst excesses in the culture.

Second, antibodies are precise. They size up the toxin before they attack it. So the lesson here is: Be knowledgeable. Do not criticize what you have not experienced. If you are a politician, take the time to see the movies whose titles pepper your speeches. If you are the sort of intellectual who takes pride in being ignorant of popular culture, then fine, do not discuss it. But if you do feel moved to make some lofty

16. "Cyber Wars," *The Economist* (January 13, 1996), p. 78.

pronouncement, bear in mind that ignorance is ignorance in every field, including popular culture. It seldom impresses, and it never persuades.

Third, antibodies are small. Consider last year's campaign against gangsta rap carried out by Bill Bennett and Senator Bob Dole. Before they weighed in, gangsta rap was getting dissed by many of its own former fans. Snoop Doggy Dogg's second album did not sell half as well as his first. A low-budget film, *Fear of a Black Hat,* subjected the genre to insider satire, the most relentless kind of criticism. But with Bennett's and Dole's attack, gangsta rap got a new lease on life. This is how the culture of transgression works. To performers who pose as the victims of the system, there is no form of publicity more welcome than being attacked by the system. They feed on the idea of persecution. Was Madonna relieved when Bennett and Dole did not mention her name? No, I daresay she was disappointed.

Antibodies also know what they are protecting. Here I would underscore the importance of affirmative cultural authority. In the humble vineyard of journalistic criticism, where I have spent a few years, you earn your living by praising as well as panning. It is important to say what is bad, but you must also find things of value, and suggest to your readers what is good about them, or you will soon burn out.

In the same vein, it is better to make comparisons, when comparisons are called for, within the same bailiwick. Too often, cultural authority has nothing to offer in place of what it deplores except some remote icon of highbrow taste. If the kids want a funky rhythm and the only place they are finding it is in *Life After Death* by the late Notorious B.I.G., play them some James Brown. Then graduate to Horace Silver. Mozart is wonderful, but there are times when Mozart is not what is needed.

This is not relativism. Built into the wise use of cultural authority is an appreciation of the process of learning. It is vital to remember that learning, and self-correction, are constantly occurring within popular culture. Despite the way it looks on a bad day, popular culture is not a realm without standards. And, to repeat, those standards are ultimately connected to the artistic standards we inherit from the past. The continuities are there, but a proper understanding of them cannot be forced.

In the end, it is this patient work of criticism, self-correction, and teaching that is most imperiled by censorship. To clumsy would-be censors wielding knives and scissors, the charlatans of transgression know just how to respond. They strike their favorite pose, that of the

Persecuted Avant-Garde Artiste. To the active, precise, intimate use of cultural authority, however, they have no defenses. All they can think of to do is cry "censorship!" and hope that Woody Harrelson will play them in the movie.

11. *Multiculturalism and the Problem of Cultural Relativism*

DINESH D'SOUZA

My topic is the troubled politics of race, an issue that has divided and perplexed this country from its very beginning and continues to define in many fundamental ways the cleavages in our culture. I will begin with the affirmative action debate and then probe a little deeper into the underlying roots of the racial and affirmative action controversy.

Proportional Representation

In the Spring of 1997, I was at the University of California in the wake of the recent debate on Proposition 209, the California Civil Rights Initiative. I approached an admissions officer at the University of California at Berkeley to pose to him this question. Imagine the case of a student applying to this fine university who has a grade average in high school of B+ to A- and an SAT, Scholastic Assessment Test score, of about 1200 out of 1600 — a good student. If this student happens to be Hispanic, what would be the chance that he or she would get into Berkeley? He replied, "The probability would be 100 percent." The student would be guaranteed admission. I then asked him to imagine the case of a student with the same grades, same test scores, same extracurricular talent, but like me the student is of Asian descent. "The chance of that student being admitted," he replied, "would be approximately 5 percent." In other words, what Berkeley has done is to estab-

lish quite clearly, quite self-consciously some form of race-based preferences in its admission policy.

Many conservative critics of Berkeley have said the university is
getting rid of merit in the application process, but this is not true.
Berkeley considers merit within racial groups. For instance, if you are
a Hispanic applicant to Berkeley, they will admit the best Hispanics. If
you are an Asian applicant, they will take the best Asians. If you are a
white applicant, they will take the best whites, and so on. But the
important thing to realize is that there is no direct competition across
racial lines. Everybody is competing to get into this fine school by
running in his or her own racial or ethnic lane.

Berkeley has established, like many other universities, a kind of
multiple-track system of race-based admissions. This may seem like a
very odd thing to do and you might ask why the University of California at Berkeley is doing this. Why are they judging students by
different sets of standards depending upon the color of their skin, why
not judge them based upon the content of their character, their academic and intellectual merits or some such other criteria? The answer
is this: studies have shown that if the University of California at
Berkeley were to be strictly colorblind, if the university were to judge
students solely based upon merit, solely based upon high school
grades and standardized test scores, virtually the entire campus would
be made up of two groups, whites and Asians. Asians and whites
together would make up over 90 percent of the Berkeley campus, the
number of Hispanics would go down quite a bit, the number of
African-Americans, American blacks, would go down a lot from the
current level of 7 to 8 percent to about 1 percent. Blacks, in fact, would
be quite scarce at Berkeley. This anticipated result is known to the
professors, the deans, the administrators, and they are profoundly
embarrassed by it.

What universities are trying to do is to balance two goals in their
admissions policy — on the one hand, merit and the equality of rights
for individuals, but on the other hand, representation and the equality
of results for groups. This is not an atrocious calculus because Berkeley
after all is a state university. It is accountable to, it is responsive to a
quite diverse, quite racially and ethnically diverse California population. And so what the University of California is trying to do is to have
a campus that, to use President Clinton's words, "looks like America,"
looks like California, that mirrors the population that surrounds it. If
Hispanics are 10 percent of the population of California, the University

of California at Berkeley would like to have roughly 10 percent Hispanics in its freshmen class.

This notion that is animating Berkeley's policies is the notion of proportional representation. You want to have a student body that broadly approximates the ethnic breakdown of the surrounding population. The concept of proportional representation, by the way, is not unique to higher education. It is in fact, and many people do not know this, the moral and legal centerpiece of our civil rights laws. If you own a company in this town and you are sued for discrimination, the federal government, the EEOC, the Equal Employment Opportunity Commission, will come to you and say, "Why is it the case that Hispanics are only 3 percent in your company when they are 9 percent in the surrounding or relevant population?" Under current law you are presumed to be guilty of illegal discrimination. Why? Because the assumption of the law is that if you are not discriminating then Hispanics, who are 9 percent of the surrounding population, would be about 9 percent in your company as well. And so quite apart from the affirmative action controversy, we have to step back and ask, "Where does proportional representation come from? What are the intellectual and moral roots of this notion of proportional representation? How did it come to be widely accepted? How did it come to be embedded in our laws?"

I want to argue that the idea of proportional representation is a logical or natural expression of the philosophy of cultural relativism. Cultural relativism is a somewhat esoteric term that can be looked at in many different ways. I am going to use it in a very clear and obvious sense. Cultural relativism simply means all cultures are basically equal. No culture is better or worse, superior or inferior to any other. This notion of cultural relativism developed in the early part of this century in the United States to oppose what can be called the "old racism."

The Old Racism and the New Relativism

Let us look at how the "old racism" developed in the West, how it gained its influence, and why cultural relativism was necessary to fight against it. The "old racism" developed essentially as an assertion of Western civilizational superiority. My point is that, in Western civilization, racism became a justification for the rise to power of the modern West.

DINESH D'SOUZA

If you lived in the year 1500, and you looked around the globe, you would see a number of impressive civilizations, of which Western civilization, then called Christendom, was only one and by no means the most powerful or the most impressive. It is probably fair to say that in the year 1500, the most advanced civilization in wealth, learning, science, exploration, technology, literature, philosophy, and so on, was the Chinese civilization. The second most advanced civilization arguably at the time was Arab-Islamic civilization. Other civilizations included the Indian civilizations; the civilizations of North Africa; in the Americas the Aztecs, the Incas, and the Mayas; and so on. At that time, Western civilization was by many people considered to be something of a relative backwater.

And yet something very interesting happened between the fifteenth century and the nineteenth century and that is that Western civilization began to grow enormously in power and influence largely because of a series of internal developments within the West — the Renaissance, the Reformation, the Enlightenment, the Scientific Revolution, the Industrial Revolution. This civilization became so powerful scientifically, intellectually, politically, militarily that by the nineteenth century the civilization of Europe could by itself subdue and conquer all the other civilizations in the world put together.

It has been estimated that about one hundred years ago, the turn of the century, Western civilization controlled about 90 percent of the real estate on this planet. It was the heyday of colonialism. Now this Western power was bound to be accompanied by a great deal of confidence, overconfidence, even hubris. In essence what the Europeans argued was: "How have we managed an achievement unprecedented in world history? How is it that we have the Cathedral of Chartres and the Cathedral of Notre Dame? How is it that we have the telescope and the microscope; we have mapped the globe and the planets? These other cultures by comparison appear to be hopelessly primitive, hopelessly far behind. The answer must be that we are in some sense naturally superior. And what is the outward mark of that superiority, but the fact that we are white. Whiteness is the most obvious, visible, noticeable, distinguishing characteristic between us and them." Whiteness in a sense becomes a symbol of Western civilizational predominance, Western civilizational superiority. That was the "old racism."

In the twentieth century, these ideas came under fierce attack in the name of cultural relativism. In essence the relativists argue as follows: "You cannot distinguish human populations as superior or infe-

168

rior. You cannot use the old categories of civilized and barbarian. All human beings live in a culture, and every culture is a kind of unique adaptation to its own surrounding environment. No culture is innately superior or inferior. In fact, these concepts of superiority and inferiority are relative — they are in the eye of the beholder. All cultures are worthy of study; all cultures are worthy of respect; and at some moral level, one could say that all cultures occupy the same level on a kind of moral plane." This was relativism.

In the first half of the twentieth century, a great debate erupted between the old racists and the new relativists. A debate that incidentally was only settled by a single event and that event was World War II. It was Hitler who discredited the "old racism." He discredits it not by proving it anthropologically false — he does show that meaningful distinctions can be made between civilization and barbarism — but by showing that concepts of civilizational hierarchy can have genocidal consequences. And so in the 1950s, if you lived in this country and said you came from a superior stock, or a superior culture, people would say that that is the kind of thinking that leads to the gas chambers. Thus, due to the event of World War II, cultural relativism established itself in the United States and more broadly in the West as the only ethical alternative to Naziism.

The Consequences of Cultural Relativism

There are two very important consequences of this triumph of cultural relativism. One is in the area of what we now call multiculturalism. But the second and far more important is in the area of the debate about merit.

The debate about multiculturalism today is only controversial for one reason. It is not controversial because people have developed an interest in studying other cultures. If hundreds of thousands of American students said, "We want to study the *Analects of Confucius;* we want to read the *Bhagavad Gita;* we want to familiarize ourselves with ancient Persian poetry," this would be uncontroversial; in fact most of us would applaud. What makes multiculturalism controversial is that it is in its very nature an attack on the idea of Western cultural superiority. In fact, multiculturalism is animated by an effort to rectify the assumption of Western cultural superiority by insisting that no culture can in any sense be said to be better or worse, superior or inferior, to any other. The controversies over multiculturalism are only understandable in this context.

A few years ago the novelist and the Noble laureate, Saul Bellow, made an interesting and provocative statement. He said, "Show me the Proust of the Papuans and I'll read him." I was at Stanford when this statement was made and countless Stanford professors jumped up and said, "This is an outstandingly racist statement."[1] Why? Was Saul Bellow saying that the Papuans are inherently or genetically incapable of producing a Proust? No, he said that to the best of his knowledge they had not. But the assumption of Western cultural superiority is what gave this controversy its racial element.

On the anniversary of Columbus, historians were coming to blows over the question of whether Columbus discovered America or did he merely encounter America.[2] That seems to be an odd semantic dispute. But it is not an odd semantic dispute because the issue in question here again was the issue of Western cultural predominance. If Columbus discovered America, it implies that Columbus and by extension the West were the acting influential agents, the subjects of history. The American Indians on the other hand were the ones discovered. The idea of Columbus discovering America implies that it is no accident that it was Columbus who arrived on the shores of the Americas and not the American Indians who arrived on the shores of Europe. On the other hand, the idea of encounter is something far more accidental. I am walking down the street, I happen to encounter you. Encounter implies interaction on a level cultural plane, it denies the idea of cultural superiority. I mention these items only in passing to get to what is my main subject and that is the influence of cultural relativism in shaping the basic premises of our thinking about race in this country today.

After the war the assumption of cultural relativism was widely imbedded in American intellectual life. The Civil Rights Movement which developed in the 1950s and 60s, led by Martin Luther King, Jr., built its basic expectations on this premise. The Civil Rights Movement was based upon the following syllogism: all cultures are basically equal and all racial groups are in some fundamental sense equal. Equal how?

1. Mary Louise Pratt, "Humanities for the Future: Reflections on the Western Culture Debate at Stanford," *South Atlantic Quarterly* 89, No. 1 (Winter 1990): 9.

2. See, e.g., Garry Wills, "Goodbye Columbus," *New York Review of Books* (November 22, 1990), p. 6; Gary B. Nash, *Red, White and Black: The Peoples of Early America* (Englewood Cliffs, N.J.: Prentice-Hall, 1974), p. 3; Ronald Takaki, *A Different Mirror: A History of Multicultural America* (Boston: Little, Brown, 1993), p. 23.

Equal in talent, equal in ability, equal in aptitude. And since racial groups are basically equal, we expect that equality of rights for individuals will over time lead to equality of results for groups. In other words, since racism has historically been a mechanism, a system of enforced group inequality, the assumption of the Civil Rights Movement is that if you can get rid of racism, outlaw it, make racial discrimination illegal, then in a reasonably short period of time, you should expect to see something resembling group equality. Remove the artificial barrier and the natural result should produce itself. What I try to argue is that, in the intervening generation of thirty years or so since Martin Luther King, Jr.'s death, what we have essentially discovered beyond a shadow of a doubt is that this syllogism is basically false. Equality of rights for individuals does not lead to equality of results for groups.

Merit Causes Inequality

In fact, I will go on to say that merit, no less than the "old racism," produces a great deal of inequality. Merit produces inequality between individuals. We all know this and expect it, but it also turns out that merit produces substantial inequality between groups. If you do not believe me let us not confine ourselves to the simple example I gave from the University of California at Berkeley and let us generalize from it in the following way. Try to imagine any measure of academic achievement and economic performance — a reading test given to a five year old, a math test given to a seventeen year old, the firefighter's test, the law school exam, the civil service test, the police sergeant's exam. You name the test. On virtually every measure of academic achievement and economic performance, if you administer this test today to one hundred randomly selected whites, blacks, Hispanics, and Asians, I will tell you in advance what the result will be. Whites and Asians will come out on the top, Hispanics will fall in the middle, African-Americans will do the least well. I know of no counterexample for the pattern I have just described. And in the entire debate surrounding my book, *The End of Racism*, there is not a single person in the United States who has been able to cite examples of measures of academic achievement which produce a different result to the one I have just described.[3] The point I am trying to make here is that merit no less than

3. Dinesh D'Souza, *The End of Racism* (New York: The Free Press, 1995), ch. 11.

the "old racism" is producing inequality and this leaves a lot of people, particularly a lot of leading civil rights activists, to suspect and to argue that merit is the new form in which the "old racism" now manifests itself. In other words, a great suspicion has now attached itself to the idea of merit because merit is seen to some degree as a camouflage for the "old racism."

Why does it seem that merit is producing so much inequality? The whole debate is not over whether this occurs; there is no doubt that it does. I know of no counter evidence that it does not occur. The whole debate is over why it occurs. Why is it the case that almost every measure of achievement produces this disparate result? There are three positions in this debate.

The first position is what one can loosely call the bell-curve position, named after the controversial book written by Charles Murray and Richard Hernstein, which argues that it is no surprise that groups perform very differently on almost every measure in the race of life.[4] The reason they perform differently is because they are different, they are naturally different, they are biologically different, and these biological differences, once accepted, immediately explain the world as we see it. This is loosely speaking the hereditarian view. It has been attacked and opposed for the better part of the century by what one can loosely call the liberal view.

The liberal view is that the reason you have group differences in academic achievement and economic performance is because society artificially manufactures those differences. According to the liberal view, it is societal intervention, societal oppression, and specifically racism that artificially creates group differences.

The liberal and hereditarian view have been dueling for the better part of a century; it is a bit of a see-saw — when one goes up the other comes down. In the first half of the century, probably the hereditarian view was predominant. In the second half of the century, probably the liberal view was predominant. The reason that the liberal view was able to prevail so easily against the hereditarian view is because the liberals in the fifties and sixties argued like this: "How can you say that group differences between blacks and whites — differences of earnings, of income, of performance, and so on — are the result of nature or of genes? Look at all of the discrimination to which blacks are subjected

4. Richard Hernstein and Charles Murray, *The Bell Curve: Intelligence and Class Structure in American Life* (New York: The Free Press, 1994).

particularly in the South." This argument was extremely plausible, extremely compelling; and the hereditarian view began to weaken. I think that what we are seeing today is something of the opposite effect.

The liberal view is now beginning to fatally weaken and we are seeing a revival to some degree of what may be called, "rumors of inferiority."[5] In fact, one of the reasons for the runaway success of *The Bell Curve,* is the belief that the book although highly controversial might be articulating in public what some people suspect to be true in private, but dare not say.

Why is the liberal view weakening? Let me cite just one example, but I could give many to illustrate my point. Look at the Scholastic Assessment Test (SAT) given to seventeen-year-olds who want to apply to college. I will concede for the purpose of argument — it is not true, but I will concede it — that the verbal section of the test may be in some ways culturally or racially biased. It asks you synonyms, antonyms, reading comprehension; the kind of questions that depend on where you grew up and so on. Ignore the verbal section of the test; throw it out. Look only at the math section in which a typical question is like this: "If an automobile can go seventy miles in a hour, how far can it go in forty minutes?" What is interesting about the math section of the SAT is that all the racial differences on the verbal section of the test are inevitably exceeded year after year by the math section. In other words, the black-white difference on the math section of the test is a lot bigger than on the verbal section of the test.

But here is the really troublesome fact that needs to be explained and is not easy to explain. Asians and whites who come from poor families, Asians and whites coming from families in this country making less than $10,000 per year, score higher on the SAT every year, verbal and math both but certainly math, than African-Americans coming from families making over $60,000 a year.[6] In other words, poor whites and poor Asians regularly do better on math tests than upper-middle-class blacks. Now, how could racism produce such a result? This is a devastating rebuttal to those who believe that these tests are merely calibrating socioeconomic privilege. In order to cope with statistics like this, to figure out their social implications, academics have been driven to a kind of flurry of explanations and largely to a flurry of denial.

5. D'Souza, pp. 441-45.
6. The College Board, "National College Bound Seniors: 1994 Profile of SAT and Achievement Test Takers" (Princeton, N.J.).

In this rather troublesome debate, my argument has been: in this duel between the genetic, hereditarian view, on the one hand, and the liberal view on the other, there is a third position that is being somewhat ignored. The third position can loosely be called the cultural position. The cultural position simply says that the reason you have differences in academic achievement and economic performance among groups is because groups differ culturally. They differ on the average but they differ in noticeable ways. This is something we observe in everyday life, this is something that can be easily measured by the techniques of social science, and this is something that can be directly correlated with academic achievement and economic performance. Let me give one example of what I mean: why is it that Asian-American students seem to be doing much better academically than other groups? Is it the case, as *The Bell Curve* hinted, that there might actually be some Asian genetic superiority, particularly in the area of mathematics and visual-spatial knowledge? Psychologist James Flynn did a comparative study of whites and Asians and he found that the two groups do not perform much differently on IQ tests administered at an early age. Asians do, however, perform far better in school and university for what Flynn concludes are largely cultural reasons: Asians come from close families, they attach a high value to education and entrepreneurship, and they study and work harder.[7] If Flynn's study is valid, and there is no reason to believe it is not, you do not have to harken to theories of genetic difference; you have right before your eyes an obvious reason — differences in academic performance are directly influenced by the amount of time invested in homework.

If it is correct that study time and academic performance are positively correlated, you can now step back and ask, "Why do Asian students study harder?" You actually have to think more carefully to give reasons for this. One reason might have to do with differences in family structure. It is certainly the case on average that a two-parent family has more time to devote to discipline and to supervising the study habits of children then a single-parent family. The illegitimacy rate in the African-American community, for example, is almost seventy percent. In the Asian-American community the illegitimacy rate is about three percent. Now these are huge differences and they would suggest that the source of the differences in academic achievement have

7. James R. Flynn, *Asian Americans: Achievement Beyond IQ* (Hillsdale, N.J.: Lawrence Erlbaum Associates, 1991).

much less to do with external racism and much more to do with differences in culture.

The Impact of Culture

This cultural diagnosis has met with a lot of hostility, a lot of hostility from many quarters, and sometimes surprising quarters. The reason for the hostility has been, since the 1960s, the notion that the cultural view wrongheadedly blames the victim. This was the title of a book written in 1971 by the sociologist William Ryan, *Blaming the Victim*.[8] The argument is that victims are not to blame for their circumstances and that, I believe, is certainly true. But if, as a result of those circumstances, a group develops a pattern of behavior that is holding it back then it seems to me that even though a victim is not to blame for being a victim, the victim might actually be in the best position to do something about that victim status. One of my critics, Bob Woodson, says, "The victim is not to blame for being knocked down, but the victim may be responsible for getting up."

The anthropologist Elijah Anderson, who studies inner-city African-Americans, argues that what we are seeing in American society and particularly in the inner city is what he calls two cultures — a black culture of decency in which you have millions of blacks who wake up in the morning, get to work, raise their kids, try to live decent lives; and what Anderson calls a culture of irresponsibility defined by crack, by drugs, by crime, by illegitimacy, and so on. No one likes to discuss it, but who can deny that that culture is also real?

And this gets me to my key point: cultural relativism, which developed in this century as a very effective mechanism for fighting the "old racism," has in some ways become a terrible obstacle. Cultural relativism is now preventing us, as a society, from saying in a clear and confident and a simple way that some cultures are in fact better than others. Cultural relativism makes it difficult for us to say out loud and to develop public policies based upon the premise that cultures of decency are simply better than cultures of irresponsibility and that in fact we need a conscious public policy that is aimed at extirpating or transforming cultures of irresponsibility and strengthening and reinforcing cultures of decency. This then becomes the irony of cultural

8. William Ryan, *Blaming the Victim* (New York: Vintage Books, 1971).

175

relativism — the solution to an old problem, the "old racism," now becomes the source of a new problem.

Conclusion

Many conservatives, in particular, focus their civil rights policy on the issue of colorblindness — let us have a colorblind public policy, they say. And I think we should too, but it is not enough for the following reason. If you simply stuck to a colorblind policy today and enforced it strictly, you would find that on virtually every elite university campus, certainly all the Ivy League schools, certainly Duke, certainly Stanford, certainly Berkeley, blacks would basically disappear. Blacks would be extremely scarce at these elite institutions. It is also probably true that blacks would be quite scarce in many of the other professional elite sectors in American life. It is a troublesome result in a racially diverse society, a society that bears a certain measure of responsibility towards blacks for the history of this country. This becomes a morally troublesome result. I would argue that colorblindness is an essential part of the strategy, but there needs to be a second part — a resistance to liberal social policy, which has since the 1960s focused primarily on the issue of redistribution — robbing Peter to pay Paul, but often without paying careful attention to the effects of this transaction on the cultural habits of Peter and Paul. In the last few years, for the first time, we see new attention to the question of not simply who is paying and who is getting the money, but how it affects responsibility, how it affects the cultural traits that are very important in determining citizenship and in determining a success.

I will end with a sentence that Martin Luther King, Jr. used, though it is not the famous line about the content of one's character. What King said is that the equality of rights under the law (the colorblind approach if you will) can only assure equality of rights, equal treatment under the law. It cannot assure much more than that.[9] According to King, every man must write for himself, with his own hand, the charter of his emancipation proclamation.[10] I think what King is saying is the law can treat us equally, but what we do with that equality and freedom,

9. Martin Luther King, Jr., *A Testament of Hope: The Essential Writings of Martin Luther King, Jr.*, ed. James Melvin Washington (Harper, San Francisco, 1986).
10. Ibid., p. 246.

what we make of our rights, how we exercise them, how we shape our own destiny, that ultimately is up to us.

12. Revolt of the Masses Revisited

RALPH McINERNY

HAVING reached the age when to read is as often as not to reread, I recently picked up José Ortega y Gasset's *The Revolt of the Masses* in the expectation of reliving some enjoyable hours.[1] My memories of the book were vague but pleasant and I opened it without any premonition of what would happen. To my surprise, I found the book appalling in its tone, in its argument, and in its assumptions. I base these remarks on it, not just to criticize it, though I shall do that, but because it raises a fundamental question about human solidarity.

Ortega begins with the sour observation that there are just too many people. The streets crawl with them, they crowd into public places, they have lowered the tone of society and tainted its culture.

> Towns are full of people, houses full of tenants, hotels full of guests, trains full of travellers, cafes full of customers, parks full of promenaders, consulting rooms are full of patients, theaters full of spectators and beaches full of bathers. What previously was, in general, no problem, now begins to be an everyday one, namely, to find room.[2]

Ortega pretty obviously despises those on whom he casts this cold and mordant eye. He was writing after World War I battlefields had seen the slaughter of millions of men that settled nothing. He could not of course have foreseen the unimaginable millions who were soon to be

1. José Ortega y Gasset, *The Revolt of the Masses* (New York: The New American Library of World Literature, Inc., Mentor Books, April of 1950).
2. Ibid., p. 7.

178

eradicated and he would doubtless have been horrified by the suggestion that the elimination of people considered subhuman was any part
of what he was suggesting. Meanwhile Stalin was starving millions of
Kulaks, eggs broken to make an omelet that never did get made. Ortega's book appeared in 1930.

It is not really a book on the population problem. It has been
said that all the people on the planet could be put into the state of
Texas, with room to spare — an observation, not a recommendation,
of course. It is not really elbow room that concerns Ortega. Rather it
is the fact that the swarming masses of whom he writes do not understand the culture on the margins of which they have been born.
What is worse, culture begins to be defined in their terms, the rare
and difficult is popularized, vulgarized, trivialized, in order that the
masses might attain it. But all this is bogus; they are incapable of it.
Nowadays, the complaint would be rephrased as the dumbing down
of the culture.

There is irony in the fact that *The Revolt of the Masses* was one of
the first mass-market paperbacks. I still have my copy. The price — new
— was thirty-five cents. It has become unglued with age — a danger of
longevity, to be sure — and if I should hand you my copy you might
wonder whether you are meant to cut or deal. It has become looseleaf.
On the front cover: *The Revolt of the Masses.* On the back cover: *Good
reading for the millions.* If Ortega is right the intended purchasers of this
paperback edition could not comprehend it. If the purchaser thought
he did comprehend it, if he enjoyed it, as I did long ago, it could only
be because he felt that he was safely included on the other side of the
line that divided Ortega and the elite from the masses. I like to remember myself reading the book at the beach, surrounded by the teeming
millions despised by the author but whom nonetheless the publisher
hoped would buy the book.

My ambivalence in thinking again of Ortega's book lies in the
fact that his distinction between those who demand much of themselves and those who do not is productive of what might be called a
moral hierarchy, a meritocracy. His division of the sheep and goats
will recall a hundred others — the *hoi polloi*, literally the many, as
opposed to the few who pursue the good; the narrow gate which few
enter as opposed to the broad road leading to destruction. And so on.
But Ortega is not merely repeating such commonplaces. He is alarmed
by a civilization that is defined from the bottom up, so to speak; one
that is controlled by the many. He sees a society in which the "un-

qualified individual" is sovereign.[3] He sounds closer to Nietzsche than to Aristotle — save when Aristotle is speaking of the perils of democracy.[4] Even when one is repelled by Ortega's condescending disdain for the bulk of mankind, one resists an indiscriminant defense of our imperfectly redeemed race.

The following remarks do several things. First, I want to meditate for a moment on Ortega's thesis and pursue one of its implications in the realm of literature. Second, I will indicate how irrelevant the pros and cons of the discussion must seem in today's cultural atmosphere. Third, I will examine John Carey's thesis that these pullulating masses came from the pens of intellectuals and are in effect a figment created by the imagination of the elite. I end on a faintly homiletic note.

"Good Reading for the Millions"

In terminals, on planes, in subway cars, wherever you go, every other person seems to be poring over a book. By and large, they pore over the chubby sort of paperback whose cover glows in the dark, but here and there you might see someone reading a title from the kind of series that introduced Ortega to the mass market. But romances, thrillers, mysteries would make up the bulk of such reading. A sign of this would be the books that show up on best seller lists around the country. Not that there is much variation between such lists in Los Angeles and Chicago and New York. The warehouse bookstores and newstands push a small selection of the books that appear at any given time, so it is not surprising that people who read at all will likely be reading those titles. The dismissive term for what the masses read is *schlock*.

We have grown up with the suggestion that there is a fundamental difference between popular writing and literature, a divide that creates a difference in kind. It is not easy to isolate the properties of literature, however. Most efforts are circular, but the note of difficulty recurs. Important reading, books really worth the effort, are demanding. There is a Kantian note in the advice that we read them: we have a duty to do so and the fact that fulfilling the duty is painful is a guarantee of the goodness of the activity. This two-storied world sometimes is

3. Ibid., p. 16.
4. It is in the *Politics* that Aristotle expresses his negative estimate of democracy.

thought to be insufficient. Dwight MacDonald once suggested three levels of culture: mass cult, mid-cult and hi-cult.[5]

Is there a qualitative difference between what the masses read and what you and I and Ortega read? Is literature for us, and all those jumbo paperbacks for the unwashed? Such a division allows for slumming, of course: Paul Tillich, for example, visiting the bistros of Harlem, or professors in general, who have been one of the surest traditional markets for mysteries. Years ago I mentioned to a colleague in the English Department that I was reading such-and-such and he fell back in his chair, clapped his forehead and cried, "I don't remember when I last read anything just for enjoyment." It was a revelation to me that he regarded "teaching" Dickens and George Eliot as a chore. But then these are literary works, not diversions. What he did not tell me was that he was a Zane Grey aficionado.

C. S. Lewis published *An Experiment in Criticism* in 1961.[6] Lewis was a professor of literature, first at Oxford, then at Cambridge. His inaugural lecture, when he was lured to Cambridge, was entitled *De descriptione temporum*.[7] He took the occasion of assuming the chair in medieval and renaissance literature to note that the Middle Ages and the Renaissance are usually thought to be historical periods radically different from one another. Oil and water, in fact. The men of the Renaissance, after all, were rescuing us from the Middle Ages by reaching back to classical times. Lewis went on to say some wise and witty things about the periodization of history, the more or less arbitrary cutting up of the temporal flow into ages and parts. He had earlier and elsewhere remarked that the Renaissance is the only historical period we allow to be defined by those who lived in it. Lewis himself was inclined to see a continuum between medieval and Renaissance literature. In the inaugural lecture, he ended with the claim that there is only one important historical division, but I will return to that.

An Experiment in Criticism begins by noting the way in which we separate the books discussed in school from that vast ocean of fiction in which, if truth were told, we spend most of our reading time. Is this merely slumming? Is an embarrassed *apologia* the only possible reaction when we are caught curled up with P. D. James, say? We would scarcely dare to say that a mystery is literature. Why? What is literature?

5. On Dwight MacDonald, see *Discriminations* (New York: Grossman, 1974).
6. C. S. Lewis, *An Experiment in Criticism* (Cambridge University Press, 1961).
7. C. S. Lewis, *De descriptione temporum* (Cambridge University Press, 1955).

Lewis first proposes a test rather than a definition. The test is this: *Literature is any book we would read again.* One is reminded of Cyril Connolly's ambition, expressed in *Enemies of Promise*, to write a book that would still be read ten years after its first appearance.[8] Lewis's test obviously leaves out some of the things we read, maybe many of them; after all, there are novels we enjoy but, having enjoyed, give away, or trade. Who would read a whodunit twice unless he forgot whodunit? This suggests that the chief, even sole, attraction of such books lies in the story, the plot, how it comes out. We swiftly turn the pages to find this out, and when we have, the book has served its purpose.

Story or plot is what Aristotle called the soul of tragedy, and perhaps we can generalize from the *Poetics*. The logic of events, thanks to which narrated events have a beginning, middle, and end, is the plot or *mythos* of stories. If evanescent reading has only plot, this should not suggest that serious fiction lacks plot. Not if Aristotle is right, as of course he is. Plot may not be reason enough to reread a story, but it is the vehicle by which the something more is conveyed to the reader. What is the something more? Aristotle speaks of language, of character, of setting as among the things beyond plot that we look for, and any of these might account for our reading something again. It is not that we have forgotten them; rather, remembering, we wish to return. In the *Book of Problems*, Aristotle asks why we like the old songs best. A pleasure relived. (He asks this twice, actually, suggesting an additional problem: why do we repeat good questions?)

One rereads Wodehouse for the crystal clarity of the prose. Judges as severe as Belloc and Waugh thought him a master of English.[9] But perhaps one would not go back to Bertie and Jeeves for much else than the pellucid prose.

Exotic settings can bring us back, the imagined landscape of *Treasure Island*, the forests of W. H. Hudson, the puritan towns of Hawthorne, the mining camps of Bret Harte, the reprise of the history of the West in *A Canticle for Leibowitz*, the Nebraska of Willa Cather. . . .

---

8. Cyril Connolly, *Enemies of Promise* (Penguin Books, 1961). The ambition expressed in the book is to write something that will still be read ten years after publication, presumably reread, thus expressing a version of Lewis's preliminary test of literature.

9. From *Nones* (New York: Random House, 1951). For Waugh on Wodehouse, see "An Angelic Doctor: The Work of P. G. Wodehouse," in *A Little Order: Evelyn Waugh A Selection from his Journalism,* ed. Donat Gallagher (Boston: Little, Brown, 1977), pp. 83-87. (There is a much ampler Penguin Books version of this collection).

The Stoic characters of Elmore Leonard's westerns can bring us back to that handful of novels for which he will be remembered; among unforgettable characters would be Heathcliff and Cathy; Emma, Silas Lapham, Gatsby. . . .

It is not that some stories have these and others do not; it is their excellence in some stories that brings the reader back. But there is something more elusive than these that enters into our ranking writers high: call it their voice or their vision, their way of seeing human life. The universe of Trollope, where money and marriage govern the characters, can bring home again the abiding importance of the division of the species into genders, the complicated and ennobling ritual whereby a man chooses a woman and a woman accepts a man. To return to Conrad is to go back to a world where the moral stakes of life are presented in an elegiac voice that drips with the *lacrimae rerum.*[10] Tolstoy provides us with meditations on the meaning of life, individually and in its sweep. Ambrose Bierce, Stevenson, Twain, F. Scott Fitzgerald, Cather, Greene, Flannery O'Connor, and Walker Percy — they all have distinctive voices and visions to which we return again and again.

Lists will differ but what they share, I think, is the fact that our favorite authors illuminate the mystery of human existence. We come away with an understanding of what it is to be human that is perhaps inarticulate at first, a mood that lingers but which, when pondered, delivers up more and more. *So we beat on, boats against the current, borne back ceaselessly into the past.* Zane Grey does not do this, nor does Tom Clancy, nor most of the authors whose works show up on lists of best sellers. We all know this. It is what we say about it that differs.

The Ortega response is that literature is for the elite and schlock is for the masses and there is a qualitative difference, a difference in kind, between the two kinds of book. The Lewis response is to suggest a continuum. There are multiple criteria for a book's being considered literature and a hierarchy can be established on the basis of a work's satisfying few or many of these criteria. The *sine qua non* of a story is story, a narrative that begins somewhere and ends somewhere, provid-

10. On Virgil's *lacrimae rerum,* see W. H. Auden's "A Walk After Dark,"

> Yet however much we may like
> The stoic manner in which
> The classical authors wrote,
> Only the young and the rich
> Have the nerve or the figure to strike
> The lacrimae rerum note.

ing a sequence of acts with the kind of closure they almost never have in life. If a story's sole interest lies in our wanting to find out how the problem is solved, the difficulty overcome, the girl won, we would not read it again. If we do, we should look for the something more than plot that brings us back.

Such a continuum provides for a good deal of principled differ-ence among readers. Some critics seek absolute hierarchies, exactly one hundred great books, say, but they do little harm and some good. Most of us shift books around on that continuum over the course of our lives. *Huckleberry Finn* may slide down the scale for years and then rebound and be restored to a higher position. The first time we read *Hamlet*, our enjoyment was based on different criteria than those that enthrall us later, or perhaps the criteria come to be more deeply appreciated. Rank-ing is not the reason for reading, of course, and Lewis suggests multiple criteria more as a defense against snobbery than as an invitation to make out lists. His is not an egalitarian view, but neither is it the elitist snobbishness of an Ortega. The Lewis view has the effect of establishing a community of readers rather than a cleavage between real readers and bogus readers. Nor is this merely a dispute between critics. The different views are based on radically different understandings of the human species and of the solidarity that ought to bind all men together.

Why This Is Irrelevant

The collision of the Ptolemaic and Copernican accounts of our planetary system once figured large in accounts of the history of science and astronomy. The ancient view took the earth to be at the center, with the other planets revolving around it. The heliocentric view put the sun at the center and recalculated the movements of the planets accordingly. Accounts of this quarrel among Catholics tend to play up the part of Galileo and the Church's alleged denial of proved scientific truth, despite the fact that proof of the movement of the earth did not come until centuries later. The judgment that the Ptolemaic account was a narrowing earthbound view of man and his destiny has to deal, but seldom does, with *The Dream of Scipio* and Dante's *Paradiso*. In any case, it is possible to look back on that controversy and see it as a kind of neighborhood quarrel, itself an indication of an incredibly — to us — limited view of the universe. Our nine planets have been swallowed up in a galaxy, there seem to be galaxies without number in an ever expanding universe. Rival ways of describing our solar system pale before the thought of the whole shebang scattering outward in all directions at the speed of light. In somewhat the same way, the opposed view of Lewis and Ortega have lost their relevance.

In effect, Ortega is arguing that only a few can appreciate efforts to plumb the mystery of human existence and a culture that retails such insights inevitably trivializes them. Lewis accords to all men the capacity to ponder the sinuous course of our days and the ability to respond to imaginative works that seek such meaning. There are gradations and hierarchy, good, better, best, and lots of books that would not hold our attention a second time, but it is universally common to human persons to reflect on the meaning of life, often through their reading, always through art of some kind. In *The Everlasting Man*, G. K. Chesterton mentioned the question that had been prompted by the caves recently discovered in France.[11] Were their inhabitants human? The discussion had gone on and on. For Chesterton the answer was simple. Look at the walls. On the walls were drawings at which anyone must marvel, line drawings of animals done with a grace that made them imaginatively present in the flickering light of the cave. Where there is art, there are human beings. Those primitive men, returned from the hunt, watched one of their number draw upon the wall what they had been pursuing all day. It is this stepping back from life, reproducing it, imitating it, in Aristotle's sense, that is an essential and ineradicable element of human existence. Its manifestations may vary, but there is a fundamental solidarity among humans based upon it.

Both the separation and the continuum views have lost their claim in a time when the very notion of objective criteria is rejected as ideological. Among the books that we read at least once are those that tell us how bad the times in which we live have become. A few years ago it was Allan Bloom's *The Closing of the American Mind;* then came Dinesh D'Souza's *Illiberal Education;* more recently Harold Bloom's *The Western Canon.*[12] Such books belong to an expanding genre in which the rotten fruits of the Enlightenment are examined.

11. G. K. Chesterton, *The Everlasting Man* was first published in New York by Dodd Mead in 1925 but will be found in *G. K. Chesterton Collected Works* (San Francisco: Ignatius Press).

12. Allan Bloom, *The Closing of the American Mind* (Simon & Shuster, 1987); Dinesh D'Souza, *Illiberal Education* (The Free Press, 1991); Harold Bloom, *The Western Canon* (Harcourt Brace, 1994).

There can be a quarrel between Ortega and Lewis only if there are standards. Both of these men appeal to standards; their disagreement is about their application or implication or range. Both think some things are not worth reading at all, others worth reading once, some worth reading again and again. Lewis thinks that human beings as such have the wherewithal to respond to works of literature, at least at some points on the continuum his analysis suggests. Ortega sees any effort to allow for the "masses" to participate in culture as its betrayal and trivialization. In short, this is a disagreement within an agreement. We have entered a time when agreement and disagreement have lost their meaning.

Jean-Paul Sartre's *Existentialism is a Humanism* is not exactly Nietzsche for the masses, but it does provide a crisp account of the philosophy that underlies a culture that denies the very assumptions of a culture.[13] A field is cultivated to actualize its potentiality, and the same is analogously true of human culture traditionally understood. Sartre shrewdly chides those figures of the Enlightenment who thought they could discard God yet everything else in society would remain the same. There would be morality at least, wouldn't there? Sartre sees this as naive.

The theist views human beings as artifacts of their creator. On the model of the artisan, God makes what he makes to be of a certain kind, to have a nature with reference to which it can be called good or bad. A knife is good or bad given what a knife is made for. To remove God is to deny that man is a creature and that he has a nature. But if a man has no nature, there is no given standard according to which he can be said to act well or badly. The theistic view would have it that essence precedes existence, that is, that nature is an antecedent measure of conduct. Atheism requires its adherents to hold that existence precedes essence; that is, any standards of appraisal are a result of choice, not prior to it. In real life, as on the wicked stage, anything goes. If God does not exist, anything is permitted, nothing is prohibited. The human agent is free all the way down.

This analysis is a continental version of the prim view set forth by G. E. Moore in *Principia Ethica*, a book embraced by Lytton Strachey

13. Jean-Paul Sartre's "Existentialism Is a Humanism" can be found in Kaufman's *From Shakespeare to Existentialism* (New York: Anchor Books, 1958); On Nietzsche, see *The Will to Power*, Friedrich Nietzsche, translated, edited with commentary by Walter Kaufman (New York: Vintage Books, 1967).

and Bloomsbury.[14] Moore put Anglo-American ethics on the road to what Alasdair MacIntyre has called Universal Emotivism.[15] Moore, influenced by Hume, introduced what he called the Naturalistic Fallacy. What does it mean to call a person or a thing good? If you recommend a food or a car, you would doubtless draw attention to its properties. A Jaguar is slim, pretty, quick, and racy. That is what you mean by calling it good. For a Jaguar to be good is for it to be SPQR. You would respond similarly to the question as to why you say that wheat germ is good. And the appraisal of human actions as good or bad would likewise be related to citing their properties. All this is a mistake, Moore tells us; indeed it is fallacious. After centuries of confusion, in 1903 we have finally gotten it right. Of course things and acts have properties, but these have nothing to do with calling them good. Anything what-soever can be called good and calling it good cannot be explained by listing its properties. There is a chasm between Fact and Value. In the case of human action, the chasm is expressed as one between Is and Ought. The pointlessness of trying to explain evaluation in terms of the properties of the thing evaluated was spelled out later, by R. M. Hare.[16] Such an attempt leads to a tautology. It is really empty. Why?

You say that a Jaguar is good because it is SPQR. For it to be good is for it to be SPQR. Good is equivalent to SPQR. "Good" = "SPQR." But then the one can be substituted for the other. Thus, "A Jaguar is good because it is SPQR" comes down to saying "A Jaguar is good because it is good." You are spinning your wheels. Any effort to account for moral goodness is similarly tautologous.

Philosophers and others have responded to this, but the corrective has not had the impact of the original mistake. In the academy and elsewhere, what McIntyre characterized as Universal Emotivism is rampant. Lewis found it in grade school textbooks decades ago. You can find it in letters to the editor in this morning's paper. Any moral judgment is taken to be private and the effort to give it public force is the imposition of one view on all. This presupposes that moral judgments are subjective.

If calling an action good or bad cannot be accounted for by citing

14. For the "naturalistic fallacy" etc. see G. E. Moore, *Principia Ethica*, which appeared in 1903 and was embraced by Lytton Strachey and Bloomsbury.
15. Alasdair MacIntyre, *After Virtue* (The University of Notre Dame Press, 1981).
16. For R. M. Hare on fact/value, see *Freedom and Reason* (New York: Oxford University Press, 1965).

the properties of the action, to what do these evaluative terms refer? If the properties of a thing are objective, evaluation is subjective. It is the objective Jaguar that is SPQR. When I call it good, the adjective refers to my feeling when confronted with such a vehicle. Let us imagine that you, standing beside me and looking at the same vehicle, say Ugh. You don't like it. If I should retort by giving the list of Jaguarian properties already mentioned, I cannot expect that this will alter your evaluation. You agree that it has them. If Moore is right, evaluations do not have their basis in such properties. Your "ugh" like my "good" refers to a subjective reaction utterly divorced from the properties of the thing reacted to. Value terms refer to emotional states, feelings.

So you and I are not really in disagreement about the Jaguar. We agree that it is SPQR, but I say good and you say ugh. That is, I feel good and you feel bad. But there is nothing to prevent my feeling pleasure while you feel pain, or vice versa. "I have excruciating sciatic pain." "I don't." This is not a contradiction, any more than "So do I" would be an agreement.

I mentioned that C. S. Lewis, in *De descriptione temporum*, told the students he was addressing that there is only one division of human history. He added that it had occurred between his youth and theirs; he addressed them, he said, as a cultural dinosaur. What had happened? What Lewis wrote of in *The Abolition of Man*.[17] In that little book he noted how the Fact/Value Dichotomy had permeated the textbooks of elementary education. Children were being taught that to call a waterfall magnificent or a sunset beautiful was not to say anything about waterfalls and sunsets. Rather, these "value terms" noted their subjective reactions to factual situations which neither justified nor precluded positive or negative reactions. This is the radical change that Lewis had in mind. Whether or not it happened between his youth and that of the addressees of his inaugural address, it does indeed divide in the dramatic way he suggests. My own suggestion is that it puts Ortega and Lewis on the same side of a divide on the other side of which all standards — and their rejection — are equally ungrounded in the way things are.

Much of Harold Bloom's distress is that those who would displace the works that have for centuries formed the basis of the learning and teaching of Western literature have no intrinsic quarrel with them. Nor are they proposing substitutes whose merits are argued for. Any

17. C. S. Lewis, *The Abolition of Man* (Oxford University Press, 1944).

critic would welcome a controversy like that: arguments against his view, arguments for the opposed view. This is the very stuff of the intellectual life. But that is not what is going on. It is not the application of certain standards that is being questioned. It is not that new standards are being proposed. What is happening is the rejection of all standards. Any book is as good or bad as any other because evaluations have no objective basis. They are proposed as power moves, as ideological weapons, and they can only be answered by countervailing power.

It was because he saw the implications of all this that Lewis could say that what divided him from the students he was addressing was the only real historical division.

The Marketing of the Masses

Despite the previous section, the difference between Ortega and Lewis is of continued importance. As I have indicated, relativism and nihilism, both moral and intellectual, can be and have been effectively countered. They can be countered in the classical manner in which one handles attacks on the obvious: by illustrating the incoherence of the attack. Logical Positivism withered away when it was observed that its canon of meaningfulness, "A sentence is meaningful if and only if it can be verified or falsified on the basis of sense experience," could not itself meet the criteria of meaningfulness. When applied to the canon itself, the canon was revealed to be a policy proposal rather than a truth, evident or otherwise. When ancient Sophists declared that it was possible for a sentence to be true and false at the same time and in the same respect, the response was that this claim itself must be both true and false, and thus pointless. Of course only the young take pleasure in the *reductio ad absurdum.* Such discourse does not establish anything as true; rather it prevents the poisoning of the wells of discourse. Moreover, refutation is not persuasion. The culture of emotivism, of moral and intellectual nihilism, will continue to feed parasitically on the culture it is destroying, much as Sophists of old made a living from the city states whose civilization their theories would destroy. There are nondenominational chapels in airports; there are non-professing professors in academe. The tide will begin to turn only when laughter begins.

Ortega cannot of course be linked with the Neo-Nietzscheans of our day. But he has a lot to answer for. Consider the thesis of John Carey's *The Intellectuals and the Masses*, published in 1992:

> This book is about the response of the English literary intelligentsia to the new phenomenon of mass culture. It argues that modernist literature and art can be seen as a hostile reaction to the unprecedentedly large reading public created by late nineteenth-century educational reforms. The purpose of modernist writing, it suggests, was to exclude these newly educated (or 'semi-educated') readers, and so to preserve the intellectual's seclusion from the 'mass.'[18]

Carey shows how the disgust with ordinary people to be found in Ortega is echoed in a host of modern authors: Wells, Eliot, Yeats, Ibsen, Flaubert, Mann, Hesse, Gide, Shaw. . . . He quotes Lawrence as wishing he had a lethal chamber on the scale of the Crystal Palace into which, to the sound of music, he could herd the sick, the halt, the maimed.

Carey explains the difficulties of modern art in terms of this dread on the part of the artist of being understood by the masses. All those subhumans, and they can read! But the masses are, Carey suggests, an invention of the intellectuals. The thought of writers dreading to be read takes some getting used to. I take Carey's thesis to be far more important for its extra-literary significance. He himself does not hesitate to draw parallels between Nazi theory and the bitter remarks of the intellectuals of whom he writes. The ranking of books and readers has moral and political implications.

So how do I express my dismay with Ortega? There is no denying that there are an awful lot of bad novels about. It is surely true that most people — not excluding you and me — read lots of things we would not read again, maybe that we should not read in the first place. And it is undeniable that a process of levelling has gone on, tugging us downward on the scale rather than upward. But the response to this ought not be to divide readers and books into two classes as if there were something inevitable and final about it. Any narrative, any story, bears a family resemblance to the best stories. The ability to respond to any story reveals a capacity, a potentiality, that can be actualized further. A literary education should link new reading to old, by showing that

18. On John Carey, see the *opus laudatum: The Intellectuals and the Masses: Pride and Prejudice Among the Literary Intelligentsia 1880-1939* (New York: St. Martin's Press, 1992), p. vii.

the same delights, and other keener ones, await one in reading the proposed book. And it should also account for the fact that nobody reads exclusively the very best. There are merits in Tarzan as well as in some mysteries. And, if Lewis is right, there is a continuum that binds books together; they have family resemblances to one another and, as we know, members of a family resemble one another in various and unusual ways.

The deeper moral and political point at issue is the recognition of every human person as possessed of dignity simply because he is a person. To be a person is to have the capacity to know, to be able to respond to the macrocosm with imaginative and cognitive microcosms that capture the essence of the real. This capacity is actualized in every person to some degree; everybody already knows things, with the help of others, of course, but on his own as well. We converse with one another on that fundamental assumption. Language obviously presupposes it. The suggestion that some uses of written language are in principle and essentially beyond the reach of the vast majority of mankind should not obscure the fact that there are others where community is actual and not merely possible. The differential of natural talent, as Kierkegaard called it, is real, but there are two areas where it is largely irrelevant: the ethical and the religious. Carey's book suggests that modernism in the arts involves a gnostic religion, with the artist as priest and the masses as objects of revulsion rather than candidates for conversion. Joyce saw himself as a priest of a substitute religion as he forged in the smithy of his soul the uncreated conscience of his race. Its actual members were caught in Dubliners and held up to scorn. It is ironic that those stories now function as nostalgia trips into a lost but regretted past.

What is wrong with contemporary society is the fault of intellectuals, not ordinary people. If there is to be a redeeming of the time, it will depend upon truths, at the disposal of the simple as well as the wise, and masses in the liturgical sense.

About the Contributors

William B. Allen is the Dean and a Professor at James Madison College, Michigan State University. He has been a Kellogg National Fellow, Fulbright Fellow, member of the National Council on the Humanities, member and Chairman of the U.S. Commission on Civil Rights (1987-92), and has received the international Prix Montesquieu for his book, published in 1993, *Let the Advice Be Good: A Defense of Madison's Democratic Nationalism.* He has edited several collections, including *George Washington: A Collection,* and the *Essential Antifederalist,* and has authored many essays on American political thought and similar topics. His interests include political philosophy, American government, jurisprudence, and political economy. Professor Allen received his Ph.D. in Government at the Claremont Graduate School.

Hadley Arkes is the Edward Ney Professor of Jurisprudence and American Institutions at Amherst College, a contributing editor to *National Review,* and a monthly columnist for *Crisis* magazine. He has been a Fellow of the Woodrow Wilson Center of the Smithsonian Institution, and the National Endowment for the Humanities. He has written five books: a book dealing with the Marshall Plan, *The Philosopher and the City, First Things, Beyond the Constitution,* and *The Return of George Sutherland.* Dr. Arkes has also written articles for newspapers and journals such as the *Wall Street Journal,* the *Washington Post, Commentary, National Review,* and *Crisis.* Arkes received his Ph.D. in Political Science from the University of Chicago.

Martha Bayles is the Literary Editor for the *Wilson Quarterly.* She has authored or contributed to nine books including *Ain't That a Shame? Censorship and the Culture of Transgression* and *Hole in Our Soul: The Loss of Beauty and Meaning in American Popular Music;* regularly contributes to columns in the *Wall Street Journal, American Spectator,* and the *New York Times Book Review;* and has written articles entitled "In Defense of Prime Time," "Fake Blood: Why Nothing Gets Done About Media Violence," and "Malcolm X and the Hip Hop Culture." She has also appeared on National Empowerment Television's *Cato Forum,* Fox Cable Network's *Under Scrutiny,* PBS's *Think Tank,* and CNN's *Showbiz Today* and *Sonya Live.* Bayles earned her Ed.M. at the Graduate School of Education at the University of Pennsylvania.

T. William Boxx is chairman and CEO of the Philip M. McKenna Foundation in Latrobe, Pennsylvania. He also serves as a fellow in culture and policy with the Center for Economic and Policy Education at Saint Vincent College in Latrobe, Pennsylvania. He is the chairman of the board of the Commonwealth Foundation for Public Policy Alternatives and is on the boards of the Intercollegiate Studies Institute and the Henry Salvatori Center at Claremont McKenna College. He and Gary M. Quinlivan are coeditors of *Culture in Crisis and the Renewal of Civil Life* (Rowman & Littlefield Publishers, 1996), *Public Life & The Renewal of Culture* (Center for Economic and Policy Education [CEPE], 1996), *Public Policy and the Restoration of a Civil Society* (CEPE, 1995), *Policy Reform and Moral Grounding* (CEPE, 1995), and *The Cultural Context of Economics and Politics* (University Press of America, 1994). He has contributed to *Religion & Liberty* (Acton Institute), *Modern Age* (Intercollegiate Studies Institute), *Essays on Civil Society* (Civil Society Project), and *Building a Community of Citizens: Civil Society in the Twenty-first Century,* edited by Don Eberly. Boxx received an M.A. in theology, summa cum laude, from Saint Vincent Seminary in 1992 and has done Ph.D. course work in theology at Duquesne University. A native of Arkansas, he received his B.A. in sociology from Arkansas State University.

Dinesh D'Souza is the John M. Olin Research Fellow at the American Enterprise Institute. He was a senior domestic policy analyst at the White House during the Reagan administration from 1987 to 1988. His expertise in the fields of social and political studies include affirmative action, cultural issues and politics, higher education, religion and public policy, and social and individual responsibility. D'Souza is the author of *The End of Racism: Principles of a Multicultural Society* and

Illiberal Education: The Politics of Race and Sex on Campus which was a *New York Times* best-seller. His articles have appeared in *Vanity Fair, Forbes,* the *Wall Street Journal* and *New York Times.* He has also been featured on numerous programs including *This Week with David Brinkley,* the *MacNeil/Lehrer News Hour, Firing Line, Good Morning America,* and *Crossfire.* D'Souza graduated Phi Beta Kappa from Dartmouth College.

Elizabeth Fox-Genovese is the Eléonore Raoul Professor of the Humanities and Professor of History at Emory University. She is currently the Director of the Project on Integrating Materials on Women into Traditional Survey Courses, and she is also the Director of Women's Studies at Emory University. Her publications include *Feminism Is Not the Story of My Life; Feminism Without Illusions: A Critique of Individualism; Within the Plantation Household: Black and White Women of the Old South;* and *The Origins of Physiocracy: Economic Revolution and Social Order in Eighteenth-Century France.* She appeared on CSPAN's *Lecture to Independent Women's Forum, Washington Journal, Firing Line,* the *Armstrong Williams Show.* She has written essays for newspapers and magazines including the *Wall Street Journal, Academe, American Enterprise, National Review, U.S. Catholic, Boston Globe,* and *Chronicles.* Fox-Genovese earned her Ph.D. at Harvard University.

Robert P. George is an Associate Professor of Politics at Princeton University, a practicing constitutional lawyer, and is currently serving a six-year term on the U.S. Commission on Civil Rights. He is general editor of a new Princeton University Press series of books on law, culture, and politics, and serves on the Editorial Board of the *American Journal of Jurisprudence,* the Academic Advisory Board of the Judiciary Leadership Development Council, and the Board of Directors of the Philosophy Education Society. He is the author of *Making Men Moral: Civil Liberties and Public Morality,* and editor of *Natural Law, Liberalism, and Morality; The Autonomy of Law: Essays on Legal Positivism;* and *Natural Law Theory: Contemporary Essays.* Professor George has received an American Bar Association Silver Gavel Award and the Federalist Society's Paul Bator Award. He is listed on the Templeton Foundation's 1997 "Honor Roll of Outstanding Professors." He is a former Judicial Fellow at the U.S. Supreme Court, where he received the Justice Tom C. Clark Award. George has a Ph.D. from Oxford University and a law degree from Harvard University.

Charles R. Kesler is the director of The Henry Salvatori Center for the Study of Individual Freedom in the Modern World and an Associate Professor of Government at Claremont McKenna College. He is a member of the Board of Editors of *Interpretation: A Journal of Political Philosophy,* a member of the Board of Directors of the California Association of Scholars, contributor to the *National Review,* and a senior fellow of the Claremont Institute. He has edited two books: *Keeping the Tablets: Modern American Conservative Thought* and *Saving the Revolution: The Federalist Papers and the American Founding,* and has written many essays related to politics within the United States. In addition, he has various professional affiliations and serves on numerous scholarly panels including *What Would Be the Elements of an Effective Public Rhetoric of Virtue Today?, Republican Sweep?* and *Natural Law and a Limited Constitution.* He has written articles for the *Wall Street Journal, Los Angeles Times, Profile,* and *National Review.* Kesler received his Ph.D. in Political Science from Harvard University.

Hilton Kramer is the editor and publisher of *The New Criterion,* a monthly review of the arts, which he founded with the late Samuel Lipman in 1982. Since 1987, he has also been the art critic for the weekly *New York Observer,* and for many years has written the "Critic's Notebook" column in *Art & Antiques* magazine. His weekly "Times Watch" column has been published in the *New York Post* since 1993. Over the years Mr. Kramer has contributed to *Commentary,* the *New Republic, National Review, New York Review of Books, American Scholar, Wall Street Journal, Atlantic, American Spectator, Partisan Review, Modern Painters, Boston Globe,* the London *Times Literary Supplement,* and the London *Sunday Telegraph.* In addition, Mr. Kramer is the author of two volumes of criticism — *The Age of the Avant-Garde* and *The Revenge of the Philistines* — and of critical monographs on the art of Milton Avery. Kramer studied in the graduate schools of Columbia University, Harvard University, Indiana University, and the New School for Social Research.

Joyce A. Little, is a Professor of Theology at the University of St. Thomas. Her books include *Toward a Thomist Methodology* and *The Church and the Culture War: Secular Chaos or Sacred Order?* She has written numerous articles for various journals and magazines, such as *Crisis, First Things, New Oxford Review,* and *Literature and Belief.* She is a member of the Writing Editorial Board of *Love and Life Newsletter,* which is published by the Pope Paul VI Institute; an Associate of the Catholic

Commission on Intellectual and Cultural Affairs; member of the Fellowship of Catholic Scholars, the National Association of Scholars, and the Walker Percy Society; a member of the Advisory Board of the Center for the Study of the Authentic Teachings of the Magisterium; and a member of the Advisory Board of the Center for NaProEthics. Little received her Ph.D. from Marquette University.

Ralph McInerny, Michael P. Grace Professor of Medieval Studies and Director of the Jacques Maritain Center (Ph.D., Laval University) is the author of *The Logic of Analogy; Thomism in an Age of Renewal; St. Thomas Aquinas; Ethica Thomistica; A First Glance at St. Thomas Aquinas: A Handbook for Peeping Thomists; Boethius and Aquinas; Aquinas on Human Action; The Question of Christian Ethics;* and *Aquinas Against the Averroists.* He is also a novelist, author of the Father Dowling and Andrew Broom mysteries, most recently *A Cardinal Offense* and *Law and Ardor.* Recipient of various fellowships — Fulbright, NEH, and NEA — he is a fellow of the Pontifical Academy of St. Thomas Aquinas and past president of the Fellowship of Catholic Scholars, the American Metaphysical Society, and the American Catholic Philosophical Association. For many years editor of The New Scholasticism, he is the founder/publisher of *Catholic Dossier;* co-founder (with Michael Novak) of *Crisis: A Journal of Lay Catholic Opinion.*

Gary M. Quinlivan is the executive director of the Center for Economic and Policy Education. He is a Professor of Economics and chairman of the economics, political science, and public policy departments at Saint Vincent College. He is the director of the center's Alex G. McKenna Series and codirector, with T. William Boxx, of the center's Religion, Culture, and Public Policy programs. Quinlivan is also the coeditor of the center's publication: *Economic Directions.* Quinlivan has several publications on international trade and finance, has authored several op ed pieces, and coedited eight books with T. William Boxx. From 1988 to 1989, Quinlivan was a Fulbright Scholar at Shandong University in the People's Republic of China. In 1997, he received an honorary professorship at Shandong University. In 1993, he received the Saint Vincent College Professor of the Year award. Since 1989, he has been an adjunct faculty member at Carnegie-Mellon University (economics department) where he teaches international trade and public finance. Quinlivan has a B.A. from the State University of New York at Geneseo and a Ph.D. in economics from the University at Albany (SUNY).

Claes Ryn is Professor of Politics at the Catholic University of America where he was also chairman of his department for six years. In 1992, the Graduate Students Association named him Outstanding Graduate Professor at Catholic University of America. His fields of teaching and research include ethics and politics; politics and the culture; and the history of Western political thought. Ryn is chairman of the National Humanities Institute and editor of the academic journal *Humanities*. Born and raised in Sweden, he is widely published on both sides of the Atlantic. His many books include *Democracy and the Ethical Life*, which is now in an expanded edition; *Will, Imagination and Reason*; and most recently, *The New Jacobinism: Can Democracy Survive?* Ryn's articles appear in leading journals, magazines, and newspapers. He lectures widely and is a frequent guest on television and radio.

Stephen Tonsor is Professor Emeritus of History at the University of Michigan, an adjunct scholar at the American Enterprise Institute, and associate editor of *Modern Age*. His past accomplishments include senior visiting research fellow at the Hoover Institution, and Consultant to President Nixon's Council of Economic Advisors. He has published dozens of articles, review articles, and reviews, including: "The Conservative as Historian: Francis Parkman," in *Modern Age*; "The Medieval Model of Social Reconstruction," in *Catholicism in Crisis*; "Revisiting Conservatism: The Foundation and the Academy," in *National Review*; "Why Democratic Technocrats Need the Liberal Arts," in *Freedom, Order and the University*; and "The Elements of the Communist Manifesto" republished as "Afterword," in Karl Marx, *Communist Manifesto*. Tonsor earned his Ph.D. at the University of Illinois.

Index